THE AFRICAN CHALLENGE TO GLOBAL DEATH PENALTY ABOLITION

THE AFRICAN CHALLENGE TO GLOBAL DEATH PENALTY ABOLITION

International Human Rights Norms in Local Perspective

Andrew Novak

intersentia
Cambridge – Antwerp – Portland

Intersentia Ltd
Sheraton House | Castle Park
Cambridge | CB3 0AX | United Kingdom
Tel.: +44 1223 370 170 | Fax: +44 1223 370 169
Email: mail@intersentia.co.uk
www.intersentia.com | www.intersentia.co.uk

Distribution for the UK and Ireland:
NBN International
Airport Business Centre, 10 Thornbury Road
Plymouth, PL6 7 PP
United Kingdom
Tel.: +44 1752 202 301 | Fax: +44 1752 202 331
Email: orders@nbninternational.com

Distribution for Europe and all other countries:
Intersentia Publishing nv
Groenstraat 31
2640 Mortsel
Belgium
Tel.: +32 3 680 15 50 | Fax: +32 3 658 71 21
Email: mail@intersentia.be

Distribution for the USA and Canada:
International Specialized Book Services
920 NE 58th Ave. Suite 300
Portland, OR 97213
USA
Tel.: +1 800 944 6190 (toll free) | Fax: +1 503 280 8832
Email: info@isbs.com

The African Challenge to Global Death Penalty Abolition. International Human Rights Norms in Local Perspective

ISBN 978-1-78068-294-5
D/2016/7849/75
NUR 828

GPRC
Guaranteed
Peer Reviewed
Content

British Library Cataloguing in Publication Data. A catalogue record for this book is available from the British Library.

FOREWORD

It is often contended that the death penalty is as old as humanity. The reason is simple. Any human society needs protection against incorrigible, dangerous and undesirable criminals. A 2011 research of the African Commission on Human and People's Rights on the *Question of the Death Penalty in Africa* states that African societies were no exception: "the death penalty existed in all precolonial African societies." The argument that the death penalty is part of the African tradition has constituted a barrier to the abolitionist movement in some parts of the continent. Abolishing the death penalty is there assimilated to abolishing customary law and, mostly, African identity. Colonial laws that were imported from apparently more "civilized" nations strengthened this view by legalizing the death penalty and formalizing its methods of execution all over Africa, except in Portuguese colonies. On the eve of independence, postcolonial governments chose to maintain the *status quo*.

The contention that the death penalty is enrooted in the African culture has become debatable. In the *Makwanyane* case, the South African Constitutional Court ruled in 1995 that the death penalty is the antithesis of the African value of *Ubuntu*. However Justice Albie Sachs stressed, in his concurring judgment, that there was an absence of authoritative materials on traditional African jurisprudence. Available sources were from historians and anthropologists. The learned Justice thus concluded, "if these sources are reliable, it would appear that the relatively well-developed judicial processes of indigenous societies did not in general encompass capital punishment for murder." The inference that the death penalty was not part of African tradition is not only seductive, it also carries the message that African ancestors, though deemed to be savage, primitive, barbaric by their colonial masters, had a greater sense of human rights than do contemporary African leaders. It would mean also that African societies started valuing the right to life and dignity long before Western societies that are still battling for complete abolition of the death penalty.

The ruling in the *Makwanyane* case has now induced legal researchers such as Andrew Novak to fill the vacuum and assess the correctness of Justice Albie Sachs' finding. In this impressive study, *The African Challenge to Global Death Penalty: International Human Rights Norms in Local Perspective*, Professor Novak distances himself from generalizations that have often led to wrong conclusions and undertakes an objective analysis. He establishes that a factual reality in one area and for some people does not lead to a general conclusion about all other Africans in other areas. Each society has conceived justice differently. The way each large or small community has defined its criminal law in terms of prohibited behavior and their punishments proves this discrepancy.

His overview of the death penalty in Sub-Saharan Africa is enriched by country studies from West to East and North to South. The Gambia, Ghana, Botswana, Lesotho, Swaziland, Zimbabwe, Kenya and Uganda, which are subjects of this study, are all former British colonies. That is not a unifying factor however. Colonial law was imported at different times and in different ways. It was superposed on customary laws whose conception of justice varied depending on the tribe concerned.

The death penalty was a valid penalty for treason among the Akan of Ghana and Ivory Coast, for disobedience and conspiracy against the rulers among the Dagaaba of Ghana and Burkina Faso, and for adultery among the Baganda of Uganda and the Ashanti of Ghana. The Baganda had an aversion to thieves of food and they sentenced them to death. The Nandi of Kenya also imposed the death sentence for repeated witchcraft.

At the same time, the Pokot of Kenya, the Iteso of Uganda, the Bemba of Zambia and Democratic Republic of Congo and the Shona of Zimbabwe and Mozambique punished adultery and non-consensual sexual intercourse with compensation. Restitution for homicide also existed among the AmaXosa, Tsonga and Nguni of South Africa, the Luo of Kenya and the Shona of Zimbabwe and Mozambique. Ostracism was also the relevant penalty for the most serious crime in precolonial Africa, namely witchcraft, among the Bantu of Kavirondo in Tanzania, the Luo of Kenya and Zimbabwean tribes.

Colonial law was superposed on these traditional plinths. In British colonies, courts regularly sentenced people to death. The abuse of the death penalty appeared to be legally authorized. Attitudes of colonial courts varied however depending on the status of the colony. Some territories were settlement. Others were protectorates or colonies. A settlement was assimilated to an overseas British territory and, there, judicial practices were not only biased but also inconsistent and arbitrary. In Kenya, offenders were at risk of receiving a death sentence where the victim was a European or an Indian. In the 1950s, the abuse of the death penalty reached its peak. It was politicized and heavily relied on in order to control the *Mau Mau* insurrection. Early before 1960, also called the year of independence in Africa, colonial powers resorted to the death penalty as a way of silencing demands for freedom.

At independence, dictatorial regimes resorted to similar techniques as the colonizer in order to keep people obedient and silent. New governments, including former Portuguese colonies that were death penalty-free under colonial rule, justified the retention of the death penalty on the grounds of stability and sovereignty. Retentionist countries in Africa view standards on the abolition or limitation of the death penalty as a threat to their sovereignty. There is no doubt that political context shapes the use of the death penalty, whether it is imposed for political offences or ordinary crimes such as voluntary homicides.

New criminal phenomena have served as a justification in some African retentionist countries for the extension of the list of capital offences. Terrorism in West Africa and East Africa has led the Nigerian and Kenyan governments to review their penal policies and reserve a death sentence to crimes related to terrorism activities. Though the Ugandan Constitutional Court struck out the anti-homosexuality act, which extended the death penalty to aggravated homosexuality, because Parliament passed it without the required quorum, the threat of this punishment being reinstated still looms. Reports indicate that Uganda is planning to table a new bill on the Prohibition of Promotion of Unnatural Sexual Practices. Gay and lesbian communities are worried that this bill contains a harsher penalty than the repealed act. Extending the death penalty is not new among retentionist countries. Even abolitionist countries have, over time, reinstated the death penalty for crimes that were previously otherwise punished. For instance, Liberia had abolished the death penalty in 2005. It immediately acceded to the Second Optional Protocol to the International Covenant on Civil and Political Rights that prohibits the reintroduction of the death penalty. However, in 2008, it passed a law punishing armed robbery, terrorism, and hijacking with the death penalty. It is still questionable whether Liberia is abolitionist or retentionist.

Nevertheless, Professor Novak proves that Africa stands as a reference for other continents where the death penalty still lingers. Progressive attitudes are rooted in customary law and in modern concepts of human rights. It should also be recalled that Botswana, the Gambia and Uganda are not only full retentionist countries. They are also parties to the Rome Statute of the International Criminal Court. These countries cannot continue to ignore that, in ratifying the Rome Statute, they joined the community of states that excluded the death penalty for the most dreadful crimes before the world's highest court in criminal matters. The African Commission on Human and Peoples' Rights has already called on African retentionist states that have ratified the Rome Statute to observe its Article 77, which provides for a maximum penalty of life imprisonment for crimes within the court's jurisdiction, rather than relying on its Article 80 which is interpreted as giving the go-ahead to the death penalty. Ghana, Kenya, Swaziland, Lesotho and Zimbabwe are among the *de facto* abolitionist states that are on the right path towards legal abolition. Eloquent lessons from this book go beyond the countries studied and constitute the basis for abolition of the death penalty in other African countries and beyond.

Dr. Aimé Muyoboke Karimunda
Justice, Supreme Court of Rwanda
Guest Senior Lecturer, University of Rwanda
Kigali, Rwanda

ACKNOWLEDGEMENTS

This book would not have been possible without collaboration and assistance from colleagues across four continents. I offer my most sincere thanks to David Johnson and Daniel Pascoe for comments on the opening chapter and to Timothy Bryant for comments on the Kenya chapter. Kuda Hove at Veritas Zimbabwe and the staff at the Death Penalty Project in London, including Annette So, Parvais Jabbar, and Saul Lehrfreund, offered documents and analysis that shaped my discussions of the pending constitutional litigation in the Kenya and Zimbabwe chapters. Joseph Middleton at Doughty Street Chambers provided inestimable assistance for the Ghana, Kenya, Uganda, and Zimbabwe chapters. The Ditshwanelo Botswana Centre for Human Rights, where I interned in the summer of 2007, was a critical source of information for the Botswana chapter. On the Gambia chapter, I would like to thank François Patuel and Sabrina Mahtani at Amnesty International's West Africa office, Jim Wormington at Human Rights Watch, and Jeffrey Smith, formerly of the Robert F. Kennedy Center for Justice and Human Rights. On these and other projects, I would also like to thank Sanaz Alasti, Lill Scherdin, Roger Hood, Sarah Lucy Cooper, Carolyn Hoyle, Sandra Babcock, Jesse Fecker, Jay Michaelson, and the staff at Intersentia. During the 2016 academic year, I did a Ph.D. by publication at Middlesex University London School of Law. I appreciate the assistance of my advisors Nadia Bernaz, William Schabas, and Alice Donald in helping me conceive a broader social and political context for my writings on the death penalty, including in Sub-Saharan Africa.

Thanks to several students in my Law and Justice Around the World class in Spring 2016 who helped me review the final proofs: Aysha Babar, Joseph Boehnlein, Angela Castaneda, Anudari Chuluundavaa, Ursula Delgadillo, Caroline Earhardt, Alexa Gohl, Won Lee, Catherine Rochon, Troy Serafin, Aleeza Stone, Christine Su, Kyle Tusing, and Jongbum Weon. Finally, I would very much like to thank Hon. Aimé Karimunda of the Supreme Court of Rwanda, not only for writing the foreword to this volume but for his detailed comments on each chapter.

CONTENTS

LIST OF ABBREVIATIONS

ACHPR	African Commission on Human and Peoples' Rights
AFPRC	Armed Forces Provisional Ruling Council (The Gambia)
CSAG	Civil Society Associations Gambia
ECHR	European Convention on Human Rights
ECOWAS	Economic Community of West African States
FLN	Front de Libération Nationale
ICCPR	International Covenant on Civil and Political Rights
KADU	Kenyan African Democratic Union
KANU	Kenyan African National Union
MDC	Movement for Democratic Change (Zimbabwe)
NARC	National Rainbow Coalition (Kenya)
NDC	National Democratic Congress (Ghana)
NGO	Non-governmental organization
NLC	National Liberation Council (Ghana)
NPP	New Patriotic Party (Ghana)
NRM	National Resistance Movement (Uganda)
PEPFAR	President's Emergency Plan for AIDS Relief (United States)
PNDC	Provision National Defence Council (Ghana)
SADC	Southern African Development Community
SERAP	Socio-Economic Rights and Accountability Project (Nigeria)
UN	United Nations
UNHRC	United Nations Human Rights Committee
ZACRO	Zimbabwe Association for Crime Prevention and Rehabilitation of Offenders
ZANU	Zimbabwe African National Union

PART I

INTRODUCTION

CHAPTER 1

AN OVERVIEW OF THE DEATH PENALTY IN SUB-SAHARAN AFRICA

1. INTRODUCTION

Sub-Saharan Africa has undergone a "remarkable transformation" in the last twenty years: the death penalty has been extinguished in law or in practice across most of the continent, a sea change from an era when authoritarian, military, and apartheid regimes extensively wielded the state power of execution.[1] With few exceptions, including a spate of recent executions in Nigeria and The Gambia and the reinstatement of the death penalty for terrorism in Chad and Cameroon, the trend across the continent has been unidirectionally toward abolition.[2] Of the 54 countries on the African continent, only ten of them, fewer than one in five, are actively retentionist, defined as a country where the death penalty is a lawful sentence and that has carried out an execution in the past ten years. An enormous swath of the continent is *de facto* abolitionist, defined as a country in which an execution has not occurred in the past ten years, including virtually all of Francophone Africa and most of the common law countries explored in this book.[3] Former colonies of Portugal have, without exception, abolished the death penalty.[4] While capital sentences across the continent number in the hundreds annually – especially where the death penalty remains mandatory upon conviction – actual executions in Sub-Saharan Africa are rare.[5]

How did a continent with such an extensive legacy of death penalty abuse transform into a vanguard of abolition? And why, in many places, does

1 Roger Hood & Carolyn Hoyle, *The Death Penalty: A Worldwide Perspective,* 89 (2015).

2 *Id.* at 95–96; *Chad Executes 10 Members of Boko Haram by Firing Squad,* The Guardian, August 29, 2015, www.theguardian.com/world/2015/aug/30/chad-executes-10-members-boko-haram-firing-squad; Ngala Killiar Chimton, *89 Boko Haram Militants Sentenced to Death in Cameroon,* CNN, March 19, 2016, http://www.cnn.com/2016/03/19/africa/cameroon-boko-haram-death-sentences.

3 For a list of African countries and their current status on the death penalty, see *infra* note 86 and accompanying text. See also Andrew Novak, *The Death Penalty in Africa: Foundations and Future Prospects,* 4 (2014).

4 *Id.* at 34–35.

5 Hood & Hoyle, *supra* note 1 at 96.

this transformation remain incomplete? In the past two decades, African governments have become more democratic, better-organized, and less economically predatory, and they possess greater capacity to respond to serious challenges, including crime. The African state may still be weak, but it no longer seems to be in crisis as it was during the 1980s when organizational failures, deep ethnic divisions, and regime fragility contributed to high rates of state executions. The death penalty in Africa south of the Sahara has never been closer to abolition precisely because of the recent success of the postcolonial African state. The erratic and political use of the death penalty is a sign of state weakness, not state strength. Improving institutional capacity of many governments does not necessarily translate into more reliable capital sentencing. Forensics and police investigations remain weak; legal aid is chronically under-resourced; and language barriers hinder due process in criminal proceedings. These realities, coupled with pressure from an increasingly global human rights movement, have contributed to the erosion, if uneven, of capital punishment across the continent.[6]

2. THE HISTORY OF THE DEATH PENALTY IN SUB-SAHARAN AFRICA

2.1. THE PRECOLONIAL PERIOD

Discerning the nature of and extent to which capital punishment was enforced by African societies prior to the colonial era is fraught with difficulty. First, scholars disagree about the nature of customary, traditional, or indigenous law – even these words themselves are subject to slippery and overlapping definitions (as is the phrase "native law and custom," frequently used by British colonial officials). Does customary law represent a primitive or "early stage" of legal development compared to European law or does it comprise a comprehensive and coherent body of law with its own values and theoretical underpinnings?[7] Second, observers have long disagreed about the extent to which precolonial legal traditions are inauthentic or invented, especially as much of the body of local law and custom was codified, preserved, and filtered by and through colonial

---

6 This book explores case studies in Sub-Saharan Africa, a continent that generally shares a unique history of human bondage, colonial domination, economic underdevelopment, and persistent political instability. In this region, the modern death penalty is largely based on European law, a holdover of the colonial period, and it is for this reason that the death penalty as applied according to Islamic religious principles and in Islamic-majority countries in North Africa and the Horn is generally outside the scope of this study.

7 L. Amede Obiora, *Reconsidering African Customary Law*, 17 Legal Stud. F. 217, 217 (1993) (describing differences among evolutionist, functionalist, and historicist approaches).

legal orders.[8] Is traditional African law actually traditional or is it a modern (re)invention dressed up to look old? This book does not attempt to resolve these debates, but the answers to these questions determine the authoritativeness of precolonial accounts of capital punishment.

Yet, precolonial attitudes toward and practices of capital punishment are relevant in the modern era because they are frequently cited in the modern death penalty debate, both by supporters of capital punishment and by opponents. Karimunda refers to the "cultural argument" as one of the barriers to abolition in Africa, namely that "the death penalty is rooted in African culture."[9] On this theory, abolishing the death penalty would mean abolishing part of local traditions, social customs, or religious beliefs. Abolition is "perceived as an attempt by former colonial powers to impose their views on independent countries," something that is un-African.[10] Undoubtedly, at least some societies practiced capital punishment in the precolonial era, as evidenced by writings of early European visitors, anthropologists and ethnologists writing during the colonial period, and later independent African governments in a search for tradition. Elias writes that death was the normal penalty for unlawful homicide more often than not, though it was often commuted to compensation when the circumstances of the murder did not vitally disturb the social equilibrium of the community.[11]

Nonetheless, something seems different between capital punishment as it existed in the precolonial era and as it developed after the onset of European colonialism. Chenwi indicates that the death penalty was an exceptional punishment in the precolonial period rather than an institutionalized one. Even if the death penalty existed prior to colonial rule, the death penalty as practiced today is not in the African tradition or practiced as it was in the precolonial period.[12] Karimunda concludes that it is "inaccurate to accuse the coloniser of introducing the death penalty to Africans," and perhaps more accurate to state that the colonial power "only legalised and extended an existing practice and introduced new methods of execution."[13] One major difference between indigenous African law and the law that was imposed during the colonial era is that indigenous law was historically unwritten and passed by traditions that

---

8 Brett R. Shadle, *"Changing Traditions To Meet Current Altering Conditions": Customary Law, African Courts, and the Rejection of Codification in Kenya, 1930–60*, 40 J. Afr. Hist. 411, 412–13 (1999) (describing criticisms of codification of customary law as inauthentic and "crystallizing" or "freezing" customary law to the disadvantage of women, children, and unmarried men).

9 Aimé Muyoboke Karimunda, *The Death Penalty in Africa: The Path Towards Abolition*, 3 (2014).

10 *Id.* at 2–3.

11 T. Olawale Elias, *The Nature of African Customary Law*, 124 (1956).

12 Lilian Chenwi, *Towards the Abolition of the Death Penalty in Africa: A Human Rights Perspective*, 18–20 (2007).

13 Karimunda, *supra* note 9 at 16.

were oral in nature, widely known but sometimes controlled by a specialized class of persons with expertise in judicial functions.[14] The laws of many ethnic groups were later reduced to writing by colonial and government officials as restatements, attracting criticism from some ethnologists and anthropologists that "codification" of these laws froze growth or preserved obsolescent legal concepts and institutions.[15] The reduction of law into writing satisfied a practical need for certainty and uniformity, but led to harmonization of diverse indigenous customs.[16]

In addition to considering whether African customary law actually constitutes "law" or authentically replicates "tradition," we might also wonder the extent to which it really is "African." Schiller writes that law based on oral tradition was not unique to Sub-Saharan Africa, but the emphasis on community harmony, settlement, and the role of the spiritual realm was unique.[17] Elias cautions against characterization of African customary law as "preoccupied with the maintenance of the social equilibrium of the community" and aiming at "restitution, not retribution."[18] He also casts doubt on the generalizations that customary law was restricted to "insiders" and was communal rather than individual, as this overstates differences between African and European law. Mengah-Brown makes a similar point with respect to the supposed "informality" of African justice proceedings and an emphasis on negotiation or mediation; true to some degree, but not necessarily different from English or European law.[19] Precolonial law had a punitive side as well as a compensatory side, and this dual nature is consistent with the maintenance or restoration of social equilibrium. The "collective" nature of African law and the emphasis on restoration to the *status quo ante* were truer of societies with a simpler or less hierarchical social organization than of societies where the clan's independence had given way to a more centralized and complex political organization.[20] In more centralized societies, as in Europe, systems of punishment were more regular and more individualized.[21] Because the overwhelming majority of homicides

---

14 A. Kodwo Mengah-Brown, *Introduction to Law in Contemporary Africa*, 23 (1976).

15 *Id.* at 25.

16 *Id.* As Ellis and ter Haar write, tradition was transmitted through religious belief and practice and depended on a perception that the spirit world had a known order. Even societies without regular codes of law could have a pervasive sense of justice and public order, and were able to reproduce over time. Stephen Ellis & Gertrude ter Haar, *Worlds of Power: Religious Thought and Political Practice in Africa*, 146 (2004).

17 A. Arthur Schiller, *Law*, in *The African World: A Survey of Social Research*, 166, 167 (Robert A. Lystad ed., 1965).

18 Elias, *supra* note 11 at 130.

19 Mengah-Brown, *supra* note 14 at 30.

20 Elias, *supra* note 11 at 130–32.

21 This only indirectly supports the point, but a centralized or hierarchical society appears to have been more likely to impose capital punishment than a stateless or non-hierarchical society. In comparing punishments for adultery among many different societies, Yehudi Cohen has documented that most centralized states punished adultery with death, while

were not premeditated, perhaps the result of drunken brawls, the emphasis on compensation to the victim's relatives rather than execution makes sense; by contrast, capital punishment would likely have been an expected punishment for the comparatively infrequent episodes of wanton homicide committed for revenge, gain, or sadism, not unlike European law.[22]

Even if not a universal norm, restoring community harmony after homicide or another serious offense was critical to African justice systems. This could include compensation from the offender to the victim, retaliatory killing or cattle raiding, or a sacrifice to the spirit world as part of the restorative process. Among the Tiv people of Nigeria and Cameroon, homicide could trigger warfare if the perpetrator and the victim were of separate lineages; to prevent this, enslavement or enforced suicide of the perpetrator could prevent war.[23] In precolonial Malawi, the Chewa people paid compensation in the form of *nkuku* (admission of guilt) and *lipo* (damages), though death by spear thrust, burning, drowning, or impalement was reserved for exceptional cases when the compensation was not paid.[24] Although Islam imposed some uniformity on the use of capital punishment in North and East Africa, *Shari'a* law was received differently in different regions, where it mixed with local customary law traditions. This could include compensation to the victim's family in the form of *diyya*, especially in the Maliki school of jurisprudence that predominated in North Africa.[25]

Undoubtedly the compensation process was intricately related to beliefs about the spirit world. Among the Jagbe peoples of Nigeria, certain offenses were seen as "crimes against the ancestors, which could provoke ancestral wrath," such as disease or natural disasters.[26] Evans-Pritchard described a ritual among the Nuer peoples of South Sudan in which a person guilty of homicide enlisted a priest to perform an animal sacrifice, which calmed the spirit of the dead man, brought the perpetrator back into the community, and prevented a retaliatory killing.[27] In Tarok society in central Nigeria, elders could order hefty compensation in the amount of rams, guinea corn, and brewed beer to the victim's family, as well as an offering and forgiveness ritual to ancestral spirits.[28] In other societies, transfer of a man or woman from the lineage group to the family of the deceased could restore harmony. Among the Bakossi of Cameroon, an offender's family had to replace a person killed by offering a girl child to the family of the deceased; she

---

very few stateless societies did. Yehudi A. Cohen, *Ends and Means in Political Control: State Organization and the Punishment of Adultery, Incest, and Violation of Celibacy*, 71 Amer. Anthropologist 658, 663 (1969).

22 Elias, *supra* note 11 at 142–43.

23 Paul Bohannan, *Justice and Judgment Among the Tiv*, 148 (1989).

24 Stacey Hynd, *Law, Violence, and Penal Reform: State Responses to Crime and Disorder in Colonial Malawi, c. 1900–1959*, 47 J. Southern Afr. Stud. 431, 431 (2011).

25 Karimunda, *supra* note 9 at 74–75.

26 Suleiman A. Quadri, *Jagbe People: Origin and Culture*, 115 (1998).

27 E.E. Evans-Pritchard, *Nuer Religion* 293–97 (1977).

28 Wilson Venbong Famwang, *The Tarok Culture*, 28–29 (c. 1998).

could never divorce the person to whom she was married in order to restore the economic loss caused to the victim's lineage. The transfer of a girl accompanied an elaborate compensation and cleansing ritual, which could be performed multiple times through an offender's life and even by his or her offspring after death.[29]

Methods of execution were also closely related to notions of death, burial, and afterlife. The kings of Dahomey "owned" the heads of their subjects and therefore performed executions by decapitation.[30] Among the Mossi people of Burkina Faso, members of the royal family were executed by strangulation, as royal blood could not be shed, while ordinary criminals were executed by sword, hanging, or beating with clubs.[31] For adultery, the Tumbuka of Malawi would carry out the slow burning of offenders in order to prevent pestilence or drought wrought by ancestral spirits.[32] In some societies, trial by ordeal was known.[33] The death penalty could also be carried out according to whichever method used by the murderer to carry out the homicide, according to some customary practices.[34]

The use or nonuse of capital punishment prior to the onset of European colonialism has been cited as a reason for abolition or retention of the death penalty in the modern period. Justice Albie Sachs of the South African Constitutional Court explained that "the relatively well-developed judicial processes of indigenous societies did not in general encompass capital punishment for murder," noting that societies such as those of the Nguni, Sotho, and Zulu only rarely executed criminals.[35] In his opinion in *Makwanyane*, which found capital punishment unconstitutional in South Africa, Sachs rejected the argument that death penalty abolition was a Eurocentric position, citing scholarship that distinguished modern capital punishment from the precolonial: "Such executions as took place in precolonial times were the frenzied, extra-judicial killings of supposed witches, a spontaneous and irrational form of crowd behavior that has unfortunately continued to this day in the form of necklacing and witch-burning."[36] The argument that the death penalty should be abolished because it is purely a construction of European colonialism is at risk of being

29 S.N. Ejedepang-Koge, *The Tradition of a People: Bakossi, A Historico-Socio-Anthropological Study of One of Cameroon's Bantu Peoples*, 231–32 (1986).

30 Robin Law, *"My Head Belongs to the King": On the Political and Ritual Significance of Decapitation in Pre-Colonial Dahomey*, 30 J. Afr. Hist. 399, 415 (1989).

31 Elliott P. Skinner: *The Mossi of the Upper Volta: The Political Development of a Sudanese People*, 41 (1964).

32 Desmond Dudwa Phiri, *History of the Tumbuka*, 51–52 (2000).

33 Yizenge A. Chondoka & Frackson Fwila Bota, *A History of the Tumbuka from 1400 to 1900*, 113–14 (2007).

34 O. Fatula, *Capital Punishment: To Be or Not To Be in Nigeria*, 14 Lesotho L.J. 97 (2001).

35 State v. Makwanyane, 1995 (3) S.A. 391 (C.C.) at ¶ 381 (Sachs, J., concurring).

36 *Id.*; *see also* William A. Schabas, *African Perspectives on Abolition of the Death Penalty*, in *The International Sourcebook on Capital Punishment*, 30, 33–34 (William A. Schabas ed., 1997).

ahistorical. After all, imprisonment was a much starker European import than capital punishment.[37]

Nonetheless, appeals to the precolonial period continue to shape the modern death penalty debate. In January 2016, an organization of traditional chiefs called for abolition of the death penalty in Zimbabwe, arguing that their ancestors never engaged in the "cruel and inhumane practice."[38] Ali Mazrui condemned public executions as simply "a perversion of the African principle of shame," whereby a culprit would traditionally be punished in front of the victim's relatives and his or her own extended family. The strategy of televising an execution for an impersonal public, as used by Nigerian military dictator Muhammedu Buhari, for instance, constituted only "a desperate bid to control rising lawlessness" and was not an extension of the traditional role of shame or ostracism.[39] As Roger Hood and Carolyn Hoyle explain, supporters have claimed that the death penalty was rooted in "customs and culture" that assume that the death penalty is the only fitting punishment for crimes such as murder.[40] According to the Botswana Court of Appeal, the people of Botswana promulgated a penal code through their elected representatives that prescribed the death penalty for murder, noting that "the death penalty has been imposed in Botswana since time immemorial, so that its abolition would be a departure from the established norm."[41]

2.2. THE COLONIAL PERIOD

Although the death penalty existed in many places prior to the onset of colonialism, modern capital punishment is overwhelmingly a colonial construction. The death penalty was used as a tool of colonial statecraft. In French Africa, executions were a dramatic show of power by the state, used to suppress a Tuareg revolt in northern Niger in 1917 and to enlist obedience from subjects in southern Gabon in the 1930s.[42] The extensive use of capital punishment in French Algeria created a cycle of revenge violence with the Front de Libération Nationale (FLN), and the high rate of executions – more than 100 per year – aroused the opposition of French intellectuals such as Nobel Literature

37 J. Read, *Kenya, Tanzania, and Uganda*, in *African Penal Systems*, 103 (Alan Milner ed., 1969).

38 Anna Chibamu, *Zimbabwe: Traditional Leaders Call for Abolition of Death Penalty*, NewZimbabwe.com, January 19, 2016 (retrieved from AllAfrica.com).

39 Ali Mazrui, *Is Africa Decaying? The View from Uganda*, in *Uganda Now: Between Decay and Development*, 336, 344 (Holger Bernt Hansen & Michael Twaddle eds., 1988).

40 Hood & Hoyle, *supra* note 1 at 98.

41 Kgafela (In re: Gabaokelwe) v. Attorney General, Crim. App. No. CLCGB-027–12 (April 27, 2012).

42 Douglas Livermore, *The Case for Azawad*, 22 Afr. Security Rev. 282, 285 (2013); Florence Bernault, *Body, Power and Sacrifice in Equatorial Africa*, 47 J. Afr. Hist. 207, 218 (2006).

Prize laureates Albert Camus and Jean-Paul Sartre.[43] Belgium allowed public executions in the Belgian Congo long after abolition in the metropolitan power. In 1922, for instance, an African man was tortured and hanged by colonial authorities before a crowd of 1,000 Europeans and 3,000 Africans.[44] By contrast, Portugal tended not to use capital punishment for ordinary crimes in its colonies; Portugal only used capital punishment intermittently since the Middle Ages and abolished it in 1849, except for military crimes during World War One.[45] This did not mean criminal justice was more enlightened in Portuguese colonies: the ruinous consequences of using its African and Indian holdings as penal colonies dragged on the Portuguese economy for decades until Antonio de Salazar ended the practice of convict labor in 1932.[46]

In former British colonies, English law was first introduced mainly for the benefit of British subjects and indigenous communities in the immediate vicinity. The British policy of "indirect rule" left much of the precolonial legal structure intact, though the colonial power typically imposed limitations on criminal jurisdiction and punishments.[47] This differed from French "direct rule," where "the body of laws applicable in French colonies in Africa emanated from the metropolis" and French criminal law "largely contained nothing adapted to the local environment."[48] Gradually, British colonial courts increased control over indigenous law and even established a "native court" system within the colonial legal system to replace customary courts. The result was the conscious elevation of colonial English law above indigenous African law.[49] Customary law was recognized by the colonial state insofar as it was not "repugnant" to natural justice, equity, and good conscience, or inconsistent with written law. Nonetheless, in the realm of the criminal customary practice was sharply curtailed: English practice prevailed in the definitions of crimes, procedures for criminal trials, and purposes of sentencing and punishment.[50] By 1935 nearly identical codes of criminal law applied to most of British colonial Africa. "These codes, which remain largely unreformed even today, were closely based on nineteenth-century English law and make few concessions to their African context."[51]

---

43 James D. Le Sueur, *Uncivil War: Intellections and Identity Politics during the Decolonization of Algeria*, 116–23 (2005); John-Paul Sartre, *Colonialism and Neo-Colonialism*, 62 (2001).

44 Stephen Peté, *A Brief History of Human Rights in the Prisons of Africa*, in *Human Rights in African Prisons*, 40, 50 (Jeremy Sarkin ed., 2008).

45 Hood & Hoyle, *supra* note 1 at 49.

46 Timothy J. Coates, *Convict Labor in the Portuguese Empire, 1740–1932*, 28 (2014); Gerald J. Bender, *Angola Under the Portuguese: The Myth and the Reality*, 74–92 (1978).

47 Mengah-Brown, *supra* note 14 at 36–37.

48 Karimunda, *supra* note 9 at 112.

49 Mengah-Brown, *supra* note 14 at 37.

50 Simon Coldham, *Criminal Justice in Commonwealth Africa: Trends and Prospects*, 44 J. Afr. L. 218, 219–20 (2000).

51 John Hatchard & Simon Coldham, *Commonwealth Africa*, in *Capital Punishment: Global Issues and Prospects*, 155, 156 (Peter Hodgkinson & Andrew Rutherford eds., 1996).

In most British colonies, the death penalty was mandatory for murder, treason, and sometimes piracy and rape, though these offenses were modified to include security and political offenses in colonies with large numbers of white settlers such as Kenya and Rhodesia.[52] Hynd states that executions were "stark enactments of colonial power intended to reinforce local order and the authority of colonial states in British Africa," though the principle extends to other colonial powers.[53] An accused was likely to face a bewildering formal justice process without defense counsel in colonial Nyasaland. The governor's prerogative of mercy on the advice of the executive council was the only recourse to avoid the gallows.[54] The colonial governor had the responsibility to confirm a capital sentence or grant a reprieve, and clemency was exercised fairly frequently.[55] In French Africa, by contrast, the death penalty was not mandatory, allowing judges to consider mitigating circumstances as early as 1832; the death penalty remained a valid punishment for ordinary crimes with aggravating factors. However, as in British Africa, separate recourse to an indigenous court system for the majority of African colonial subjects allowed imposition of criminal punishments (though not the death penalty) without the safeguards of French law.[56]

Apartheid South Africa had a much more robust tradition of capital punishment during the colonial period than most other colonies. From the creation of the Union of South Africa in 1910 until a moratorium on executions in 1990, about 4,200 people were hanged in South Africa.[57] Although the country adopted the doctrine of extenuating circumstances in 1935, allowing judges to substitute a lesser sentence depending on the circumstances of the offense, capital punishment took on the racial and gendered characteristics of the apartheid state.[58] Judicial discretion resulted in wide sentencing disparities, and defendants were denied the automatic right of appeal and frequently had no legal representation.[59] By the 1980s, South Africa's capital punishment industry was in crisis as death sentences mounted as did the length of time on death

---

52 *Id.* at 157.

53 Stacey Hynd, *Killing the Condemned: The Practice and Process of Capital Punishment in British Africa, 1900–1950s*, 49 J. Afr. Hist. 403, 403 (2008).

54 Stacey Hynd, *"The Extreme Penalty of the Law": Mercy and the Death Penalty as Aspects of State Power in Colonial Nyasaland, c. 1903–47*, 4 J. East Afr. Stud. 542, 544–45 (2010).

55 Hatchard & Coldham, *supra* note 51 at 157.

56 Karimunda, *supra* note 9 at 112–18.

57 Novak, *supra* note 3 at 31.

58 Robert Turrell, *White Mercy: A Study of the Death Penalty in South Africa*, 236–37 (2004); Criminal Procedure and Evidence (Amendment) Act 46 of 1935 §61.

59 T.P. McNally, *Capital Punishment: An Orange Free State Perspective*, 2 S. Afr. J. Crim. Just. 239, 249 (1989); Christina Murray, Julia Sloth-Nielsen & Colin Tredoux, *The Death Penalty in the Cape Provincial Division: 1986–1988*, 5 S. Afr. J. Hum. Rts. 154, 159 (1989); Laurel Angus & Evadné Grant, *Sentencing in Capital Cases in the Transvaal Provincial Division and Witwatersrand Local Division: 1987–1989*, 7 S. Afr. J. Hum. Rts. 50, 51 (1991).

row.[60] In 1990, President F.W. de Klerk announced a moratorium on executions, a concession to Nelson Mandela and the African National Congress. Later that year, parliament launched a sweeping reform of the death penalty, including the abolition of the doctrine of extenuating circumstances in favor of a pure discretionary sentencing regime and the institution of automatic rights of appeal and review.[61] Abolition of the death penalty altogether in 1995 accompanied South Africa's transition to democratic rule.

2.3. THE INDEPENDENCE PERIOD

The colonial era ended rapidly and dramatically by the 1960s, and ambitious new governments took the reins of power for the first time. Virtually everywhere, the new governments inherited a colonial-influenced constitutional and legal order without interruption. Former British colonies adopted meticulously-drafted constitutions at independence that generally replicated British parliamentary democracy and even maintained the Queen as the head of state for a period.[62] In French-speaking Africa, the Constitution of the Fifth Republic served as a model for independence constitutions that were approved in popular referenda.[63] Public input into this process was minimal, but new nationalist elites such as Jomo Kenyatta in Kenya, Ahmadou Ahidjo in Cameroon, and Kenneth Kaunda in Zambia played critical roles in determining the structure of the head of state, the scope of executive power, and the content of the Bill of Rights.[64]

One thing that did not change at independence was the structure of the criminal law regime. Despite emphasis on African values and traditions, newly-independent governments made few real attempts to amend penal codes in line with such values or with criminological advances from elsewhere in the world, reflecting a "marked continuity with the colonial period."[65] As emerging African democracies drifted toward one-party or military rule by the end of the 1960s, the death penalty emerged as a tool of state repression. Judicial independence declined as inter-party competition reduced incentives to check powerful executives. The judiciary suffered from a lack of resources, corruption, and political manipulation, with severe consequences for the criminal justice

60 Janos Mihalik, *The Death Penalty in Bophuthatswana: A New Deal for Condemned Prisoners?*, 107 S. Afr. L.J. 465, 473–75 (1990); McNally, *supra* note 59 at 247.

61 Criminal Procedure Amendment Act 107 of 1990, §§19–20, E. Grant & L. Angus, *Capital Punishment*, 2 S. Afr. Hum. Rts. Y.B. 1, 2–8 (1991).

62 William Dale, *The Making and Remaking of Commonwealth Constitutions*, 42 Int'l & Comp. L.Q. 67, 67–70 (1993).

63 John Mukum Mbaku, *Effective Constitutional Discourse as an Important First Step to Democratization in Africa*, 31 J. Asian & Afr. Stud. 39, 43–44 (1996).

64 John Hatchard, Muna Ndulo & Peter Slinn, *Comparative Constitutionalism and Good Governance in the Commonwealth*, 18–19 (2004).

65 Hatchard & Coldham, *supra* note 51 at 157.

system and individual fundamental rights.[66] In Nigeria, the death penalty could be imposed by special tribunals at both the federal and state levels to try armed robbery and economic offenses under summary procedures, often by judges without legal training and without review by a higher court.[67]

The United States and the Soviet Union propped up client regimes with foreign and defense aid, fighting a global bipolar war by proxy. In Zaire, a client state of the United States, military officers under strongman Mobutu Sese Seko were agents of gratuitous violence, including torture and extrajudicial killings. Mobutu carried out state executions against persons perceived as orchestrating anti-regime activity.[68] President Siad Barre of Somalia introduced the death penalty for homicide, replacing the customary practice of reconciliation. He turned the threat of state executions on political opponents, including of eleven Islamic leaders who opposed modernization reforms, even though the death penalty was prohibited by the national constitution.[69] The death penalty even became a tool of racial or ethnic repression. In the Rwandan revolution of 1959, on the eve of independence from Belgium, the Hutu government executed prominent members of the Tutsi elite who were accused of having "a guilty relationship with the enemy" as part of a broader ethnic cleansing campaign that led to 2,000 murders that year and 20,000 extrajudicial killings of Tutsi by 1973.[70]

Political prosecutions were especially prolific in countries that had a long history of instability. In Sierra Leone, the first executions after independence took place in 1971 when four soldiers were executed for treason; fifteen more hangings occurred in 1975. In 1989, President Joseph Momoh had the vice president and eleven others executed for high treason. With his overthrow in 1992, another round of summary executions occurred.[71] In Liberia, Samuel Doe killed President William Tolbert and publicly executed twelve members of his government upon taking power in 1980. In 1990, Doe himself was video recorded as he was tortured and executed by rebel faction leader Prince Johnson.[72] In Equatorial Guinea, murderous dictator Macías Nguema jailed, executed, tortured, or exiled his opponents, their families, and sometimes their

66 Jennifer Widner, *Building the Rule of Law: Francis Nyalali and the Road to Judicial Independence in Africa*, 100 (2001).

67 Fatula, *supra* note 34 at 102–03.

68 Michael G. Schatzberg, *The Dialectics of Oppression in Zaire*, 58 (1991).

69 Florence Ssereo, *Clanpolitics, Clan Democracy, and Conflict Regulation in Africa: The Experience of Somalia*, 2 Global Rev. Ethnopolitics 25, 36–37 (2003).

70 Aimé Muyoboke Karimunda, *The Death Penalty in Rwanda: Surrounding Politics and the ICTR's Battle for Abolition*, in *The Politics of the Death Penalty in Countries in Transition*, 128, 132–33 (Madoka Futamura & Nadia Bernaz eds., 2014).

71 Mohamed Suma, *The Politics of the Death Penalty in Post-Conflict Sierra Leone: An Opportunity for Reform or a Missed Opportunity?*, in *The Politics of the Death Penalty in Countries in Transition*, 163–65 (Madoka Futamura & Nadia Bernaz eds., 2014).

72 David Harris, *From "Warlord" to "Democratic" President: How Charles Taylor Won the 1997 Elections*, 37 J. Mod. Afr. Stud. 431, 433–34 (1999).

entire villages. By 1974 more than two-thirds the members of parliament had been executed or missing, as were a host of other government diplomats and officials. Nguema himself was executed after toppling in a coup in 1979.[73]

The oil crisis of 1973 forced authoritarian governments to borrow heavily and incur substantial amounts of external debt. This in turn led African governments to seek financial assistance from the World Bank, International Monetary Fund, and Western governments, that came with strings attached, including economic liberalization and reduction in the size of the state.[74] Resource constraints led to erosion in police, judicial, and correctional capacity, including prison overcrowding and maltreatment.[75] The economic crisis increased crime rates, including violent crimes such as armed robbery and economic crimes such as embezzlement or corruption, as well as drug trafficking. Governments responded harshly. In Nigeria, the death penalty was implemented for sabotage of oil extraction facilities and drug trafficking.[76] Armed robbery became a capital offense in Nigeria due to a spate of attacks in the 1980s.[77] Guinea added the death penalty for theft in 1976 to stem an increase in looting state resources.[78] As rulers surrendered sovereignty to international financial institutions, they became possessive of their remaining state powers. In Nigeria, Major-General Muhammadu Buhari authorized detention without trial, prohibited all political activities, and punished even common crimes with death in order to compensate for the erosion of state capacity.[79]

---

73 Randall Fegley, *The U.N. Human Rights Commission: The Equatorial Guinea Case*, 3 Hum. Rts. Q. 37–38, 40–41 (1981).

74 Yusuf Bangura & Peter Gibbon, *Adjustment, Authoritarianism and Democracy in Sub-Saharan Africa*, in *Authoritarianism, Democracy and Adjustment: The Politics of Economic Reform in Africa*, 7, 11–14 (Peter Gibbon, Yusuf Bangura & Arve M. Ofstad eds., 1992).

75 Yash Vyas, *Alternatives to Imprisonment in Kenya*, 6 Crim. L.F. 76, 80 (1995).

76 Silvia Federici, *The Debt Crisis, Africa, and the New Enclosures*, Midnight Notes 10, 16 (1990); Anita Kalunta-Crumpton, *Drugs, Victims and Race: The Politics of Drug Control*, 123 (2006).

77 Oluyemisi Bamgbose, *Towards the Global Abolition of the Death Penalty: Comparing the Criminal Laws in the United States of America and Nigeria*, 13 E. Afr. J. Peace & Hum. Rts. 30, 37 (2007).

78 Victor Azarya & Naomi Chazan, *Disengagement from the State in Africa: Reflections on the Experience of Ghana and Guinea*, 29 Comp. Stud. Soc. & Hist. 106, 123–24 (1987).

79 Yusuf Bangura, *Structural Adjustment and the Political Question*, 37 Rev. Afr. Pol. Econ. 24, 30 (1986). The focus of this book is on judicial executions, not extrajudicial state killing, even though the numbers of persons killed due to extrajudicial violence far exceed those put to death lawfully. However, as the Nigerian example shows, the boundary between judicial and extrajudicial executions is not clearly defined: is a situation in which a person is executed for a crime without due process safeguards a judicial or extrajudicial execution? Judicial executions presumably require the existence of a state, but what relevance is this where the state has collapsed or the government is itself illegal or criminalized? Prior to the imposition of the nation-state on Sub-Saharan Africa, were all executions "extrajudicial" even if political authority was legitimate? These questions are outside the scope of this book, but studying the death penalty in Sub-Saharan Africa adds new dimensions to global research on state killing.

2.4. THE DEMOCRATIC ERA

By the early 1990s, the African continent experienced a thaw: regimes changed, constitutional orders were renegotiated, and market-oriented economies opened. The continent-wide democratic transition occurred because of a combination of external and internal factors. The end of the Cold War and the advancement of good governance agendas by Western governments and NGOs no doubt played some role, as did opposition to human rights abuses by local religious groups, protests by trade unions and civilians, and advocacy by the learned professions.[80] Once powerful leaders such as Hastings Banda in Malawi, Kenneth Kaunda in Zambia, Hissène Habré in Chad, André Kolingba in Central African Republic, and Mengistu Haile Mariam in Ethiopia, among others, were overthrown, left office, or were defeated at the polls. Not all was progress: the institutional capacity of some states, such as Liberia, Sierra Leone, Somalia, and Zaire, eroded and collapsed, while protracted civil wars and mass violence engendered enormous refugee crises in countries like Angola and Rwanda. But, by and large, the 1990s brought conditions for change unmatched since independence. "The era of one-partyism, statistically implausible electoral margins of victory, and unaccountable life presidents is over for now," one scholar optimistically wrote as the decade closed.[81]

With constitutional change came new prospects for renegotiating capital punishment, either in the text of the new constitution itself, as in Namibia, or in human rights litigation. In 1995, the Constitutional Court of South Africa unanimously found the death penalty unconstitutional, holding that judicial executions violated the right to life and human dignity and the freedom from cruel, inhuman, or degrading punishment.[82] The decision was notable for its searching analysis of comparative jurisprudence from Canada, India, the United States, and the European Court of Human Rights, among others. According to Chief Justice Arthur Chaskalson, the death penalty was inherently arbitrary given the small fraction of prisoners sentenced to death and the even smaller number executed, a lottery without rationalization.[83] William Schabas called the *Makwanyane* judgment in South Africa "a marvelous and eloquent decision that will serve as a precedent for courts throughout the world."[84]

---

80 John Mukum Mbaku, *Constitutionalism and the Transition to Democratic Governance in Africa*, in *The Transition to Democratic Governance in Africa: The Continuing Struggle*, 113–116 (John Mukum Mbaku & Julius Omozuanvbo Ihonvbere eds., 2003).

81 Jean-Germain Gros, *Introduction: Understanding Democratization*, in *Democratization in Late Twentieth Century Africa: Coping with Uncertainty*, 1, 18–19 (Jean-Germain Gros ed., 1998).

82 State v. Makwanyane, 1995 (3) S.A. 391 (C.C.).

83 *Id.* at 418–19.

84 William A. Schabas, *African Perspectives on Abolition of the Death Penalty*, in *The International Sourcebook on Capital Punishment: 1997 Edition*, 30, 30 (William A. Schabas ed., 1997).

Only six months after the promising decision of the South African Constitutional Court, the execution of environmental and minority rights activist Ken Saro-Wiwa and his colleagues led to the isolation of the Sani Abacha military regime, the suspension of Nigeria from the Commonwealth, and eventually Nigeria's return to civilian rule. Saro-Wiwa, a prominent author and poet, was president of the Movement for the Survival of the Ogoni People, which protested the degradation of the Niger Delta region by Royal Dutch Shell Petroleum and other oil companies.[85] Saro-Wiwa and the other Ogoni activists were tried for suspected involvement in civil disturbances that led to the deaths of four local leaders, without appeal to an impartial judicial tribunal. The resulting death sentences were quickly confirmed by the military leadership and the executions were carried out on November 10, 1995.[86] Upon taking office after Nigeria's return to civilian rule, President Olusegun Obasanjo announced a moratorium on executions and called for abolition, though subsequent constitutional challenges to capital punishment failed.[87] Change was coming, even here.

The pace of death penalty abolition has consistently progressed.[88] At least seventeen countries on the African continent have abolished capital punishment altogether, with the date of abolition in parentheses: Angola (1992), Benin (2012), Burundi (2009), Cape Verde (1981), Côte d'Ivoire (2000), Djibouti (1995), Gabon (2010), Guinea-Bissau (1993), Mauritius (1987), Mozambique (1990), Namibia (1990), Rwanda (2007), São Tomé e Principe (1990), Senegal (2004), Seychelles (1993), South Africa (1995), and Togo (2009). Another twenty-six have not carried out executions in the past ten years, a category to which Uganda and Zimbabwe now belong but Chad no longer does with the reinstatement of executions for terrorism in 2015 (date of last execution in parentheses): Algeria (1993), Burkina Faso (1989), Cameroon (1997), Central African Republic (1981), Comoros (1997), Republic of Congo (1982), Democratic Republic of the Congo (2003), Eritrea (1982), Ghana (1993), Guinea (2001), Kenya (1987), Liberia (2000), Lesotho (1995), Madagascar (1958), Malawi (1992), Mali (1979), Mauritania (1989), Morocco (1993), Niger (1976), Sierra Leone (1998), Swaziland (1989), Tanzania (1994), Tunisia (1981), Uganda (2006), Zambia (1997), and Zimbabwe

85 G.N.K. Vukor-Quarshie, *Criminal Justice Administration in Nigeria: Saro-Wiwa in Review*, 8 Crim. L.F. 87, 87–90 (1997).

86 Misty L. Bastian, *"Buried Beneath Six Feet of Crude Oil": State-Sponsored Death and the Absent Body of Ken Saro-Wiwa*, in *Ken Saro-Wiwa: Writer and Political Activist*, 127, 134–35 (Craig W. McLuckie & Aubrey McPhail eds., 2000). In 2009, Shell Oil settled a pending human rights lawsuit over the executions for $15 million. Ed Pilkington, *Shell Pays Out $15.5m over Saro-Wiwa Killing*, The Guardian, June 9, 2009.

87 Fatula, *supra* note 34 at 99; Bamgbose, *supra* note 77 at 38.

88 The statistics compiled in this paragraph come from a composite of sources, some of which conflict slightly. See Karimunda, *supra* note 9 at 197–98; Hood & Hoyle, *supra* note 1 at 89–98; Death Penalty Worldwide Database (retrieved at DeathPenaltyWorldwide.org).

(2005).[89] Equatorial Guinea has announced an official moratorium even though it carried out executions more recently than ten years ago. This leaves ten countries out of fifty-four that still actively retain capital punishment: Botswana, Chad (for terrorism), Egypt, Ethiopia, The Gambia, Libya, Nigeria, Somalia, South Sudan, and Sudan.

3. AFRICAN RESISTANCE, AFRICAN ACCOMMODATION

Undoubtedly, global death penalty abolition bears a strong European imprint. The new wave of death penalty abolition has its origins in the post-World War Two era, as "acceptance of international human rights principles created a climate that advocated, in the name of democracy and freedom, the protection of citizens from the power of the state and the tyranny of the opinions of the masses."[90] Abolitionist thought can be traced back to Enlightenment philosophy and the liberal utilitarian and humanistic ideas that swept through Europe at the end of the eighteenth century.[91] As part of the postwar European integration project, organizations such as the Council of Europe, the guardian of the European Convention on Human Rights, have constructed death penalty abolition as an aspect of a "European" conscience or identity.[92] Even though European abolition was comparatively recent and not without opposition, the Council of Europe and European Union have woven a narrative that death penalty abolition is an essential part of Europe's heritage and intellectual tradition. European institutions and European-based organizations such as Amnesty International, Hands Off Cain, Community of Sant'Egidio, and Ensemble contre la peine de mort have taken the abolition campaign global –

---

89 Dr. Daniel Pascoe at Hong Kong City University has made the interesting suggestion that the category of *de facto* abolition may not be analytically useful, as it combines countries that have an official or unofficial policy against carrying out executions with countries that do not have such a policy. Therefore, one cannot make assumptions about the propensity of a country to carry out executions in the future. As this book notes, The Gambia unexpectedly carried out executions in 2012, despite its status as *de facto* abolitionist; Nigeria did the same in 2013. To this end, the book's case studies could largely be divided between those countries that have an international posture that is conducive to abolition and where political elites appear unwilling to reactivate the death penalty, even if no moratorium is in place (Ghana, Zimbabwe, Kenya, Lesotho, and Swaziland), and those countries where international posture favors retention and the dominant political elites support future executions (Botswana, Uganda, and The Gambia). These analytical categories roughly correspond to Amnesty International's designation of "retentionist" and "*de facto* abolitionist," but Pascoe's broader point is well-taken.

90 Hood & Hoyle, *supra* note 1 at 22.

91 *Id.* at 49.

92 Jon Yorke, *The Evolving Human Rights Discourse of the Council of Europe: Renouncing the Sovereign Right of the Death Penalty*, in *Against the Death Penalty: International Initiatives and Implications*, 43, 65–66 (2008).

in media coverage, diplomatic pressure, and financial support – to retentionist countries in Asia, Africa, the Caribbean, and, of course, the United States.[93]

Viewing the global human rights agenda as driven by European governments and institutions is not unique to the realm of capital punishment (though the longstanding divide between Europe and the United States on the issue is certainly peculiar).[94] Considering abolition of the death penalty in the actively retentionist countries of Asia, David Johnson and Franklin Zimring ask whether the conditions for death penalty abolition in Europe might be exceptional in themselves and, derivatively, whether East Asia and Southeast Asia in particular lack those same prerequisites.[95] They note, however, that the continent of Africa is not as economically or culturally autonomous from Europe as countries such as Singapore and China – here, Europe's magnetism is stronger.[96] Roger Hood and Carolyn Hoyle explain that a number of retentionist nations, especially in the Islamic world but also including Singapore and others, have at times characterized European-driven efforts on death penalty abolition as a form of "cultural imperialism, dictating a particular set of values."[97] To the extent that the death penalty abolition movement is seen as European-driven, it will engender resistance from the Global South.

As with the Asian continent or the Islamic world, of course, Sub-Saharan Africa is not monolithic and does not hold a single view on the death penalty. African political leaders have expressed a range of views on the abolition of capital punishment and have responded to European lobbying in different ways. Among the countries studied in this book, The Gambia maintains the most obstinate retentionist stance on the death penalty, as confrontational President Yayeh Jammeh is locked in a diplomatic battle over his human rights record and increasingly authoritarian rule. Similarly, the passage in Uganda of the Anti-Homosexuality Act of 2014, explored further in Chapter 8, occurred over the near-unanimous objections of the Global North, including prominent aid donors and intergovernmental organizations. By contrast, countries such

---

93 Evi Girling, *European Identity and the Mission Against the Death Penalty in the United States*, in *The Cultural Lives of Capital Punishment: Comparative Perspectives*, 112, 114–18 (Austin Sarat & Christian Boulanger eds., 2005).

94 Martti Koskenniemi, *The Case for Comparative International Law*, 20 Finnish Y.B. Int'l L.1, 4–5 (2009). "The view that there is a single, universal international law with a homogeneous history and an institutional-political project emerges from a profoundly Eurocentric view of the world … The vocabularies of statehood, sovereignty, self-determination and human rights refer back to European thinkers and jurists, and events placed in Europe or dictated by Europeans – which is not to say that they could not resonate elsewhere, too." *Id.* at 4.

95 David T. Johnson & Franklin E. Zimring, *The Next Frontier: National Development, Political Change, and the Death Penalty in Asia*, 8–9, 11 (2009).

96 *Id.* at 12. The role of the United States of America is harder to pinpoint. While European influence on former colonies in Africa is likely stronger than American influence, the fact that the United States, a respectable industrialized democracy, still carries out executions is not lost on retentionist African governments.

97 Hood & Hoyle, *supra* note 1 at 44.

as Ghana and Kenya have accepted death penalty abolition at least in principle in public fora such as the UN General Assembly and the UN Human Rights Council's Universal Periodic Review.[98] Even within these countries, political elites are not unanimous; public opinion appears conflicted; and momentum is not unidirectional. Some countries accommodate the European-driven agenda of abolition. Equatorial Guinea, which carried out executions as recently as 2014, placed a moratorium on executions shortly after in order to join the Community of Portuguese-Speaking States due to the promise of trade and investment with Portugal, Brazil, and Angola.[99] Karimunda notes that Rwanda likely would not have abolished the death penalty without the insistence of the International Criminal Tribunal for Rwanda, which then was in the process of trying perpetrators of the 1994 genocide.[100]

Nor is resistance to European-driven death penalty abolition solely limited to Africa. Writing of Belarus, Charnysh explains how the Council of Europe's overt attempts to abolish the death penalty in Europe's last remaining holdout actually feeds into the government's narrative of resistance to European domination and has the counterproductive consequence of driving Belarus closer to Russia.[101] Abolitionist countries such as Australia, Canada, New Zealand, and most of Latin America are not strictly "European," but the dynamic of death penalty abolition as a Western-driven agenda is similar. Before carrying out executions in April 2015, Indonesian President Joko Widodo decried the meddlesome intervention of Australia, an abolitionist country that sought to rescue two of its nationals from death row. Facing domestic criticism at home, Widodo felt forced by his political circumstances to stand up to Australia by ultimately letting the executions go forward.[102] Undoubtedly, similar anti-European sentiment has even arisen from time to time in the United States over European campaigning against the death penalty.[103]

Like the death penalty, colonial-era laws that criminalize consensual sex between partners of the same gender have triggered resistance to a human rights agenda that some African leaders have perceived to be imposed by the Global North. Writing of Uganda, Kristen Cheney describes the anti-gay rhetoric of evangelical pastor Martin Ssempa, whose appeal lies in his

98 See, e.g., UN Third Committee, *Moratorium on the Use of the Death Penalty*, A/C.3/67/L.44/Rev.1 (November 19, 2012), www.un.org/en/ga/third/67/docs/voting_sheets/l.44.Rev.1.pdf.

99 CPLP Ministers Support Equatorial Guinea Membership, Agência de Informação de Moçambique, February 21, 2014 (retrieved from AllAfrica.com).

100 Karimunda, *supra* note 70 at 150–51.

101 Volha Charnysh, *Transnational Networks and Norm Compliance: Stopping Executions in Belarus*, in *Capital Punishment: New Perspectives*, 229, 243, 246–47 (Peter Hodgkinson ed., 2013).

102 Deasy Simandjuntak, *Spectacle of the Scaffold? The Politics of Death Penalty in Indonesia*, Eurasia Review, September 17, 2015, www.eurasiareview.com/17092015-spectacle-of-the-scaffold-the-politics-of-death-penalty-in-indonesia-analysis.

103 Girling, *supra* note 93 at 118–21.

assertion and independence from foreign pressure and his vehement rejection of homosexuality as a violation of Uganda's cultural traditions. Even United States President Barack Obama, otherwise popular in the region, is vilified for undermining the traditional family and Ugandan autonomy.[104] Diverse precolonial attitutes toward homosexuality notwithstanding, the colonial origins of anti-sodomy laws in common law Africa, India, and the Caribbean mirror the colonial origins of the mandatory death penalty for murder. Both were part of the uniform penal codes adopted in British Africa and retained after independence.[105] Opposition to a (perceived) European-driven human rights agenda may be local and situational, rather than comprehensive and transnational, but it is real. Death penalty abolition and repeal of anti-sodomy laws, when they occur, must occur on African terms.

4. THE AFRICAN CONTRIBUTION TO GLOBAL DEATH PENALTY JURISPRUDENCE

But abolition *is* taking place on African terms. Even if the death penalty abolition movement is perceived as having its center of gravity on the European continent, the continent of Africa is not simply a passive recipient of human rights norms. Rather, the continent is an active contributor to an emerging global body of human rights jurisprudence. Although national courts have long cited and applied international norms in their own domestic contexts, "judicial globalization" on human rights issues is "a much more diverse and messy process of judicial interaction across, above and below borders, exchanging ideas and cooperating in cases involving national as much as international law."[106] What defines this process is not just the reception of international law in domestic legal systems, but the active contribution that domestic courts make in solidifying and expanding international legal norms. Domestic courts are not "passive conduits through which fixed and immutable international law norms become part of domestic law," but rather "mediators between international and domestic legal norms" that play an active part in creating, enforcing, and shaping the international norms themselves.[107]

---

104 Kristen Cheney, *Locating Neo-Colonialism, "Tradition," and Human Rights in Uganda's "Gay Death Penalty"*, 55 Afr. Stud. Rev. 77, 82 (2012).

105 Michael Hollander, *Gay Rights in Uganda: Seeking to Overturn Uganda's Anti-Sodomy Laws*, 50 Va. J. Int'l L. 219, 225–26 (2009); Douglas E. Sanders, *377 and the Unnatural Afterlife of British Colonialism in Asia*, 4 Asian J. Comp. L. 1, 12 (2009).

106 Anne-Marie Slaughter, *Judicial Globalization*, 40 Va. J. Int'l L. 1103, 1104 (2000).

107 Melissa A. Waters, *Mediating Norms and Identity: The Role of Transnational Judicial Dialogue in Creating and Enforcing International Law*, 93 Geo. L.J. 487, 490 (2005). Based on a suggestion from Dr. Alice Donald at Middlesex University, I admit that this process of norm-creation may not always be an unqualified good thing. The result of this "sharing" process is that countries that did not consent to an international norm (e.g., a treaty) may still end up

Courts in Sub-Saharan Africa are active contributors to this global body of human rights norms. Judges in developing or democratizing states may adopt rulings of international and foreign courts in order to gain legitimacy for both the rulings and the legal system as a whole, or they may resist foreign jurisprudence to please a domestic constituency or to emphasize local values.[108] Countries in the Global South may look to human rights jurisprudence from international tribunals and foreign courts frequently, possibly because regional human rights frameworks are more fragile in these regions and a tradition of domestic constitutionalism is less robust.[109] The mutually-reinforcing synergy between comparative constitutional law and international customary law serves as a critical component in the crystallization of international legal norms:

> Comparative law dialogue among domestic courts helps to harmonize state practices and to encourage courts to declare the emergency of a new international norm on a given issue. The emerging norm in turn informs and shapes ongoing judicial dialogue, further reinforcing and entrenching the norm in domestic and international legal systems.[110]

Developing international norms on the abolition of the death penalty "provide an especially strong example of the growing globalization of human rights norms."[111] African courts are part of a global conversation that is actively shaping international law.

The Constitutional Court of South Africa joined the European Court of Human Rights, Supreme Court of Canada, and UN Human Rights Committee (UNHRC), among others, in forging a new consensus that both reflected and reinforced abolitionist state practice against extradition to retentionist states.[112] The emerging norm against the death row "syndrome" or "phenomenon" – the theory that delay or conditions of death row could render an otherwise constitutional sentence cruel and degrading – developed in a similar way. The Supreme Courts of Zimbabwe and Uganda have made prominent rulings that accord with decisions of the Supreme Court of India, Judicial Committee of the Privy Council, and European Court of Human Rights that delay in

---

bound by it. This may have the consequence of threatening local autonomy, legal pluralism, and even the development of an indigenous African constitutionalism.

108 See Erik Voeten, *Borrowing and Nonborrowing Among International Courts*, 39 J. Legal Stud. 547, 549–57 (2010).

109 Mirna E. Adjami, *African Courts, International Law, and Comparative Case Law: Chimera or Emerging Human Rights Jurisprudence?*, 24 Mich. J. Int'l L. 103, 131 (2002).

110 Waters, *supra* note 107 at 527.

111 Paolo Carozza, *"My Friend Is a Stranger": The Death Penalty and the Global* Ius Commune *of Human Rights*, 81 Tex. L. Rev. 1031, 1034 (2003).

112 *Id.* at 532–35. See also Soering v. United Kingdom, (1989) 11 E.H.R.R. 439; Kindler v. Canada, [1991] 2 S.C.R. 779 (Can.); United States v. Burns, [2001] 1 S.C.R. 283 (Can.); Judge v. Canada, Comm. No. 829/1998, UN Doc CCPR/L/78//D/829/1998 (2003); Mohamed v. President of the Republic of South Africa, (2001) 3 S.A. 893 (C.C.).

execution of a death sentence could render an otherwise constitutional sentence unconstitutional.[113] "Moreso than perhaps any other issue," Schabas writes, "the death row phenomenon has generated a tremendous synergy among international and domestic courts."[114] Such global consensus is now firmly enshrined in international human rights law, cited by the UNHRC and by other international organizations.[115]

The abolition of the mandatory death penalty in common law East Africa has reinforced a global trend that includes the United States, South Asia, and the Caribbean.[116] Courts in Malawi, Kenya, and Uganda have abolished the mandatory death penalty for murder, decisions that have been cited as far away as India and Bangladesh. Although the Kenyan decision is in limbo, the Malawian and Ugandan decisions have succeeded in extinguishing large death rows and resentencing prisoners to terms of imprisonment. The Malawian court's ruling that the mandatory death penalty infringes on a defendant's right of access to the justice system for the resolution of disputes was a novel holding that drew from Malawi's experience as a one party state.[117] The Ugandan court's holding that the mandatory death penalty was an unconstitutional violation of the separation of powers because it constrained judicial sentencing discretion raised a new ground for constitutional challenge that was rejected in the Caribbean but followed in subsequent decisions in India and Bangladesh.[118] Finally, the Kenyan court's finding that the mandatory death penalty violated the right to life because it was not saved by the constitution's death penalty "savings clause" reflected the contentious debate in Kenyan politics over the right to life clause and its

---

113 Soering v. UK, (1989) E.H.R.R. 439; Catholic Commission for Justice and Peace v. A.G., (1993) L.R.C. 277 (Zim. S.C.); Triveniben v. State of Gujarat, (1989) 1 S.C.J. 383 (India); U.S. v. Burns, [2001] 1 S.C.R. 283 (Can.); Pratt and Morgan v. A.G., (1993) UKPC 1 (appeal taken from Jam.); A.G. v. Kigula, [2009] 2 E.A.L.R. 1 (Uganda S.C.); Lackey v. Texas, 514 U.S. 1045 (1995) (Stevens, J., dissenting to denial of cert.); Knight v. Florida, 528 U.S. 990, 993 (1999) (Breyer, J., dissenting to denial of cert.).

114 William A. Schabas, *The Death Penalty as Cruel Treatment and Torture: Capital Punishment Challenged in the World's Courts*, 127 (1996).

115 See Draft General Comment No. 36 on Article 6: Right to Life, United Nations Human Rights Committee, CCPR/C/GC/R.36/Rev.2, at ¶ 42 (September 2, 2015) ("Extreme delays in the implementation of a death penalty sentence, which exceed any reasonable period of time necessary to exhaust all legal remedies, may also involve the violation of articles 6 and 7 of the Covenant, especially when the conditions of detention are exceptionally harsh or stressful, and when the individual in question is particularly vulnerable due to factors such as age or mental state").

116 Andrew Novak, *The Global Decline of the Mandatory Death Penalty: Constitutional Jurisprudence and Legislative Reform in Africa, Asia, and the Caribbean* (2014).

117 Kafantayeni v. Attorney General, [2007] MWHC 1, 14, citing Malawi Const. art. 41(2). See also, Peter Forster, *Law and Society Under a Democratic Dictatorship*, 34 J. Asian & Afr. Stud. 275, 286 (2001).

118 Attorney General v. Kigula, et al., [2009] UGSC 6 at 45. This decision was most recently cited in Bangladesh Legal Aid and Services Trust (BLAST) v. Bangladesh, 1 S.C.O.B. [2015] A.D. 1 (May 5, 2015) (Supreme Court Online Bulletin Law Report) and State of Punjab v. Dalbir Singh, A.I.R. 2012 S.C. 1040 (India).

application to issues as diverse as abortion and environmental protection.[119] This transnational body of global death penalty jurisprudence has "created both a dynamic interstate constitutionalism and a rich body of international law" as a result of this sharing process.[120] African courts have undoubtedly made a contribution to the evolution of international legal norms.

Decisions of African regional tribunals have also made unique contributions to the global body of death penalty jurisprudence. Although the African Commission on Human and Peoples' Rights has shied away from direct challenges to capital punishment, one of its most remarkable contributions to this global corpus of case law is its emphasis on fair trial rights and procedural benchmarks in capital cases.[121] The Commission has ruled that a proceeding in which a defendant does not have access to a legal representative or in which the representative is harassed during the trial violates the African Charter.[122] Similarly, denying the right to appeal in a death penalty case is also a violation of a state party's treaty obligations.[123] The Commission has found that execution after an unfair trial constitutes an arbitrary deprivation of the right to life, as in the executions of 24 soldiers in Sierra Leone and of environmental activist Ken Saro-Wiwa and his colleagues under the Nigerian military regime.[124] Chenwi notes that these holdings are in accord with rulings of the UNHRC and other regional human rights tribunals.[125] The African Commission was the first tribunal to find that a defendant and his or her family and legal representative were entitled to be notified of a pending execution, a right that now appears in the African Commission's General Comment on the Right to Life under Article 4 of the African Charter.[126] While other regional tribunals in Africa have yet to make as significant a contribution to death penalty jurisprudence as the African Commission, this is likely to change as tribunals such as the Economic

119 Mutiso v. Republic, Crim. App. No. 17/2008 (Kenya Ct. App., July 30, 2011), at 24.

120 Margaret A. Burnham, *The Death Penalty in East Africa: Law and Transnational Advocacy*, in *Human Rights NGOs in East Africa*, 263, 274 (Makau Mutua ed., 2009).

121 Lilian Chenwi, *Taking the Death Penalty Debate Further: The African Commission on Human and Peoples' Rights*, in *Against the Death Penalty: International Initiatives and Implications*, 75, 81–82 (Jon Yorke ed., 2008).

122 Amnesty International (on behalf of Orton and Vera Chirwa) v. Malawi, Comm. Nos. 68/92 and 78/92 (ACHPR 1995); Constitutional Rights Project (on behalf of Zamani Lekwot) v. Nigeria, Comm. No. 87/93, [2000] A.H.R.L.R. 183 (ACHPR 1995).

123 Forum of Conscience v. Sierra Leone, Comm. No. 223/98, [2000] A.H.R.L.R. 293 (ACHPR 2000).

124 *Id.*; International Pen (on behalf of Ken Saro-Wiwa) v. Nigeria, Comm. Nos. 137/94, 139/94, 154/96, 161/97, [2000] A.H.R.L.R. 212 (ACHPR 1998).

125 Chenwi, *supra* note 121 at 92–93.

126 Interights (on behalf of Mariette Sonjaleen Bosch) v. Botswana, Comm. No. 240/2001, (2003) A.H.R.L.R. 55 (ACHPR); Spilg (on behalf of Lehlohonolo Kobedi) v. Botswana, Comm. No. 277/03 [2011] A.H.R.L.R. 3, 4 (ACHPR 2011); African Commission, Draft General Comment No. 3 on the African Charter on Human and Peoples' Rights: The Right to Life (Article 4), at ¶ 26 (November 4–18, 2015).

Community of West African States (ECOWAS) Community Court of Justice and the East African Court of Justice have expanding human rights jurisdiction.[127]

5. LOCAL NORMS IN COMPARATIVE PERSPECTIVE

Whether due to funding pressure, convenience, or vanity, Hodgkinson writes that "many abolitionists are reducing abolition to its most rudimentary terms, ignoring country-specific nuances, disregarding negative repercussions and often entrenching bad law for the sake of expedience."[128] This book aims to provide some level of country-specific nuance, while providing enough material for comparison across systems. This book is comprised of eight country studies over seven chapters, each of which attempts to provide social, political, and historical context for capital punishment from precolonial times to the present. The book cannot claim to be comprehensive or even necessarily representative of Sub-Saharan Africa. The fact that all the case studies are of common law countries alone makes them unrepresentative even though former British colonies are among the most actively retentionist in the region. Former colonies of France, Belgium, and Portugal, by contrast, do not generally use capital punishment for ordinary crimes, notwithstanding recent death sentences for terrorism in Chad and Cameroon. Similarly, only one case study in this book, The Gambia, has a majority Islamic population. Nonetheless, the case studies themselves cover important and heretofore under-researched political systems.

Of the eight countries explored over the next seven chapters, only two of them – The Gambia and Botswana – have carried out executions in the past ten years. Of these, only Botswana is likely to do so in the near-term future, if only because President Yayeh Jammeh pardoned most of The Gambia's death row in July 2015, though the country's political volatility makes predictions difficult. The other six countries, Ghana, Lesotho, Swaziland, Zimbabwe, Kenya, and Uganda, remain in limbo with an official or unofficial moratorium on executions even as their death rows continue to expand, which make them representative of the majority of countries in Sub-Saharan Africa. Yet, even these six *de facto* abolitionist (but officially retentionist) countries show considerable variation as to international and domestic posture toward death penalty abolition. Ghana seems the closest to abolition if the country carries through on an expected referendum on a series of constitutional amendments that would include abolition of the death penalty;

127 See James Thuo Gathii, *African Regional Trade Agreements as Legal Regimes*, 279–282 (2013).
128 Kerry Ann Akers & Peter Hodgkinson, *A Critique of Litigation and Abolition Strategies: A Glass Half Empty*, in *Capital Punishment: New Perspectives* (Peter Hodgkinson ed., 2013).

public survey polling shows majority support for abolition.[129] In Zimbabwe, too, the momentum appears on the side of abolitionists, with powerful figures in the ruling party calling for abolition and a number of constitutional challenges to capital punishment pending. Lesotho and Swaziland are harder to classify, as neither seems likely to abolish the death penalty soon, but their geographic position vis-à-vis South Africa makes executions extremely unlikely. Kenya and especially Uganda are still further from abolition though both countries have made recent efforts to restrict the scope of capital punishment. In neither country does the government appear to have the political will to reinstate executions.

This selection of case studies necessarily omits others, but a number of Sub-Saharan African countries have recently been the subject of excellent studies that provide significant local nuance and global context to assist both the national and the comparative researcher. Mohamed Suma has recently written a comprehensive chapter on the death penalty in Sierra Leone, another *de facto* abolitionist state, where he describes the death penalty on the backdrop of the country's transition after civil war and gross human rights violations during the 1990s.[130] Suma notes that the country's last execution occurred in 1998, of 24 coup plotters convicted of overthrowing President Ahmed Tejan Kabba. Subsequently, the ruling party announced an official moratorium on executions and has taken steps to redress the arbitrary executions that took place during the civil war.[131] Sierra Leone has a history of political executions dating to the early 1970s, many of which were carried out for high treason by a series of military and authoritarian regimes. *De facto* abolition of the death penalty is part of a range of transitional justice reforms, including establishment of an international tribunal to prosecute human rights violators during the civil war and a truth and reconciliation commission, that has helped the country recover from internal armed conflict.[132]

Liberia is another country that verges on abolition, providing many of the same transitional and post-conflict considerations as Sierra Leone. Unlike Sierra Leone, however, Liberia actually took steps to abolish the death penalty in law and then retreated, ratifying the Second Optional Protocol to the International Covenant on Civil and Political Rights (ICCPR) in 2005 but without abolishing the death penalty in domestic law. In a recently-published country study, Jessie Munton provides a comprehensive perspective on Liberia's paradox in which death sentences continue to be passed for first-degree murder even though Liberia has made international treaty commitments to abolish capital

129 See Justice Tankebe, Kofi E. Boakye & Atudiwe P. Atupare, *Public Opinion on the Death Penalty in Ghana: Final Report* (2015).
130 Suma, *supra* note 71 at 154.
131 *Id.* at 155–56, 165–66.
132 *Id.* at 162–64, 166.

punishment.[133] Three years after acceding to the Second Optional Protocol, the legislature passed an amendment to the penal code authorizing the death penalty for armed robbery, "a symptom of a profoundly dysfunctional justice system" that lacked public support.[134] Munton explains that Liberia's post-conflict transition created the opportunities for an increase in crime rates while depriving the government of effective means of responding, which has reduced the durability of Liberia's initial commitment to abolition.[135]

Aimé Muyoboke Karimunda has tackled the complex case of the Democratic Republic of the Congo, another *de facto* abolitionist state, in his 2014 book, *The Death Penalty in Africa: The Path Towards Abolition*. As Karimunda writes, the number of capital offenses in the Democratic Republic of the Congo (previously, Zaire) resembles the colonial emergency laws imposed by Belgian officials, and includes a mandatory death sentence for murder, armed robbery, and certain political offenses.[136] During Mobutu's thirty-year reign, the death penalty was used extensively for political crimes, including of political rivals, as late as the 1990s. Extrajudicial executions and enforced disappearances also took place, including summary executions of university students, protestors, and religious communities.[137] If anything, Mobutu's successor Laurent Kabila relied even more heavily on the death penalty as a political tool, executing 236 people between 1996 and 2000, while his son, President Joseph Kabila, executed 215 between 2002 and 2006, including many secret executions. Due to the regime's refusal to provide information about capital punishment, the last execution likely occurred in January 2003, though secret executions may have continued until 2006.[138]

Malawi, a resource-constrained country highly leveraged on donor aid, has been the subject of several recent case scholarly analyses, in part because of the country's apparent willing acceptance of global human rights norms. In 2007, the Malawian Constitutional Court struck down the mandatory death penalty as unconstitutional, citing a range of foreign and international jurisprudence.[139] In a groundbreaking chapter, Sandra Babcock and Ellen Wight McLaughlin acknowledge the positive consequences of this decision, including the great reduction in the number of prisoners sentenced to death, but they also detail the slow progress of resentencing a large number of prisoners; the logistical challenges of developing a new capital sentencing procedure; and stresses on the penal system due to an increase in life imprisonment sentences.[140] Babcock

---

133 Jessie Munton, *The End of the End: Understanding the Paradox of Capital Sentencing in Liberia*, in *Capital Punishment: New Perspectives*, 319 (Peter Hodgkinson ed., 2013).

134 *Id.* at 328–29.

135 *Id.* at 332–33.

136 Karimunda, *supra* note 9 at 154–55.

137 *Id.* at 160–61.

138 *Id.* at 162–63.

139 Kafantayeni v. Attorney-General, [2007] MWHC 1.

140 Sandra Babcock & Ellen Wight McLaughlin, *Reconciling Human Rights and the Application of the Death Penalty in Malawi: The Unfulfilled Promise of* Kafantayeni v. Attorney General, in *Capital Punishment: New Perspectives,* 181 (Peter Hodgkinson ed., 2013).

and McLaughlin conclude that death penalty abolitionists must be conscious of resource constraints and the potential for broader structural justice reform for abolition to be durable.[141] The link between judicial and extrajudicial state killings is perhaps most pronounced in a resource-limited legal system such as Malawi's, to the extent that it reflects a broader respect of the right to life, where the judiciary has attempted to restrain law enforcement from giving effect to a "shoot-to-kill" policy for apprehending criminals.[142]

In attempting to analyze the political and social contexts that lead to death penalty abolition, country studies on abolition may be as useful to the comparative researcher as studies of retention. The abolition of the death penalty in Rwanda has been the subject of several recent country studies, especially in the context of the Rwandan genocide and the post-conflict process of reconciliation.[143] Namibia's independence in 1990 also provided an occasion to renegotiate the constitutionality of capital punishment, particularly after emerging from apartheid rule and civil war. The country's troubled history of capital punishment and its absolutist constitution, which prohibits the death penalty in a provision that cannot be amended, have been the subject of several recent articles.[144] Except for Rwanda, English-language scholarship on the death penalty in French-speaking Africa is unusual. More could be said about all of these countries, and others. Little scholarly literature on the death penalty in South Sudan exists, even though the country has carried out executions as recently as 2012, a year after independence.[145] Nonetheless, South Sudan voted in favor of UN resolutions calling for a moratorium on executions in November 2012 and December 2014, signifying uncertainty about death penalty retention.[146] The country is in a protracted state of instability and still operates under a transitional constitution, Article 21 of which authorizes the death penalty for the most serious crimes and for persons over the age of eighteen and under the age of seventy, except for pregnant or lactating women.[147] Other countries that are ripe for future study include Ethiopia, Zambia, and Tanzania.

---

141 *Id.* at 204. See also Msairŵale Chigaŵa, *The Death Penalty Under the Laws of Malawi and the Law of Human Rights*, 3 Malawi L.J. 70 (2009).

142 Esther Gumboh, *"Roving Executioners"? The Use of Lethal Force in Malawi and Warnings from* R. v. Cheuka, 57 J. Afr. L. 234, 234 (2013).

143 Karimunda, *supra* note 70 at 151–53; Jamil Ddamulira Mujuzi, *Issues Surrounding Life Imprisonment After the Abolition of the Death Penalty in Rwanda*, 9 Hum. Rts. L. Rev. 329 (2009); Audrey Boctor, *The Abolition of the Death Penalty in Rwanda*, 10 Hum. Rts. Rev. 99 (2009).

144 S.S. Terblanche, *Sentencing in Namibia: The Main Challenges Since Independence*, 26 S. Afr. J. Crim. Just. 21 (2013); Nikki Kalbing, *A Matter of Life and Death: Criminal Law and the Death Penalty in South West Africa Under South African Rule, 1915–1939*, 66 S. Afr. Hist. J. 249 (2014).

145 Death Penalty Worldwide, *South Sudan*, retrieved from DeathPenaltyWorldwide.org (current as of April 26, 2013).

146 Hood & Hoyle, *supra* note 1 at 98.

147 S. Sudan Interim Const. art. 21 (2011).

While Ethiopia is actively retentionist, Zambia and Tanzania share many similarities with most of the countries explored in this volume: a common law colonial heritage with a period of authoritarian rule after independence, coupled with a lack of commitment to carry out executions.

Nigeria is a complex case that merits in-depth analysis. First, its strong federal system means that both the states and the federal government can carry out executions in their respective domains. Second, the installation of *Shari'a* law in twelve northern states extends the death penalty to offenses under Islamic legal principles, including adultery, sexual offenses, and robbery, and authorizes methods of execution to include crucifixion, decapitation, and stoning.[148] This is true even though Nigeria has, in principle, a federal constitution respecting freedom of religion. The Court of Appeal has successfully prevented most of these executions, Karimunda writes, and the *Shari'a* courts are now viewed as instruments of oppression.[149] Nigeria had one of the highest rates of execution in the world per capita for the duration of military rule and, because the death penalty is mandatory for homicide, still sentences large numbers of people to death. At least 1,233 prisoners were on death row in 2015.[150] Nigeria's federal system makes even an official moratorium difficult to achieve.

6. ABOUT THIS BOOK

The next seven chapters in this book trace the death penalty in The Gambia (Chapter 2), Ghana (Chapter 3), Botswana (Chapter 4), Lesotho and Swaziland (Chapter 5), Zimbabwe (Chapter 6), Kenya (Chapter 7), and Uganda (Chapter 8). The chapters focus primarily on the following themes:

- *Precolonial or colonial-era use:* While empirical proof is lacking, use of capital punishment during the precolonial and colonial periods may have some relationship with the retention and use of the death penalty in modern times. The death penalty existed in Botswana and Uganda in precolonial times, though generally not in Zimbabwe, Swaziland, or Lesotho, which largely corresponds to the modern practice. In addition, Zimbabwe and Kenya suffered significant abuses of state executions during the late colonial period, where capital punishment fell heavily on African nationalists. Neither country currently carries out executions. This potential correlation is explored in later chapters.
- *Mandatory or discretionary sentences:* Three of the countries in this book have mandatory death penalty regimes for murder and other crimes: The Gambia,

148 Karimunda, *supra* note 9 at 174.
149 *Id.* at 175–76.
150 Hood & Hoyle, *supra* note 1 at 95.

Ghana, and Kenya. By contrast, Swaziland, Uganda, and Zimbabwe have pure discretionary regimes that require the prosecutor to prove the existence of an aggravating factor that merits the special punishment of death. These regimes, however, are new: in Swaziland since 2005, Uganda since 2009, and Zimbabwe since 2013. Botswana and Lesotho have something of a hybrid, the doctrine of extenuating circumstances, in which death is the presumptive sentence unless mitigating factors exist in the defendant's case. Whether a death penalty is mandatory or discretionary is related to the number of death sentences in a country (and consequently, the size of death row). Where the death penalty is not mandatory, the chapters describe how courts weigh mitigating and aggravating factors in murder cases and levy appropriate sentences of imprisonment. The mandatory or discretionary nature of the death penalty also reflects different roles for prosecutors, sentencing judges, appellate courts, and clemency authorities.

- *The number of capital offenses:* The countries explored in this book vary considerably in the number of capital offenses authorized by the constitution or the penal code. Some, like The Gambia and Zimbabwe, restrict the death penalty only to aggravated forms of murder. Others, like Uganda, permit the death penalty for a very large number of crimes, in violation of prevailing international law norms, including Article 6 of the ICCPR. Although the range of capital offenses in Africa has generally declined, as in other regions (for instance, the abolition of the death penalty for drug offenses in The Gambia and Nigeria, and for crimes other than aggravated murder in Zimbabwe), the recent expansion of the death penalty for terrorism crimes merits further analysis.
- *Restrictive constitutional provisions:* Former British colonies typically had a death penalty savings clause in their independence constitutions; where these constitutions remain intact, such as in Botswana, the death penalty is largely preserved from constitutional challenge. However, more recent constitutions restrict the scope of capital punishment further than the original template used at independence, based on Article 2 of the ECHR.[151] In the constitutions of Swaziland and Zimbabwe, the mandatory death penalty is not permitted, while in the Gambian constitution the death penalty may only be used for poisoning or murder with violence. Kenya's provision waters down the original death penalty savings clause to create a circular provision, one that will undoubtedly be the site of future constitutional litigation.
- *Prospects for abolition:* Every chapter includes a section on the prospects for death penalty abolition, including the country's international posture,

---

151 Art. 2(1), Convention for the Protection of Human Rights and Fundamental Freedoms ("European Convention on Human Rights"), 213 U.N.T.S. 222, entered into force September 3, 1953. This provision states in whole: "Everyone's right to life shall be protected by law. No one shall be deprived of his life intentionally save in the execution of a sentence of a court following his conviction of a crime for which this penalty is provided by law." *Id.*

statements from political elites, an assessment of public opinion, and the activity of local NGOs or local branches of large human rights organizations.

- *Responses to pressure from the Global North*: Finally, the chapters discuss the extent to which the countries explored in this book resist or accommodate the European- or Western-driven death penalty agenda. On the one hand, the proposed laws punishing with death "aggravated homosexuality" in Uganda or rape with HIV/AIDS transmission in Lesotho and Swaziland generated significant controversy and reinforced a narrative of confrontation between African governments and the Global North. On the other hand, the international postures of most Sub-Saharan African countries have undoubtedly shifted in the past fifteen years, as evidenced by statements to the UN Human Rights Council's Universal Periodic Review and by the biannual votes in the UN General Assembly calling for a moratorium on executions on which even ardently retentionist states such as Nigeria and Uganda abstained in 2014. Whether leaders in Sub-Saharan Africa generate political capital by resisting or accepting the abolitionist agenda may determine whether continent-wide abolition will take place in the next generation.

PART II
COUNTRY STUDIES

CHAPTER 2
THE GAMBIA

1. INTRODUCTION

Of the countries analyzed in this volume, The Gambia maintains the most resistant and obstinate stance on death penalty abolition. Although The Gambia has a post-independence history of vibrant democracy, authoritarian rule after 1994 has led to eroding human rights standards.[1] The criminal justice system has suffered. The Gambia abolished the death penalty in 1993, but the post-coup regime of Yayeh Jammeh reinstated the penalty and prior death sentences in 1995 in violation of international law.[2] In 2012, The Gambia carried out nine executions to widespread global condemnation.[3] As a result of the executions, The Gambia was the subject of two complaints at the Community Court of Justice of the Economic Community of West African States (ECOWAS) and now faces the prospect of a constitutional referendum to broaden the scope of capital punishment. Although the country currently appears unwilling to carry out more executions due to international pressure, Jammeh's dictatorship is volatile. Until a moratorium is announced as official policy, the country must be considered actively retentionist.

The Republic of The Gambia grew out of the British post of Bathurst, which was built in 1816 in present-day Banjul to control commerce on the Gambian River and to suppress the slave trade.[4] The death penalty appears to have been known before the slave trade era among the Mande-speaking peoples of West Africa, which include the Mandinka, the largest ethnic group in The Gambia.[5] The country's postcolonial stability was punctured in 1994 when the Armed

---

1. Abdoulaye Saine, *The Gambia's "Elected Autocrat, Poverty, Peripherality, and Political Instability," 1994–2006: A Political Economy Assessment*, 34 Armed Forces & Soc. 450 (2008); Abdoulaye Saine, *The Paradox of Third-wave Democratization in Africa: The Gambia Under AFPRC-APRC Rule, 1994–2008*, 1 (2009).
2. Death Penalty (Restoration) Act of 1995, sec. 2, 3 L. of Gambia Ch. 13 (2009), reversing Death Penalty (Abolition) Act of 1993.
3. *Gambia 'Executes Nine Prisoners,'* The Guardian, August 25, 2012, www.theguardian.com/world/2012/aug/25/gambia-executes-nine-prisoners.
4. Mark Davidheiser & Niklas Hultin, *Policing the Post-Colony: Legal Pluralism, Security, and Social Control in The Gambia*, in *Policing in Africa*, 123, 125 (David J. Francis ed., 2012).
5. For the death penalty in other Mande-speaking societies in West Africa, see T.C. Anwyl, *The Timne and Other Tribes of Sierra Leone*, 16 J. Royal Afr. Soc. 36, 46 (1916).

Forces Provisional Ruling Council (AFPRC) under Jammeh deposed President Dawda Jawara, the country's first republican head of state.[6] "Until a military coup d'état in 1994 ushered in a two-year interregnum of military rule, The Gambia arguably held the record as the longest surviving multiparty democracy in Africa."[7] By 1994, however, public support for Jawara's ruling People's Progressive Party was eroding as persistent resource constraints and poor government performance led to a reduced standard of living and low levels of development.[8] While Jammeh initially rode a wave of public discontent to carry out populist reforms, declining human rights standards and media censorship have hampered the democratization process.[9]

Constitutionally, Gambia operated under a Westminster system for the first five years after independence, with Queen Elizabeth II as head of state as represented in the colony by a governor-general.[10] In April 1970, a new Republican constitution installed a system of checks and balances, with a president as head of state and a unicameral House of Representatives.[11] Significant infringements were imposed on civil liberties imposed after a 1981 coup attempt.[12] However, the prosecutions that followed, including a high-profile acquittal of an opposition leader, were a testament to The Gambia's judicial independence.[13] In 1982, in the wake of the coup attempt and instability in Senegal's Casamance region, Senegal and Gambia united to form the Senegambia Confederation with the intention of creating an integrated political union.[14] Senegambia, however, failed to make significant progress toward integration and the two countries went their separate ways in 1989.[15] Senegal, for its part, has not carried out an execution since 1967 and abolished the death penalty in 2004.[16] In 1997, a new Gambian constitution strengthened executive power, ousted the jurisdiction of the Privy Council in London as the country's highest court, created a new Supreme Court, and replaced the House of Representatives with a National Assembly.[17]

---

6 Abdoulaye S. Saine, *The Military and "Democratization" in The Gambia: 1994–2002*, in *Political Liberalization and Democratization in Africa: Lessons from Country Experiences*, 179, 179 (Julius Omozuanvbo Ihonvbere & John Mukum Mbaku eds., 2003).

7 Ousman A.S. Jammeh, *The Constitutional Law of The Gambia 1965–2000*, 3 (2011).

8 Saine, *supra* note 6 at 180–81.

9 Abdoulaye Saine, *The Gambia's 2006 Presidential Election: Change or Continuity?*, 51 Afr. Stud. Rev. 59, 61–71 (2008).

10 Jammeh, *supra* note 7 at 21 (2011).

11 *Id.* at 18.

12 *Id.* at 23.

13 *Id.* at 23–24.

14 Jeggan C. Senghor, *The Politics of Senegambian Integration, 1958–1994*, 213 (2008).

15 *Id.* at 253–62.

16 Roger Hood & Carolyn Hoyle, *The Death Penalty: A Worldwide Perspective*, 89 (5th ed., 2015).

17 See Jammeh, *supra* note 7, at 3–4.

2. THE DEATH PENALTY AND THE GAMBIAN CONSTITUTION

The 1970 Constitution of Gambia contemplated the continued existence of the common law mandatory death penalty through a savings clause of the right to life provision at Article 14(1), modeled on a similar clause in the European Convention on Human Rights (ECHR):[18]

> No person shall be deprived of his life intentionally save in execution of the sentence of a court in respect of a criminal offence under the law of The Gambia of which he has been convicted.[19]

The 1970 Constitution also included a provision for the executive prerogative of mercy, allowing the president to pardon and commute sentences at Article 54.[20] Article 55 established an Advisory Committee on the Prerogative of Mercy to advise the president on the clemency power.[21] The president alone appointed the Advisory Committee and it served at his pleasure.[22]

By contrast, the 1997 Constitution provided a more detailed right to life clause that altered the scope of the death penalty. The relevant portions of Article 18 of the 1997 Constitution of The Gambia read:

> (1) No person shall be deprived of his or her life intentionally of right to life except in the execution of a sentence of death imposed by a court of competent jurisdiction in respect of a criminal offence for which the penalty is death under the Laws of The Gambia as they have effect in accordance with subsection (2) and of which he or she has been lawfully convicted.
> (2) As from the coming into force of this Constitution, no court in The Gambia shall be competent to impose a sentence of death for any offence unless the sentence is prescribed by law and the offence involves violence, or the administration of any toxic substance, resulting in the death of another person.
> (3) The National Assembly shall within ten years from the date of the coming into force of this Constitution review the desirability or otherwise of the total abolition of the death penalty in The Gambia.[23]

---

18 Art. 2(1), Convention for the Protection of Human Rights and Fundamental Freedoms ("European Convention on Human Rights"), 213 U.N.T.S. 222, entered into force September 3, 1953; Jennifer Widner, *Building the Rule of Law: Francis Nyalali and the Road to Judicial Independence in Africa,* 161 (2001); William Dale, *The Making and Remaking of Commonwealth Constitutions*, 42 Int'l & Comp. L.Q. 67 (1993).

19 Gambia Const. art. 14(1) (1970).

20 Gambia Const. art. 54 (1970).

21 Gambia Const. art. 55 (170).

22 Gambia Const. art. 56(1)–(2) (1970) ("There shall be an Advisory Committee on the Prerogative of Mercy which shall consist of such persons not being less than two nor more than four as may be appointed by the President. A member of the Advisory Committee shall hold office during the pleasure of the President").

23 Gambia Const. art. 18 (1997).

A simple comparison between the text of the 1970 Constitution and the 1997 Constitution indicates a desire to restrict the scope of the death penalty from the original common law mandatory death penalty. This intention is manifest in three ways. First, the additional provision at Article 18(2) prohibits the death penalty for any crime other than an "offence involv[ing] violence, or the administration of any toxic substance, resulting in the death of another person,"[24] which appears to extinguish the death penalty for rape, armed robbery, treason, and other capital crimes that do not result in death. Second, the provision at 18(3) mandates a ten year review of the death penalty, with the hope of encouraging the abolition of the death penalty.[25] To date, no such review has occurred. Finally, the provision at Article 82(2) concerns the Committee on the Exercise of the Prerogative of Mercy.[26] Unlike the 1970 Constitution, the 1997 Constitution does not leave the membership of the Committee solely to the executive, but instead requires that the National Assembly confirm members.[27] Under Article 82 of the 1997 Constitution, the mercy committee is composed of the attorney general and three persons appointed by the president and confirmed by the National Assembly. The president is required to consult with the committee, but is not bound by the body's recommendation.[28] Although The Gambia complies with international law in establishing a clemency mechanism in death penalty cases, President Jammeh vowed never to pardon anyone condemned to death, effectively nullifying death row prisoners' right to seek clemency.[29] Such a policy contradicts the prevailing interpretation of the right to life under the International Covenant on Civil and Political Rights (ICCPR), which requires capital clemency proceedings to be genuine and effective.[30]

3. THE LEGAL STATUS OF THE DEATH PENALTY IN THE GAMBIA

Until 1997, the highest court in The Gambia was the Court of Appeal, which appealed to the Privy Council in London. After that date, a new Supreme

24 Gambia Const. art. 18(2) (1997).

25 Gambia Const. art. 18(3) (1997).

26 Gambia Const. art. 82(2) (1997).

27 Compare Gambia Const. art. 82(2) (1997) ("There shall be a Committee on the exercise of the prerogative of mercy consisting of the Attorney General and three other persons appointed by the president subject to confirmation by the National Assembly"), with Gambia Const. art. 55(2) (1970) ("A member of the Advisory Committee shall hold office during the pleasure of the President").

28 Gambia Const. art. 82(1)–(2) (1997).

29 Hood & Hoyle, *supra* note 16 at 313.

30 United Nations Human Rights Committee (UNHRC), CCPR Draft General Comment No. 36, ¶ 49 (September 2, 2015).

Court became the highest judicial body in the country.[31] The Supreme Court has some tradition of asserting judicial independence, including, for instance, invalidating an anti-corruption law that limited the right of an accused to appeal.[32] Courts have also set boundaries on the application of the death penalty. Because the death penalty is mandatory for a conviction of murder, Gambian courts have expansively interpreted defenses to reduce a murder conviction to manslaughter, such as where "reasonable doubt" existed that the defendant had been provoked.[33]

Hassan B. Jallow, who later became a Gambian Supreme Court justice and the chief prosecutor at the International Criminal Tribunal for Rwanda, reflected on the abolition of the death penalty during the final year of Jawara's presidency and its reinstatement under the AFPRC military government in 1995.[34] According to Jallow, 87 death sentences had been handed down between independence in 1965 and abolition in 1993, of which 23 were for murder and another 64 for treason from the 1981 coup attempt.[35] These resulted in only a single execution since independence in 1965 until 2012, of an army general for murder committed during the 1981 coup attempt. "By and large … the tradition had developed, and with it a public expectation, of the President commuting to life imprisonment or to a lesser term all sentences of death on the recommendation of the Advisory Committee on the Prerogative of Mercy."[36] Jallow believed that the death penalty was incongruous with the internationally recognized right to life, and that the letter of the law should reflect the country's customary practice.[37] He lamented that, because of the events to follow, abolition had been performed only by statute and not by constitutional amendment.[38] Almost precisely two years after abolition, the AFPRC military regime reinstated the death penalty and all previously enacted death sentences. To date, The Gambia is one of only three countries, and the only one in Africa, to abolish and reinstate the death penalty for ordinary crimes, along with the Philippines and Papua New Guinea.[39]

---

31 Gambia Const. sched. 2, art. 7(3)(b) (1997) (transitional provision indicating that appeals will continue to the Privy Council until the Supreme Court is established).

32 Alhaji Ousainou Jeng v. Gambia Commercial and Development Bank, Civil Appeal No. 4/1999 (SC).

33 Williams v. State, (1960–1993) Gam.L.R. 407, 409 (May 28, 1993).

34 See Hassan B. Jallow, *Journey for Justice*, 344–46 (2012).

35 *See id.* at 345–46.

36 *See id.* at 346.

37 *See id.* at 337.

38 *See id.* at 346–47.

39 Hood & Hoyle, *supra* note 16 at 20. In addition, Liberia reinstated capital punishment for armed robbery, terrorism, and hijacking resulting in death in 2008, although it is unclear that Liberia formally abolished the death penalty in domestic law when it acceded to the Second Optional Protocol of the ICCPR in 2005. See Death Penalty Worldwide, *Liberia*, www.deathpenaltyworldwide.org/country-search-post.cfm?country=Liberia (last updated July 8, 2015).

Gambia is a party to the ICCPR, which states that the death penalty may only be reserved "for the most serious crimes."[40] Gambia has not ratified the Second Optional Protocol to the ICCPR, which commits state parties to the abolition of the death penalty. Nonetheless, the United Nations Human Rights Committee (UNHRC) has, as early as 1982, held that the ICCPR "strongly suggest[s] ... that abolition is desirable."[41] The UNHRC generally holds that a limitation on rights must be established by law, must not be applied in a discriminatory manner, must not be applied in a manner that would undermine the substance of the right, and must be directly related and proportionate to the specific need on which the limitation is predicated.[42] According to the UNHRC 2015 Draft General Comment on Article 6, the Right to Life, the term "most serious crimes" must be read restrictively.[43] The African Commission on Human and Peoples' Rights (ACHPR) has come to a similar conclusion and permits limitations only when "strictly proportionate with and absolutely necessary" for the advantages derived from the limitation.[44] As the ACHPR explained in a general principle applicable to all fundamental rights, "[g]overnments should avoid restricting rights, and have special care with regard to those rights protected by constitutional or international human rights law."[45] In November 2015, the ACHPR adopted a new general comment on the right to life, stating in starker terms that a country that abolished the death penalty should not reinstate it and that countries should only use capital punishment for intentional killing.[46] The comment also stated that the death penalty should not be mandatory and the "right to life should not be interpreted narrowly."[47] The implication of these principles is that constitutional provisions providing for the death penalty should be restrictively construed since the death penalty limits the fundamental right to life.

The repeal of the death penalty for drug trafficking offenses in The Gambia accords with the plain reading of Article 18(2) of the 1997 Constitution, prohibiting the death penalty for crimes not resulting in death.[48] In October 2010, the National Assembly passed the Drug Control (Amendment) Act, providing a mandatory death sentence for anyone possessing more than 250

---

40 International Covenant on Civil and Political Rights (ICCPR), art. 6(2), 99 U.N.T.S. 85, entered into force March 23, 1976. The Gambia ratified the ICCPR on March 22, 1979.

41 UNHRC, CCPR General Comment No. 6, ¶ 6 (April 30, 1982).

42 See *id.* at ¶¶ 6–7. *See generally* UNHRC, CCPR General Comment No. 22, ¶ 1 (July 30, 1993) (referring to limitations on the freedom of thought, conscience, and religion, imposing a kind of strict scrutiny on limitations of this fundamental right).

43 UNHRC, CCPR Draft General Comment No. 36, ¶ 36 (September 2, 2015).

44 Media Rights Agenda v. Nigeria, [2000] A.H.R.L.R. 200, ¶ 69 (ACHPR 1998).

45 *Id.* ¶ 65.

46 African Commission on Human and Peoples' Rights (ACHPR), General Comment No. 3 on the African Charter on Human and Peoples' Rights, adopted during 57th Session, November 4–18, 2015, ¶¶ 22–26.

47 *Id.* at ¶¶ 6, 24.

48 See Gambia Const. art. 18(2) (1997).

grams of cocaine or heroin.[49] The Gambia is increasingly a transit point for drugs en route from Latin America to Europe because the country's administrative softness and substantial tourist trade allow couriers to easily travel on commercial flights.[50] Massive drug busts, including the June 2010 seizure of two metric tons of cocaine worth about USD $1 billion, lent urgency to the country's efforts to combat the drug trade.[51] Critics have said that the drug enforcement agency is too "cozy" with alleged traffickers.[52] Given that drug trafficking was not a crime that resulted in death, the death penalty provisions under the Drug Control Act were constitutionally inoperable under Article 18(2), and the Gambian bar raised protests to the passing of death sentences.[53] In April 2011, the legislature abolished the death penalty for drug trafficking by substituting "life imprisonment."[54] The legislature also increased the monetary penalties in the Drug Control Act, but did not alter the Act's lesser penalties, including a minimum ten year sentence for trafficking smaller amounts of drugs and a presumption of trafficking where a person is found in possession of one gram of heroin or cocaine, ten grams of cannabis resin, or two kilograms of cannabis.[55] The legislative abolition of the death penalty for drug trafficking is additional evidence that the death penalty for crimes other than premeditated murder is deemed to be unconstitutional under the Gambian constitution.

4. CONSTITUTIONAL CHALLENGES TO THE DEATH PENALTY IN THE GAMBIA

As noted above, the constitution of The Gambia prohibits the death penalty unless "the offence involves violence, or the administration of any toxic substance, resulting in the death of another person."[56] In January 2012, the High Court refused to sentence a former government minister to death for treason,

---

49 Andrew Novak, *Legislative Note: The Abolition of the Death Penalty for Drug Offenses in The Gambia*, 38 Commonw. L. Bull. 63, 63 (2012).

50 Stephen Ellis, *West Africa's International Drug Trade*, 108/431 Afr. Affairs 171, 171–72 (2009).

51 Novak, *supra* note 49 at 63.

52 Peter Clottey, *Gambian Lawyer Concerned About Death Penalty for Drug Offenses*, Voice of America News (October 8, 2010), www.voanews.com/content/Gambian-lawyer-concerned-about-death-penalty-for-drug-offenses – 104537659/156005.html.

53 *Gambian Lawyer Faults Legislation on Drug Trafficking*, JollofNews (November 21, 2010) http://jollofnews.com/human-rights/1503-gambian-lawyer-faults-legislation-on-drug-trafficking.

54 Drug Control Act, 3 L. of Gambia Ch. 13 (2009), amended by Drug Control (Amendment) Act of 2011, art. 44, ¶ 4 (October 2011); *Gambia: Death Penalty for Drug Offenses Abolished*, Libr. of Cong. – Global L. Monitor (April 11, 2011), www.loc.gov/lawweb/servlet/lloc_news?disp3_l205402619_text.

55 Drug Control Act, 3 L. of Gambia Ch. 13 (2009), amended by Drug Control (Amendment) Act of 2011, art. 44, ¶ 4 (October 2011).

56 Gambia Const. art. 18(2) (1997).

believing such a sentence was not constitutionally permissible.[57] In October 2012, however, a five-member bench of the Gambian Supreme Court upheld the death penalty for treason in a challenge by convicted coup plotter Lieutenant General Lang Tombong Tamba and his accomplices.[58] Such a ruling explicitly contradicts the text of Article 18(2). Tamba's failed constitutional challenge against the death penalty for treason was surprising in light of both the plain text of Article 18(2) and the unanimous repeal of the mandatory death penalty for drug trafficking in April 2011.[59] Tamba sought reconsideration of his case from the seven-member full bench of the Supreme Court in November 2014.[60] He appeared before the Court in April 2015 before he was curiously pardoned on July 3, 2015, and released on July 24, 2015.[61]

On January 17, 2012, High Court Judge Emmanuel Nkea sentenced former Information Minister Amadou Scattred Janneh to life imprisonment for treason for distributing t-shirts reading "End Dictatorship Now." According to one witness, these t-shirts were "capable of inciting contempt, hatred and disaffection against the democratically elected government of The Gambia and the person of the President."[62] Janneh and his accomplices were convicted of unlawfully conspiring and endeavoring to overthrow the government. In determining the judgment to be passed on Janneh, Judge Nkea noted that, "[s]ection 35 of the Criminal Code provides for both the death penalty and life imprisonment for treason. The death penalty would have been the proper sentence for this offence."[63] He reasoned, however, that Article 18(2) reserved the death penalty for homicides and that the transitional provision at Schedule 16, Article 2, which substitutes the penalty of life imprisonment for any Criminal Code provision authorizing the death penalty, was outside the scope of Article 18(2).[64] Judge Nkea's ultimate sentence for Janneh was life imprisonment with three years' hard labor:

> My understanding of the above is that for a court to be competent to impose a death sentence, it must be shown that the offence committed by the convict involved

---

57 Sanna Jawara & Sidiq Asemota, *Life Sentence for Scattred Janneh*, Daily Observer (Gambia) (January 18, 2012), http://observer.gm/africa/gambia/article/life-sentence-for-scattred-janneh allafrica.com/stories/201201190272.html.

58 Badjie v. State, (2012) SC Criminal Appeal 1–7/2011 (Gambia). Col. Lamin Bo Badjie and Lt. Gen. Lang Tombong Tamba were among the seven appellants in the case.

59 Novak, *supra* note 49 at 63.

60 Mamadou Dem, *Supreme Court Reviews Sentence of Lang Tombong & 6 Others*, Foroyaa Newspaper, November 5, 2014, www.foroyaa.gm/archives/2210.

61 *Lang Tombong Tamba, Sarjo Fofana Appear Before Supreme Court*, Daily Observer, April 28, 2015, http://allafrica.com/stories/201504300825.html; Lamin Jahateh, *President Jammeh Pardons Treason, Death Row Convicts*, The Point, July 23, 2015, http://allafrica.com/stories/201507231882.html.

62 State v. Janneh, Crim. Case No. HC/323/11/CR/101/AO at 4 (January 17, 2012) (Gambia H.C.).

63 *Id.* at 37.

64 *Id.* at 37–38.

> violence or the administration of toxic substance which in any case results in the death of another.
>
> These constitutional limitations warrant this Court to spare the 1st convict [Janneh] his life; I have no option than to follow the Constitution.[65]

Judge Nkea's interpretation of Article 18(2) is the correct one even if imposing life imprisonment for printing t-shirts is otherwise objectionable. Amnesty International considered Janneh, a dual citizen of Gambia and the United States, a prisoner of conscience.[66] He was ultimately released and granted asylum in the United States after international pressure, including a personal plea by Rev. Jesse Jackson, resulted in his pardon.[67]

Following the High Court's ruling in the Amadou Janneh matter, the Supreme Court had an opportunity to interpret Article 18 in its October 2012 decision in the treason trial of Lang Tombong Tamba and six co-defendants.[68] The High Court imposed a death sentence for Tamba for plotting a coup attempt against Jammeh's regime and the Court of Appeal subsequently affirmed the sentence. Tamba's conviction was based on testimony that he and the other appellants sought to procure arms and train mercenaries.[69] However, Tamba and the others did not bring a constitutional challenge to the death penalty for treason until after their conviction at the trial court level.

After upholding the merits of the convictions, the Court addressed the constitutional challenge by first turning to the definition of "violence" in Article 18(2). According to the Court, "violence" was a constitutional element that must be proven in lieu of poisoning to trigger the death penalty.[70] Lawyers for the appellants argued that the crime did not involve actual violence that resulted in the death of another person. After some discussion of the definition of the word "violence," the Court found that violence "does not have to be actualized; it is sufficient if violence is intended" to satisfy the requirements of Article 18(2).[71] It may be reasonable to question whether one could ever commit homicide without violence, though the provision notably separates out poisoning ("administration of a toxic substance") as being *non*-violent. This makes it likely that the drafters intended the death penalty to only apply to a type of aggravated homicide (i.e., homicide with violence) and premeditated homicide (poisoning).

---

65 *Id.* at 38. See also Sanna Jawara & Sidiq Asemota, *Life Sentence for Scattred Janneh*, Daily Observer, January 18, 2012, http://observer.gm/africa/gambia/article/life-sentence-for-scattred-janneh.

66 Amnesty Int'l, *Dr. Amadou Scattred Janneh – Serving Life Imprisonment for the Printing and Distribution of T-shirts in The Gambia*, AFR 27/004/2012 at 1 (July 2012), available at www.amnesty.org/fr/library/asset/AFR27/004/2012/fr/d99cd4a8-b7a7–4f31-b627–87699c189c27/afr270042012en.pdf.

67 Adam Nossiter, *Jesse Jackson Helps Free 2 From Gambia Prison*, N.Y. Times, September 22, 2012, at A7.

68 Badjie et al. v. State, [2012] SC Criminal Appeal 1–7/2011 (Gambia).

69 State v. Lang Tombong Tamba, [2010] Crim. Case No. HC/153/10/CR/058/AO (Gambia).

70 Badjie et al. v. State, [2012] SC Criminal Appeal 1–7/2011 at 14 (Gambia).

71 *Id.* at 15.

As to the appellants' objection that Article 18(2) only permits the death penalty where the "death of another person" has resulted from the poisoning or violent act, the Court's decision is critically flawed. As Justice Raymond Sock writes (paying special attention to his placement of the commas):

> Counsel's argument that the violence must result in the death of another person is in my opinion a misinterpretation of section 18(2) arising from a misconstruction of the word "or." There are in my opinion two conditions that must be met under the section, to wit, (i) the sentence of death must be prescribed by law for the offence and (ii) the offence must involve violence "or" the administration of any toxic substance, resulting in the death of another person.[72]

Even if this construction is reasonable under a fair reading of Article 18(2), this holding violates ordinary principles of constitutional interpretation, international customary law on fundamental rights, and legislative intent as expressed in the repeal of the mandatory death penalty for drug offenses.

As a textual matter, this holding violates ordinary principles of constitutional interpretation because it manipulates the commas to merge two distinct clauses. In essence, Justice Sock removed the second comma from the clause by writing that Article 18(2) permitted the death penalty where an offense "involves violence, or the administration of any toxic substance[] resulting in the death of another person" (second comma removed). To restate this, according to the Court, Article 18(2) permits the death penalty where an offense (a) involves violence, *or* (b) involves poisoning that results in the death of another person. Furthermore, Justice Sock's misquoted the actual text by writing "the offence must involve violence 'or' the administration of any toxic substance, resulting in the death of another person."[73] By failing to use the first comma, and by placing the word "or" in quotes, he ignored the importance of the *second* comma that set apart the poisoning clause and clearly linked the phrase "involves violence" to the phrase "resulting in the death of another person."

The Supreme Court's interpretation of Article 18(2) does not accord with international law as expressed by the UNHRC's and ACHPR's general comments on the right to life. Assuming that Article 18(2) is ambiguous, the position that more narrowly infringes on fundamental rights is preferred where two interpretations of a clause are possible.[74] Because the ICCPR restricts the penalty

---

72 *Id.* at 15.

73 Compare *id.* with Gambia Const. art. 18(2) (1997).

74 Elizabeth Wicks, *The Meaning of "Life": Dignity and the Right to Life in International Human Rights Treaties*, 12(2) Hum. Rts. L. Rev. 199, 201 (2012). Although the right to life may seem "primary" in some sense, that is not formally the case in international instruments and the right is less absolute than, for instance, prohibitions on torture and slavery in international law. See Paul Sieghart, *The International Law of Human Rights*, 130 (1983). But even though some balancing is contemplated by the right due to competing considerations such as self-defense, as with all fundamental rights, derogations and limitations must be looked at with a skeptical eye.

only to the "most serious crimes," the Court should have read Article 18(2) in a manner that would have been most consistent with an expansive interpretation of the right to life and a narrow interpretation of the limitation on the right.[75] Indeed, the death penalty for crimes other than homicide or serious bodily injury is heavily disfavored in international law.[76] The death penalty for treason warrants the strictest of limitations because such prosecutions, like Tamba's, could be politically motivated. The Court's holding in Article 18(2) also conflicted with legislative intent after the repeal of the mandatory death penalty for drug trafficking in April 2011, only eighteen months after the provision became law. The legislature, supported by the Gambian bar, believed death sentences for crimes other than murder were unconstitutional. The Supreme Court's decision could open Article 18(2) to allowing the death penalty for crimes of violence even where those crimes do not result in death, an interpretation that does not accord with customary international law on the right to life.

The Court next addressed a novel argument raised by appellants' counsel concerning the problem posed by Article 18(3). Article 18(3) says that, "[t]he National Assembly shall within ten years from the date of the coming into force of this Constitution review the desirability or otherwise of the total abolition of the death penalty in The Gambia."[77] The Court acknowledged that this constitutionally required review never took place. In 2007, a Gambian newspaper columnist questioned whether the National Assembly had abdicated its responsibility in letting the ten-year deadline pass.[78] Appellants' representatives argued that the death penalty was abolished in Gambian law as a consequence of this sunset provision. However, Justice Sock wrote that the failure of the legislature to comply with this provision "cannot by any stretch of the imagination equate to an abolition of [the] death penalty in The Gambia."[79] He reasoned that outcome of such a review could have been either retention or abolition, which therefore made it impossible to guess what the outcome would have been.[80] However, the simple existence of the constitutional clause in the first place shows that the drafters had some discomfort with the death penalty.[81] A decision giving due weight to the drafters' intentions may not have dismissed the argument so easily.

---

75 ICCPR, art. 6, 999 U.N.T.S. 85; see also Second Optional Protocol to the ICCPR, art. 1(2), 1642 U.N.T.S. 414, entered into force July 11, 1991 ("Each State Party shall take all necessary measures to abolish the death penalty within its jurisdiction.").

76 Elizabeth Wicks, *The Right to Life and Conflicting Interests*, 70 (2010).

77 Gambia Const. art. 18(3) (1997).

78 Ousman Njie, *The Death Penalty, When Will There Be A Review?*, Foroyaa, October 1, 2007, www.foroyaa.gm/editorial/732-gambia-news-archive.

79 Badjie v. State, [2012] SC Criminal Appeal 1–7/2011 at 16 (Gambia).

80 *Id.* at 16–17.

81 See Lamin J. Darbo, *The Constitution Vs. The Killer President*, The Gambia Echo (September 17, 2012), http://thegambiaechos.com/index.php/permalink/3380.html. Darbo argues that the death penalty in The Gambia became unconstitutional on January 17, 2007, ten years after the coming into force of the 1997 Constitution, as the National Assembly never performed the ten-year review.

Chief Justice Emmanuel Akomaye Agim came to substantially the same conclusions as Justice Sock in his concurring opinion. In his analysis of Article 18(2), Chief Justice Agim explained that the word "or" is a disjunctive that separates the preceding clause from the clause that follows. "There is nothing in that provision requiring that the offence involving violence must result in death," he explained.[82] The only requirement that applies to both violent crimes and poisoning is that they be prescribed by law. He also agreed with Justice Sock that treason for coup plotting was a crime involving violence even though no actual physical violence had occurred in Tamba's case. "The use of violence is inherent in the nature of the offences," he wrote.[83] He also confirmed that the National Assembly's failure to review the death penalty's legality under Article 18(3) within ten years did not make the death penalty unconstitutional, because the drafters would have included such a provision if that was their intention.[84] The other three justices on the five-justice panel of the Supreme Court, Ade Renner-Thomas, Henrietta Abban, and Emmanuel Abeyi, concurred with the two opinions.

5. THE AUGUST 2012 EXECUTIONS

Late in the night on August 23, 2012, nine death row inmates were executed at the notorious Mile 2 Central Prison in The Gambia to broad international condemnation.[85] Of the nine, three were convicted of treason, a notoriously politicized charge in a country under Jammeh's authoritarian hybrid civilian-military rule.[86] Prior to this, The Gambia had only carried out a single execution since its independence from Great Britain in 1966: Mustapha Danso, for the murder of an army commander during the 1981 coup attempt.[87] At the time of

82 Badjie v. State, [2012] SC Criminal Appeal 1–7/2011 at 46 (Gambia).

83 *Id.* at 48.

84 *Id.* at 49.

85 See Andrew Novak, *Nine Judicial Executions in The Gambia Undermine the Rule of Law*, AfricLaw (August 30, 2012), http://africlaw.com/2012/08/30/nine-judicial-executions-in-the-gambia-undermine-the-rule-of-law/; *Death Row / Gambia: "Stop Arbitrary Stream of Executions," Says UN Expert*, U.N. Human Rights (August 28, 2012), www.ohchr.org/EN/NewsEvents/Pages/DisplayNews.aspx?NewsID=12461&LangID=E. Much of the controversy centered on Foreign Minister Mamburay Njie, who was demoted to Minister for Higher Education hours before the executions took place due to his opposition. See Pa Nderry M'Bai, *Jammeh Executed First Bunch of Prisoners Friday!*, Freedom Newspaper, August 24, 2012, www.freedomnewspaper.com/Homepage/tabid/36/mid/367/newsid367/7830/Gambia-Breaking-News--Jammeh-Executed-First-Batch-Of-Death-Row-Inmates-Friday-/Default.aspx.

86 Adam Nossiter, *Gambia Leader Declares Plans for Mass Executions*, N.Y. Times, August 24, 2012, www.nytimes.com/2012/08/25/world/africa/president-yahya-jammeh-of-gambia-warns-of-mass-executions.html?_r=0; Novak, *supra* note 85 (showing that three of those executed were convicted of both murder and treason).

87 Saikou Jammeh, *Death Penalty Alive and Well*, Inter-Press Serv. News Agency, December 14, 2010, www.ipsnews.net/2010/12/death-penalty-alive-and-well-in-the-gambia/.

the August 23 executions, 47 inmates were on death row.[88] Two of those executed were Senegalese nationals and at least one was placed on death row prior to the enactment of The Gambia's current constitution in 1997.[89] The executions came as a shock to the international community, with sharp condemnation from the European Union, the African Union, and ECOWAS.[90]

The executions in August 2012 raised several constitutional issues. First, the Ministry of the Interior issued a press release afterwards stating that the executions were carried out by firing squad rather than hangings.[91] Executions by firing squad are exceptionally rare in common law Africa, though they appear to be legal under the Gambian penal code.[92] Second, two of the executed were entitled to certain internationally recognized diplomatic rights because they were Senegalese nationals.[93] Because the executions were carried out secretly and suddenly, the lack of warning to diplomatic officers, families, and attorneys of the prisoners violated ACHPR rulings.[94] After the executions, none of the bodies were returned to relatives for burial.[95]

---

88 Jo Adetunji, *Gambia 'Executes Nine Prisoners'*, The Guardian, August 25, 2012, www.guardian.co.uk/world/2012/aug/25/gambia-executes-nine-prisoners.

89 Novak, *supra* note 85. The execution of a prisoner sentenced prior to the enactment of the 1997 constitution is constitutionally problematic. See Gambia Const. sched. 2, art. 16 (1997) (holding that all capital punishment laws that conflicted with the new Constitution were construed to read "life imprisonment").

90 Both Nigerian President Goodluck Jonathan and Beninois President Thomas Yayi Boni, the current chairs of ECOWAS and the African Union, respectively, have lobbied Jammeh. Jonathan intervened on behalf of two Nigerians on death row. See Bubacarr Sowe, *Jammeh's Execution Threat 'Would Mean A Genocide,'* The Dispatch (Gambia), August 24, 2012, http://gambiadispatch.com/jammehs-execution-threat-would-mean-a-genocide/ (also noting early condemnation by French government).

91 *9 Death Row Inmates Executed*, Daily Observer, August 28, 2012, http://observer.gm/africa/gambia/article/9-death-row-inmates-executed.

92 The penal code states that the Minister of Justice may choose the method of execution, though historically hanging was the method used. See Gambia Criminal Code, art. 28(1), Act No. 25 of 1933, as amended through to 2009, 3 L. of Gambia, Ch. 10:01 (2009).

93 Vienna Convention on Consular Relations art. 37(a), 596 U.N.T.S. 261, entered into force April 24, 1963 (protecting the consular notification rights of death row prisoners who are foreign nationals in the country in which they are to be executed). See, e.g., Howard S. Schiffman, *The LaGrand Decision: The Evolving Legal Landscape of the Vienna Convention on Consular Relations in U.S. Death Penalty Cases*, 42 Santa Clara L. Rev. 1099 (2002). The Gambia did not accede to the Vienna Convention on Consular Relations until March 28, 2013, after the August 2012 executions.

94 See, e.g., Interights v. Botswana, 2005 A.H.R.L.R. 55, 60–61 (ACHPR 2003). One challenge in this case was that failure to give reasonable notice of the date and time of execution amounts to cruel, inhuman, and degrading punishment. The ACHPR stated that "a justice system must have a human face in matters of execution" by affording a prisoner an opportunity to arrange his affairs, be visited by family members, and receive spiritual advice. *Id.* at p. 61, ¶ 41. A violation of international law could occur, for instance, if the prisoner had not exhausted appeals or had not had an opportunity to seek clemency or pardon. See, e.g., Aitken v. Jamaica, Case No. 12.275, Report No. 58/02, Inter-Am. C.H.R., Doc. 5, rev. 1 ¶¶ 113–14 (2002) (finding violation of Inter-American Convention on Human Rights for failure to permit defendant the opportunity to seek clemency, mercy, or pardon).

95 Hood & Hoyle, *supra* note 16 at 219.

Most importantly, one of those executed had been on death row since 1988, prior to the new constitutional provisions at Article 18 and Schedule 2 of the 1997 Constitution.[96] Schedule 2 of the 1997 Constitution states at Article 16:

> Where any law makes provision for a sentence of death in any case other than that provided for in section 18 (2), the law shall have effect as if imprisonment for life were substituted for that penalty.[97]

Because the prisoner in question, Lamin Darboe, had been on death row since 1988, his death sentence would have been automatically substituted for life imprisonment if his case involved a death sentence "other than that provided for in section 18 (2)." He was convicted of murder carried out in a violent fashion, so as a technical matter his death sentence was not inconsistent with Article 18(2) of the 1997 Constitution. However, when the then House of Representatives abolished the death penalty in 1993, all prisoners on death row had had their sentences commuted to life imprisonment.[98] Those death sentences were unconstitutionally reinstated in August 1995 when an AFPRC decree again legalized capital punishment.[99] Certainly, even if Darboe's death sentence could be interpreted as constitutional, his reinstatement to death row when Gambia reinstated the death penalty in 1995 was not in accordance with the ICCPR or customary international law.[100]

Although Darboe's execution was the most constitutionally problematic of the nine, several others raised additional concerns. A word must be said about the mental torture or distress that takes place in the mind of a prisoner as he or she awaits final execution.[101] Courts around the world have recognized that

---

96 Pa Nderry M'Bai, *The Gambia: The Untold Dictator Yahya Jammeh's Story*, 54, 65–66 (2012). M'Bai is the former editor of *Freedom Newspaper* and lives in exile in the United States. *Id.*, at 180; *Gambia Leader Vows to Execute Death Row Prisoners*, NPR (August 30, 2012, 12:00 PM), www.npr.org/2012/08/30/160314862/gambia-leader-vows-to-execute-death-row-prisoners (critiquing the government's press release following the executions).

97 Gambia Const. sched. 2, art. 16 (1997).

98 Halifa Sallah, *Gambian Opposition Leader Writes to President Jammeh*, Jollofnews (August 27, 2012), www.jollofnews.com/human-rights/3470–20120827gambian-opposition-leader-writes-to-president-jammeh.

99 *Id.*

100 See UNHRC, Draft General Comment No. 36, *supra* note 43 at ¶ 36. This paragraph states: "States parties may not transform an offence, which upon ratification of the Covenant, or at any time thereafter, did not entail the death penalty, into a capital offence. Nor can they remove legal conditions from an existing offence with the result of permitting the imposition of the death penalty in circumstances in which it was not possible to impose it before." *Id.*

101 See Stuart Grassian & N. Freidman, *Effects of Sensory Deprivation in Psychiatric Seclusion and Solitary Confinement*, 8 Int'l J. L. & Psychiatry 49 (1986) (originally defining death row syndrome based on Grassian's research on the mental deterioration of fourteen death row inmates who were held in solitary confinement); see also Caycie D. Bradford, Note, *Waiting To Die, Dying To Live: An Account of the Death Row Phenomenon from a Legal Viewpoint*, 5 Interdisc. J. Hum. Rts. L. 77, 82 (2010) (exploring the vast literature and case law that

delays longer than several years or demeaning conditions on death row could turn an otherwise constitutional death sentence into a sentence that is cruel, inhumane, and degrading.[102] Four of those executed in August 2012 had been on death row for more than ten years, and six of them for about five years or more.[103] These executions did not accord with the emerging international consensus that undue delay on death row constitutes cruel and degrading punishment.[104]

The executions precipitated two complaints to the ECOWAS Community Court of Justice in Abuja, Nigeria, a supranational tribunal with expanding jurisdiction to hear human rights complaints from its West African members. Established by treaty in 1975, the ECOWAS Community Court is relatively dynamic and has fairly broad jurisdiction compared to other African regional tribunals.[105] The Gambia, however, has a record of failing to enforce judgments from the Court and has refused to honor the judgments awarded to two journalists, Musa Saidykhan and Chief Ebrima Manneh, who were illegally arrested and tortured in The Gambia.[106] Jammeh's regime does engage with ECOWAS in other forums, but it risks sanctions since a failure to enforce the judgments violates the ECOWAS Treaty.[107]

The first suit against the government of The Gambia was brought by the Socio-Economic Rights and Accountability Project (SERAP), based in Lagos, Nigeria, in September 2012, on behalf of two Nigerians on death row in The

---

developed around the death row syndrome since Grassian's article). According to Bradford, the death row syndrome has both a temporal component (the length of time a prisoner spends on death row) and a physical one (the harsh conditions to which an individual is subject on death row). *Id.* at 79.

102 See, e.g., Soering v. United Kingdom, Eur. Ct. H.R. (ser. A) No. 161 (July 7, 1989), reprinted in 28 I.L.M. 1053 (1989); Triveniben v. State of Gujarat, (1989) 1 S.C.J. 383 (India); Catholic Comm'n for Justice & Peace v. Attorney-Gen., (1993) L.R.C. 277 (Zimb. S.C.); Pratt v. Attorney-Gen. of Jam., (1993) UKPC 1, [1994] 2 AC 1 (PC); United States v. Burns, [2001] 1 S.C.R. 283, 353 (Can.); Attorney Gen. v. Kigula et al., [2009] UGSC 6 at 63–64 (Uganda). Justice Stephen Breyer of the United States Supreme Court has recognized the death row phenomenon may be a violation of the Eighth Amendment of the United States Constitution. See Knight v. Florida and Moore v. Nebraska, 528 U.S. 990, 120 S.Ct. 459, 462 (1999) (Breyer, J., dissenting from a denial of certiorari).

103 *9 Death Row Inmates Executed*, *supra* note 91 (quoting government press release and giving the lengths of time the executed prisoners spent on death row).

104 Courts have come to differing conclusions as to when unconstitutional delay on death row begins. Compare *Kigula*, [2009] UGSC, Constitutional Appeal No. 03/2006 (Uganda) (arguing that the delay begins from the time all appeals were exhausted) with Catholic Comm'n v. Attorney-Gen. of Zim., (1993) L.R.C. (Zim.) (arguing that the delay begins from the time the sentences were initially handed down). In this case, however, ten years would be too long under either standard, and five years may be as well.

105 James Thuo Gathii, African Regional Trade Agreements as Legal Regimes 279–282 (2011).

106 Andrew W. Maki, *Gambia's Compliance with the ECOWAS Court*, Hum. Rts. Brief (March 16, 2010), http://hrbrief.org/2010/03/africacourts-17-3-1/.

107 *ECOWAS Sanctions Against Gambia Looms*, Daily News (Gambia) (August 8, 2012), http://dailynews.gm/africa/gambia/article/ecowas-sanctions-against-gambia-looms.

Gambia.[108] SERAP argued that the two Nigerian nationals did not exhaust their rights of appeal and risked secret execution. SERAP sought an order of perpetual injunction restraining The Gambia from carrying out the executions of the Nigerian nationals.[109] The second suit was brought by the Civil Society Associations Gambia (CSAG) in October 2012 on behalf of all death row prisoners and on behalf of the families of the executed, who sought monetary damages and the return of the deceased prisoners' bodies.[110] Both suits claimed that The Gambia violated the right to life, the prohibition on cruel and degrading punishment, the right to a fair trial, and other provisions of the African Charter and the ICCPR.[111] A hearing date of May 7, 2013, was set in the SERAP challenge, after the presiding judge, Anthony Benin, rejected the initial jurisdictional challenges and found that the Court's human rights jurisdiction was proper.[112]

On February 14, 2014, the ECOWAS Community Court of Justice issued a decision in *Gomez v. Republic of The Gambia*, a consolidated petition that included one from CSAG and several other individual complaints from persons on death row and family members of the executed prisoners.[113] Amnesty International filed an amicus curiae brief arguing that a clear trend existed toward death penalty abolition, both globally and on the African continent. The Court rejected the claim that international law prohibited the death penalty, noting that the African Charter and other international instruments permitted the death penalty in narrow circumstances.[114] The Court was unable to discern a "universally accepted norm in favour of abolition of the death penalty as yet."[115] Interestingly, the Court noted that the death penalty "is a cruel and inhuman punishment and is inconsistent with the right to life," but stated that it was "constrained to make a definite pronouncement on its illegality in view of Article 4 of the African Charter which permits States to carry out the death penalty if due process is observed."[116] More troublingly, however, the Court failed to address the due process shortcomings in the Gambian capital

---

108 *Nigerians on Death Row: SERAP Drags Gambia to ECOWAS Court*, Nigerian Compass (September 13, 2012), www.compassnewspaper.org/index.php/component/content/article/90-front-page-/7596-nigerians-on-death-row-serap-drags-gambia-to-ecowas-court.

109 SERAP v. The Gambia, ECW/CCJ/AAP/11/12 (ECOWAS September 2012) (Nigeria), http://serap-nigeria.org/the-filed-court-paper/.

110 Press Release, Civil Society Associations Gambia (CSAG), CSAG Sues Gambia Government over Execution of Death Row Inmates (October 12, 2012), http://civilsociety-gambia.org/csag-sues-gambia-government-over-execution-of-death-row-inmates/.

111 See *id.*

112 *ECOWAS Court to Review Death Sentence on Two Nigerians by Gambian Court*, Premium Times (Nigeria), February 5, 2013, http://allafrica.com/stories/201302061024.html?viewall=1.

113 Gomez v. Republic of The Gambia, Suit No. ECW/CCJ/APP/18/12 (February 14, 2014).

114 *Id.* at 14–18.

115 *Id.* at 17.

116 *Id.* at 23.

sentencing process. The Court found that the plaintiffs had not proven that the Gambian government carried out executions of persons who had not exhausted their appeals, and the government denied doing so.[117] The Court also denied that the African Charter and other international instruments required the return of prisoners' bodies to their families.[118] The Court also accepted the government's arguments that one of the prisoners who was executed in August 2012 had not been executed at all and remained alive (despite news reports to the contrary) and that the government restricted access to prisoners by family and legal counsel.[119]

The ECOWAS Community Court of Justice missed a valuable opportunity to develop international law on the death penalty. For instance, the Court did not address the mandatory nature of The Gambia's death penalty, which has been clearly interpreted to violate Article 6 of the ICCPR.[120] The Gambia has not squarely faced a constitutional or international challenge to its mandatory death penalty, though the mandatory nature of the death penalty was confirmed in a recent High Court ruling.[121] Nor did the Community Court of Justice address the propriety of President Jammeh's statements that he would not grant clemency to death row prisoners, which violates Article 6 of the ICCPR.[122] The Court failed to reach some of the more troubling due process aspects of the August 2012 executions, including the execution of a prisoner whose sentence was commuted and reinstated; the executions of foreign nations who were denied consular notification rights; and the delay of ten years or more in carrying out the executions.

6. PROSPECTS FOR ABOLITION OF THE DEATH PENALTY

Since the August 2012 executions, The Gambia has maintained a hostile posture toward death penalty abolition, reflecting the regime's internal paranoia and international isolation. Yet, despite its rhetoric, the government has not taken concrete steps to carry out additional executions, indicating that international pressure on the regime has taken its toll. In a report to the UN Human Rights

117 *Id.* at 19.

118 *Id.* at 20.

119 *Id.* at 20–21.

120 UNHRC, Draft Comment No. 36, *supra* note 43 at ¶ 39.

121 Dawda Bojang v. State, Case No. HC/332/07/CR/081/B0 (July 30, 2010) (HC), *cited in* Death Penalty Worldwide, *The Gambia*, www.deathpenaltyworldwide.org/country-search-post.cfm?country=Gambia (last accessed December 28, 2015).

122 Hood & Hoyle, *supra* note 16 at 313; UNHRC, CCPR Draft General Comment No. 36, *supra* note 43 at ¶ 49 (September 2, 2015) (noting that the right to clemency cannot be rendered "ineffective").

Council, the UN Secretary-General reported that the August 2012 executions occurred after breaches of fair trial rights.[123] In November 2014, the UN Special Rapporteurs for Torture and Extrajudicial Executions, respectively, conducted their first joint visit to The Gambia. Although the rapporteurs insisted that their visits to places of detention and interrogations should be unrestricted, unaccompanied, and unsupervised, they were not allowed in to the "Security Wing" of Mile 2 Central Prison where death row inmates were held. The rapporteurs noted reports that inmates in this wing were held in prolonged or indefinite solitary confinement. In addition, the rapporteurs objected to the Supreme Court's decision expanding the death penalty for murder with "violence" to crimes including attempted violence or violence not resulting in death, which violated customary international law by interpreting the right to life exception more broadly than necessary. The report also noted, with concern, reports of torture and enforced disappearances.[124] Reflecting the country's weak commitment to the rule of law, in April 2015, a military court handed down death sentences after a secret trial to three coup plotters from an attempted coup d'état in December 2014.[125] Such death sentences, like those of Lang Tombong Tamba and the other suspected coup plotters, violate Article 18(2) of the Gambian constitution.

Curiously, President Jammeh pardoned 227 prisoners in July 2015, including all prisoners convicted of treason before 2013 as well as persons convicted of murder who had served ten years' imprisonment, with three exceptions for particularly notorious murderers.[126] Persons convicted of rape, robbery, economic crimes, abuse of office, sedition, and other offenses were also released. These prisoners included Lang Tombong Tamba and most of his accomplices, as well as former government ministers and other officials who fell out of favor with Jammeh.[127] In total, 26 treason convicts were released, as were fourteen persons convicted of murder, six of armed robbery, and at least 171 persons convicted of drug trafficking and possession offenses.[128] On August 7, 2015, Tamba

123 Hood & Hoyle, *supra* note 16 at 266–67.

124 Office of the High Commissioner for Human Rights, Press Release, *End of visit statement of the Special Rapporteur on extrajudicial, summary or arbitrary executions, Christof Heyns, and the Special Rapporteur on torture and other cruel, inhuman and degrading treatment or punishment, Juan Mendez, The Gambia: UN team prevented from completing torture and killing investigations*, November 7, 2014, www.ohchr.org/EN/NewsEvents/Pages/DisplayNews.aspx?NewsID=15265&LangID=E#sthash.wyM8RwJt.dpuf.

125 Amnesty International, *Soldiers Sentenced to Death in Secret Trial Must Not Be Executed*, April 1, 2015, https://www.amnesty.org/en/latest/news/2015/04/gambia-soldiers-sentenced-to-death-in-secret-trial-must-not-be-executed.

126 Lamin Jahateh, *President Jammeh Pardons Treason, Death Row Convicts*, The Point, July 23, 2015, http://allafrica.com/stories/201507231882.html.

127 Muhammed Sailu Bah, *227 Prisoners Released Today*, Foroyaa, July 24, 2015, http://allafrica.com/stories/201507260205.html.

128 *Id.*; Halimatou Ceesay & Bakary Samateh, *More Than 200 Pardoned Convicts Released From Prison*, The Point, July 27, 2015, http://allafrica.com/stories/201507272001.html.

wrote a letter to President Jammeh that was published in *The Daily Observer*, a Gambian newspaper, thanking him for the pardon and pledging loyalty to the current regime.[129] These events are certainly odd, though they must be seen in light of President Jammeh's resistance to the economic and political agenda of Western powers and the UN. A mass pardon of prisoners, including those on death row, portrayed Jammeh as benevolent and merciful while complying with international pressure not to carry out executions on his own terms. The mass pardon allowed Jammeh to implicitly accept the death penalty abolition agenda while continuing his confrontational stance with European and American leaders.

Despite the pardons, the Jammeh regime has continued to actively resist death penalty abolition, portraying it as something European leaders were attempting to impose on the country. In July 2015, at the same time the pardons were in progress, President Jammeh pledged to reinstate firing squads and vowed to hold a referendum on a constitutional amendment to broaden the list of death-eligible offenses.[130] The amendment would allow provision of the death penalty to crimes other than those involving actual violence or poisoning. Opposition leaders and human rights activists roundly condemned the proposal.[131] Because Article 18 on the right to life is "entrenched" in the Gambian constitution, it can only be amended by supermajority (75%) in a public referendum with at least 50% voter turnout.[132] In addition, President Jammeh has made numerous statements calling for application of *Shari'a* (Islamic) law in The Gambia, including for criminal offenses. He repeated the calls in December 2015.[133] The Gambian constitution prohibits establishment of a state religion or the establishment of a one-party state.[134] Such proposals, like the death sentences imposed for treason, send the signal that the Gambian government is not seriously committed to the rule of law, including application of its own constitution. The country's resistance to the global death penalty abolition agenda, perceived to be led by European-based institutions and organizations, feeds into the Jammeh regime's confrontational stance with global leaders in many economic, political, and legal realms.

---

129 *Former CDS Tamba Writes to the President*, Daily Observer, August 7, 2015, http://allafrica.com/stories/201508071578.html.

130 *Gambia to Reinstate Firing Squads: President*, Agence France Press, July 18, 2015, http://news.yahoo.com/gambia-reinstate-firing-squads-president-162216521.html.

131 Lamin Jahateh, *Gambia: Hamat Bah to Campaign Against Broadening of Death Penalty*, The Point, June 22, 2015, http://allafrica.com/stories/201506221953.html.

132 Gambia Const. ch. 12, arts. 226(4), 226(7) (1997) (indicating that fundamental rights provisions cannot be amended without a referendum).

133 *Gambia Now an "Islamic State," Says President*, Vanguard Media (Nigeria), December 12, 2015, www.vanguardngr.com/2015/12/gambia-now-an-islamic-state-says-president.

134 Gambia Const. art. 100(2) (1997).

7. CONCLUSION

Death penalty abolition in The Gambia has become part of a political narrative of confrontation between the regime of Yayeh Jammeh on the one hand and European and American leaders on the other. The Jammeh regime resists the Western-driven human rights agenda, portraying it as imposed by the Global North. However, recent executions in The Gambia in August 2012 underscore the softness of the rule of law in the country. A recent Gambian Supreme Court decision contradicted the plain text of the constitution, purporting to expand the constitutionality of the death penalty despite the requirement in international law that exceptions to the right to life be narrowly construed. Nonetheless, The Gambia has avoided sanction thus far from international tribunals, including the ECOWAS Community Court of Justice, even though several aspects of the Gambian death penalty regime, such as the death penalty's mandatory nature, contradict international human rights norms. Challenging the mandatory nature of the death penalty in domestic and regional courts in the future might be a more effective strategy than challenging the death penalty directly. Nonetheless, the country will remain a slippery target for death penalty abolitionists so long as the Jammeh regime opts for a policy of confrontation with the West.

CHAPTER 3
GHANA

1. INTRODUCTION

In sharp contrast to The Gambia, Ghana has long observed a moratorium on the death penalty and has expressed a commitment in principle to abolition in both domestic and international fora. Ghana routinely abstains on the periodic UN General Assembly resolutions calling for a global moratorium, and the government of current President John Dramani Mahama has preserved his predecessor's White Paper proposing a constitutional amendment abolishing capital punishment. The Ghanaian electorate is likely to go to the polls to vote on a series of constitutional amendments during 2016. However, not all is progress: the Ghana Supreme Court upheld the constitutionality of the mandatory death penalty in a confusing and legally unsound opinion, though a subsequent petition to the UN Human Rights Committee (UNHRC) resulted in a finding that Ghana's mandatory capital punishment regime was out of compliance with Ghana's ratification of the International Covenant on Civil and Political Rights (ICCPR).[1] Ghana remains in the familiar moratorium limbo, though it is likely the retentionist country closest to abolition in Commonwealth Africa.

Ghana, the former British colony of Gold Coast and previously the site of an important slaving post, is a small country in West Africa bordered by Côte d'Ivoire, Togo, and Burkina Faso with a population of about 25 million people.[2] Members of the Akan ethnic group comprise about half the population, though the Akan community is divided into a number of smaller subgroups.[3] One of these subgroups is the Ashanti, who possessed a powerful state in the early nineteenth century that resisted British rule. In postcolonial times Ashanti has become a stronghold of conservatism while other Akan groups formed alliances with the Ga and the Ewe and other minority ethnicities to balance Ashanti power.[4] These alliances were on display even in the 2012 general election, in which the Ashanti region voted heavily for the New Patriotic Party (NPP), the

---

1 Dexter Johnson v. Republic, (2011) 2 S.C.G.L.R. 601; Johnson v. Ghana, Comm. No. 2177/2012, UN Doc. CCPR/C/110/D/2177/2012 (March 27, 2014) (UNHRC).

2 International Business Publications, *Ghana: A Country Study Guide*, 9 (4th ed., 2012).

3 Rachel Naylor, *Ghana: Oxfam Country Profile*, 7–8 (2000).

4 John E. Flint, *Nigeria and Ghana*, 23–24 (1966).

party of former President John Kufour, while the northern, coastal, and eastern regions supported the ultimately-victorious National Democratic Congress (NDC), the party of former Presidents Jerry Rawlings and John Atta Mills and current president Mahama.[5]

2. THE DEATH PENALTY IN THE PRECOLONIAL AND COLONIAL PERIODS

As in every society, death, burial, and the afterlife in Ghana were culturally embedded processes, accompanied by often intricate funerary rituals and beliefs.[6] A death caused or intended by another person produced significant social dislocation. Among the Kwahu subgroup of the Akan, for instance, suicide or accidental death was treated very differently from death due to natural causes or the death of a woman during childbirth, though these traditional rituals underwent significant change as a result of colonial rule and the spread of Islam and Christianity.[7] The list of capital crimes varied by community, and could include spiritual crimes such as witchcraft, sorcery, referring to the death of the king, growing long hair, or refusing to eat.[8] Methods of punishment in precolonial Ghana included decapitation, burying alive, banishment, and sale into slavery.[9] Minor cases were handled by lineage heads and elders, while chief's courts handled major cases involving murder, stealing, and adultery. Important due process rights were enforced in these proceedings: laws had to be published before they could be enforced and appeals were permitted. Trials were public. However, other aspects of the precolonial justice system did not comply with modern fair trial norms, as troublemakers, rabble-rousers, or loners could face severe punishments even if they had not committed a crime in the modern sense.[10]

Capital punishment was intimately tied to the religious and spiritual life of the community. For the Akan people, the traditional justice ritual in cases

---

5 Martin W. Lewis, *Ethnicity and Political Division in Ghana*, GeoCurrents Blog (February 22, 2013), www.geocurrents.info/geopolitics/elections/ethnicity-and-political-division-in-ghana.

6 See, e.g., Clive Seale & Sjaak van der Geerst, *Good and Bad Death: An Introduction*, 58 Soc. Sci. & Medicine 883, 883 (2004) ("Death, at one level, is a problem that all humans must face, yet there is great variety across cultures (and over time) in people's explanations for why death must occur, in perceptions of what it is to die well or badly, and in how bereaved individuals are expected to respond").

7 Sjaak van der Geest, *Dying Peacefully: Considering Good Death and Bad Death in Kwahu-Tafo, Ghana*, 58 Soc. Sci. & Medicine 899, 904–05 (2004) (describing the difference between "good death" and "bad death" in Kwahu society).

8 Aimé Muyoboke Karimunda, *The Death Penalty in Africa: The Path Towards Abolition*, 13 (2014).

9 A.O. Atiemo, *Religion and the Inculturation of Human Rights in Ghana*, 121–22 (2013).

10 *Id.* at 120–21.

involving murder, witchcraft, and land disputes, among others, involved oath-taking, incantations, and curses. Traditional and spiritual leaders supervised the ritual, and in particularly complex cases the parties appealed to the spiritual world for resolution of disputes. Perjury could result in serious misfortune, the consequences of which could extend to an entire family, lineage, or village.[11] The Akan also used the death penalty for treason.[12] In addition, early methods of incarceration were known. A person guilty of theft could be held in a compound that formed part of the chief's residence where he or she would have to perform compulsory labor in the chief's household, such as collecting firewood and drawing water.[13] The existence of a known spirit world was linked to the belief that harm could befall the entire group if harmony were not restored after an offense.[14] Among the minority Ewe of Eastern Ghana, the death penalty (along with slavery or banishment) was used for homicide, assault, theft, attacks on elders, and crimes of similar gravity, as these were crimes in which the entire community could suffer spiritual harm.[15] Retaliation, perhaps in the form of burning of a house or field, was permitted, and a reconciliation ritual was performed for the spirits of the dead or the wronged.[16]

Despite the communal nature of punishment, some aspects of criminal justice in the precolonial period mirrored the modern. For instance, the Ashanti legal order recognized a distinction between civil and criminal cases. Chiefs prosecuted political offenses, sorcery, and crimes against the person and received any fines paid. By contrast, plaintiffs prosecuted all other cases and were able to keep any fines paid; the chiefs had no right to the award.[17] The Ashanti also recognized a distinction between murder and manslaughter.[18] Nonetheless, aspects of the precolonial justice system perceived as exotic by Europeans were misunderstood, vilified, and suppressed by the colonial state. Early European visitors to Ashanti commented on elaborate rituals in which a person was killed, writing sensationalist accounts of human sacrifice.[19] While some of those killed may have been members of the royal court at the death of

---

11 Charles-Radu Chereji & Charles Wratto King, *West Africa: A Comparative Study of Traditional Conflict Resolution Methods in Liberia and Ghana*, 5 Conflict Resolution Q. 3, 16 (2013).

12 Karimunda, *supra* note 8 at 17.

13 C.A. Ackah, *Akan Ethics: A Study of the Moral Ideas and the Moral Behavior of the Akan Tribes in Ghana*, 102 (1988).

14 See Stephen Ellis & Gertrude ter Haar, *Worlds of Power: Religious Thought and Political Practice in Africa*, 146 (2004). As Ellis and ter Haar write, many Ghanaians perceived the presidents of modern Ghana as possessing similar spiritual qualities as the precolonial rulers of Ashanti. *Id.* at 90–91.

15 Veronika Bendt, *Some Aspects of Legal Minority in the Tradition of the Anfoe Ewe, Ghana*, 104 Zeitschrift für Ethnologie 155, 160 (1979).

16 *Id.*

17 T. Olawale Elias, *The Nature of African Customary Law*, 113 (1956).

18 *Id.* at 142.

19 See Clifford Williams, *Asante: Human Sacrifice or Capital Punishment? An Assessment of the Period 1807–1874*, 21 Int'l J Afr. Hist. Stud. 433, 433 (1988).

an Asatehene (king) or other dignitaries, more commonly they were criminals or prisoners of war, blurring the line between so-called "human sacrifice" and capital punishment.[20] Two thousand war prisoners were sacrificed at the funeral of the Asantahene's mother in the early nineteenth century, and another 2,000 Gyaman war prisoners were slaughtered in 1818 and 1819.[21] The sensationalist accounts of human sacrifice were widely disseminated in Europe and provided further justification for the colonial mission.[22]

Like punishment, law enforcement was also collective. In precolonial Ghana, the bureaucratic and strongly centralized Ashanti Empire had a nascent equivalent of a police force, though it was not salaried or permanent; the maintenance of law and order fell to the community at large, especially individual kinship networks.[23] Like other societies with strong political organizations and sophisticated administrative machinery such as the Yoruba and Benin kingdoms in Nigeria, the Bunyoro and Buganda kingdoms in Uganda, and the Zulu and Matabele chiefdoms in Southern Africa, the Ashanti had a system of public officials who performed police duties, such as capturing wanted offenders and producing them before the king or chiefs.[24] Because punishment was collective – an entire family, lineage, or community could suffer the negative consequences of a wrongdoer's actions – all persons had a role to play in law enforcement. By contrast, the colonial state separated police from society and created a disciplined, uniformed unit that exercised violence and social control on behalf of the state.[25] During the colonial period, police were "an 'alien' institution, imposed on an unwilling but helpless populace," closely identified with the colonial state, unpopular and resented.[26] After independence, this social distance did not improve: policemen served to suppress civil liberties and political freedoms in the era of one-party and military rule, and complaints of misconduct and corruption persist even to the present.[27]

The legal system that developed in Ghana was characteristically English, a product of colonial rule. "The substantive criminal laws remain basically those of the common law, the assumptions of the penal system are British, and the machinery implementing the assumptions is modelled on the British pattern."[28] British rule in Ghana was formally established in 1844 with the first agreement

20 See Ivor Wilks, *Asante: Human Sacrifice or Capital Punishment? A Rejoinder*, 21 Int'l J. Afr. Hist. Stud. 443, 443 (1988).

21 Karimunda, *supra* note 8 at 33.

22 Robin Law, *Human Sacrifice in Pre-Colonial West Africa*, 84 Afr. Aff. 53, 54–55 (1985).

23 Justice Tankebe, *Colonialism, Legitimation, and Policing in Ghana*, 36 Int'l J. L., Crime & Just. 67, 68 (2008).

24 Elias, *supra* note 17 at 216.

25 Tankebe, *supra* note 23 at 69–70.

26 *Id.* at 75.

27 *Id.* at 76, 78–79.

28 Robert B. Seidman & J.D. Abaka Eyison, *Ghana*, in *African Penal Systems*, 59, 83 (Alan Milner ed., 1969).

with one of the coastal kingdoms, and the defeat of Ashanti in 1874 opened up the interior to colonization as the Gold Coast.[29] As in other former British colonies, murder and manslaughter were brought within the jurisdiction of British courts. The West African Offences Act of 1871 applied to citizens of Gold Coast, along with Sierra Leone, Gambia, and Lagos, establishing jurisdiction over murder, robbery, and other violent offenses and prohibiting human sacrifice.[30] The Queensland penal code inspired the Ghanaian criminal code of 1892, which included a large list of capital crimes and sparked opposition among the educated African intelligentsia. However, despite the harshness of punishments in the code, colonial Ghanaian courts were not inclined to issue death sentences. Clemency was granted in almost half the cases, and between 1950 and 1955 only 30% of those convicted of capital crimes were executed. Courts frequently used their discretionary power to reduce a charge of murder to manslaughter so as to avoid the mandatory death penalty under the criminal code.[31] Beginning in 1948, however, criminal law, including the death penalty, was used to quell African nationalist activities.[32]

The Criminal Code, as originally adopted in 1892 in similar form as other British colonies, codified the theory of criminal guilt in English common law, including the *mens rea* doctrine of responsibility.[33] The Criminal Offences Act of 1960 is substantively the same, though it does not authorize corporal punishment, which was rarely used in colonial Gold Coast except for juveniles.[34] However, subsequent Nkrumah-era legislation greatly stiffened criminal penalties and provided minimum sentences for an array of crimes, particularly those involving economic crimes and habitual or repeat offenses.[35] Even in the early years of independent Ghana, the death penalty was used relatively infrequently, with thirty death sentences and thirteen executions between 1950 and 1951, 31 death sentences and nine executions in 1953 and 1954, nine death sentences and zero executions in 1959, and fifteen death sentences and sixteen executions in 1962.[36] During the colonial and independence periods, imprisonment has been the principal form of punishment, with wild fluctuations in sentencing policy and a trend in the early years of independence toward sharp lengthening of sentences.[37]

The rough edges of British colonial justice were on display in the sensational trial of the eight persons suspected in the murder of an Akan chief in southern

29 Maxwell Opoku-Agyemang, *Constitutional Law and History of Ghana*, 65–67 (2009).
30 Karimunda, *supra* note 8 at 89.
31 *Id.* at 106–07.
32 *Id.* at 108.
33 Seidman & Eyison, *supra* note 28 at 68–69.
34 *Id.* at 68.
35 *Id.* at 70.
36 *Id.* at 75.
37 *Id.* at 76–78.

Ghana in February 1944, which resulted in numerous appeals to the Judicial Committee of the Privy Council in London, a bitter vote in the House of Commons, the resignation of the colonial governor, and a political crisis in colonial Gold Coast that contributed to nationalist uprisings in the late 1940s.[38] The eight perpetrators were tried by a jury composed of six members of one of Ghana's minority ethnicities and one European bank clerk and the dramatic trial was hampered by coached witnesses, bewildering language barriers, and a lack of direct evidence as to the existence of a "joint enterprise" among the co-defendants.[39] The executions of some of the convicted and the reprieves of others exacerbated the bitter political divisions triggered by the murder. British justice, though ragged, was meticulously well-documented, and the contradiction between the obsessive due process rights guaranteed to defendants and the undemocratic nature of the colonial state was not lost upon Britain's African subjects.[40]

3. THE DEATH PENALTY AND STATE POWER AFTER INDEPENDENCE

Ghana was the first country in Sub-Saharan Africa to receive independence from British rule, nine years after riots by cocoa farmers and war veterans swept the country in 1948 and first caught the colonial government off guard.[41] This early unrest metastasized into a nationalist movement for self-government under the Convention People's Party and its leader, Kwame Nkrumah, who triumphed in the first universal elections for the legislative assembly in 1951 and became prime minister upon independence in 1957.[42] Under Nkrumah Ghana experimented with periods of both socialism and capitalism, but the initial promise of rapid economic development faded in the early years of independence and Nkrumah fell to a military coup under Lieutenant General Joseph Ankrah in 1966.[43]

In the post-independence period, Ghana suffered from prison overcrowding and overly harsh criminal sentences, including mandatory life imprisonment after three convictions or for cultivation of marijuana.[44] Because Ghana's 1957

---

38 Recounted in Richard Rathbone, *Murder and Politics in Colonial Ghana, passim* (1988).

39 *Id.* at 99–102.

40 See David Anderson, *Histories of the Hanged: The Dirty War in Kenya and the End of Empire*, 7 (2005) (on Kenya, but generally applicable).

41 John D. Hargreaves, *Toward the Transfer of Power in British West Africa*, in *The Transfer of Power in Africa: Decolonization, 1940–1960*, 117, 136 (Prosser Gifford & Wm. Roger Louis eds., 1982).

42 Dennis Austin, *The British Point of No Return?*, in *The Transfer of Power in Africa: Decolonization, 1940–1960*, 225, 233 (Prosser Gifford & Wm. Roger Louis eds., 1982).

43 Ruth First, *Power in Africa*, 173–177, 366, 371.

44 R.E.S. Tanner, *Penal Practice in Africa: Some Restrictions on the Possibility of Reform*, 10 J. Mod. Afr. Stud. 447, 451, 453 (1972).

Constitution did not contain a Bill of Rights, it established a troubling tradition of parliamentary supremacy, especially with the passage of the notorious Preventive Detention Act less than a year after independence, which permitted indefinite detention without charge.[45] Although Nkrumah did not generally use the death penalty against his political opponents, several noted human rights activists died in detention.[46]

Unlike the constitution of 1957, the constitution of 1960 contained a bill of rights, but it was rendered non-enforceable or non-justiciable after the Supreme Court's decision in *Re Akoto*, which held that the provisions of Article 13 designating certain "fundamental" guarantees that the president "should" pledge to uphold were legally inconsequential as a restraint on the president's conduct. The Supreme Court upheld a law permitting the president to arrest and detain persons without trial.[47] The 1960 constitution was suspended by the National Liberation Council (NLC) after the military coup of 1966, and the NLC military council commissioned the drafting of a new constitution that decentralized political power and re-established a Westminster-style parliamentary regime.[48] The subsequent constitutions of 1969 and 1979 provided an enforceable bill of rights and judicial review of unconstitutional laws.[49] The pendulum swing between the strong presidential system and a Westminster-style parliamentary system found balance in the Constitution of the Fourth Republic, enacted in 1992. The 1992 constitution follows the American model of three branches of government with checks and balances and a single executive as both head of state and head of government.[50]

The death penalty became a tool of repression during the period of military rule in Ghana. Decisions of customary courts and military courts were not subject to judicial review, and corruption and favoritism in the judicial system were rife.[51] In 1982, when Flight Lieutenant Jerry Rawlings and the Provisional National Defence Council (PNDC) assumed power after deposing the brief presidency of Dr. Hilla Limann, a new system of civilian and military tribunals was created to stamp out profiteering, corruption, and other economic crimes, as well as gross military indiscipline.[52] During the first two years, these Public Tribunals had jurisdiction to prosecute crimes such as robbery without judicial

---

45 A. Kodzo Paaku Kludze, *Constitutional Rights and Their Relation with International Human Rights in Ghana*, 41 Isr. L. Rev. 677, 689–90 (2008).

46 *Id.* at 691–92.

47 Re Akoto, [1961] G.L.R. 523. See also H. Kwasi Prempeh, *The Ghanaian Judiciary and the 1992 Constitution: A Problem of Asymmetrical Jurisprudence*, 6 (1999). *Atoko* is today "discredited as precedent." *Id.*

48 Opoku-Agyemang, *supra* note 29 at 94–97.

49 S.K.B. Asante, *Reflections on the Constitution, Law and Developmen,t* 26–28 (2002).

50 Opoku-Agyemang, *supra* note 29 at 103–04.

51 Baffour Agyeman-Duah, *Ghana, 1982–6: The Politics of the P.N.D.C.*, 25 J. Mod. Afr. Stud. 613, 626 (1987).

52 *Id.* at 625–26.

review. In 1984, an Appeals Tribunal Board was created to hear such appeals.[53] Although these parallel tribunals were intended to address the abuses of the prior military regime by establishing judicial review of the death penalty, providing legal aid, and opening proceedings to the public, the new tribunals fell victim to many of the same excesses.[54]

With the creation of the parallel judicial system under military rule, the scope of the death penalty was broadened. In 1983, the Public Tribunals began to sentence armed robbers to death. One of the first cases involved an armed robber named "Padmore," who was executed three days after his sentence was handed down. That year, the chairman of the tribunals advocated the death penalty for cocoa smuggling.[55] Those involved in the abduction and murder of three High Court justices in June 1982 and the abortive coup attempt in July 1983 were quickly executed after their sentences.[56] The tribunals punished businessmen engaged in illicit financial dealings with sentences of imprisonment as long as sixty years, heavy fines, and confiscation of assets, with informal procedures that failed to protect due process rights in the interest of efficiency and fused the roles of prosecutor and judge.[57] In 1985, the Public Tribunals sentenced 58 people to death, almost doubling the number for 1984. The tribunals tended not to sentence people to death for cocoa smuggling as this practice was too widespread, but rather opted instead to pass harsh terms of imprisonment even for smuggling of minor quantities.[58] The death penalty was reinstated for "economic sabotage" by 1986.[59]

The parallel justice system suffered a crisis of legitimacy by the end of the 1980s. The tribunals were perceived to be political weapons of the ruling military council against competing capitalist interests.[60] Amnesty International reported that no safeguards from torture or ill-treatment of detainees existed under the PNDC, and torture, disappearances, and death in state custody were reported.[61] The abuses of the Public Tribunals were a flashpoint during the constitution drafting process in 1991 and their authority formally ended on January 7, 1993. Thereafter, the tribunals' functions were folded into the ordinary court system.[62]

---

53 Joseph Appiahene-Gyamfi, *Violent Crime in Ghana: The Case of Robbery*, 26 J. Crim. Just. 409, 415 (1998).

54 Agyeman-Duah, *supra* note 51 at 627.

55 Roger Gocking, *Ghana's Public Tribunals: An Experiment in Revolutionary Justice*, 95 Afr. Aff. 197, 207 (1996).

56 *Id.* at 207–08.

57 Darko K. Opoku, *Political Dilemmas of Indigenous Capitalist Development in Africa: Ghana under the Provisional National Defence Council*, 55 Afr. Today 25, 43–45 (2008).

58 Gocking, *supra* note 55 at 212–13.

59 Agyeman-Duah, *supra* note 51 at 628.

60 *Id.* at 629. See also Rita J. Simon & Dagny A. Blaskovich, *A Comparative Analysis of Capital Punishment: Statutes, Policies, Frequencies, and Public Attitudes the World Over*, 24 (2002).

61 Mike Oquaye, *Politics in Ghana, 1982–1992: Rawlings, Revolution and Populist Democracy*, 399, 407–11 (2004).

62 Gocking, *supra* note 55 at 220.

During the military rule of Jerry Rawlings from 1982 until 1993 when he was democratically elected to the first of his two civilian terms, the death penalty by firing squad in Ghana was most often used to punish political dissidents, sometimes sentenced in absentia.[63] The second largest category of executions was for those convicted of robbery or theft – particularly white collar and other economic crimes.[64] Nearly half of the 281 people sentenced to death in absentia or executed were armed robbers.[65] The period of military rule under Jerry Rawlings and the PNDC was characterized by economic austerity under a structural adjustment loan from the International Monetary Fund, which resulted in social dislocation caused by unemployment and shortages of foodstuffs and essentials.[66] At least 100 people were executed during the Rawlings regime.[67]

Ghana's return to civilian rule began in 1992. Ghana possesses a modern constitution, ratified in 1992, that includes elaborate human rights provisions that sharply contrast with the violations of human rights that took place after independence.[68] The constitutional protections extend to economic, educational, and cultural rights and not solely civil and political rights, and include protections for vulnerable groups such as women, children, the sick, and persons with disabilities.[69] However, according to some critics, the Constitution may not have been a fully representative document, as public participation was only consultative, drawn heavily from the "revolutionary" ruling class.[70] Since shortly after the return to civilian rule in 1993, Ghana has not carried out any executions, though more than 400 prisoners remained on death row as of 2009.[71] The death penalty's legacy of abuse has undoubtedly contributed to abolitionist sentiment in the country.

The transition to democracy led to an increase in crime rates. Murder rates rose from 275 in 1990 to 401 by 2002, numbers that included a rise in domestic murders between husbands and wives.[72] In the modern era, many

---

63 Appiahene-Gyamfi, *supra* note 53 at 412.

64 *Id.* at 415.

65 *Id.* at 412.

66 *Id.* at 410.

67 Karl Maier, *Ghana: Party Politics*, 37(4) Afr. Rep. 34, 35 (1992).

68 Kludze, *supra* note 45 at 683.

69 Asante, *supra* note 49 at 38.

70 Kludze, *supra* note 45 at 684. For a contrary perspective see Kwado Afari-Gyan, *The Making of the Fourth Republican Constitution of Ghana*, 27–28 (1995). According to Afari-Gyan, one of the nine members of the Committee of Experts, the PNDC defended the arrangements as fully representative. *Id.*

71 Joseph Appiahene-Gyamfi, *Crime and Punishment in the Republic of Ghana: A Country Profile*, 33 Int'l J. Comp. & Applied Crim. Just. 309, 320 (2009). See also Oswald K. Seneadza, *The Death Penalty in Ghanaian Law and Practice: Can Its Retention in Contemporary Time Be Justified?*, 37 Commonw. L. Bull. 115, 130 (2011) (also noting that mass commutations have taken place).

72 Mensah Adinkrah, *Women Who Kill Their Husbands: Mariticides in Contemporary Ghana*, 33 Aggressive Behavior 526, 528 (2007) (notice the enormous variation in factual circumstances of the case studies of homicide described in the article).

of these domestic homicides occurred by husbands against wives as a form of enforcing patriarchal gender norms in the household, aggravated by the limited "exit" options available to victims of violence or abuse.[73] Men who killed their wives had a relatively high rate of suicide once the murder took place, possibly "to escape judicial punishment" as the death penalty remains mandatory for homicide.[74] Because the victim and perpetrator are known to one another, domestic murders may have higher conviction rates (and therefore, higher rates of death sentences) than other forms of homicide, and yet they often possess mitigatory factors that distinguish them from, for instance, cold-blooded murder or murder for hire.[75]

As Ghana's position in the global drug trade increased in prominence, a product of increasing wealth and economic development, the country has stiffened sentences significantly, though unlike Nigeria or The Gambia it has never experimented with a death sentence for large-scale drug traffickers.[76] By 2006, rates of drug offenses and murder were in marked decline: only 87 murders and 98 drug offenses were reported in the first quarter that year.[77] As elsewhere, crime in Ghana correlates with changing demographics, patterns of urbanization, inequalities of wealth, and neighborhoods: northern Ghana has a lower crime rate than the south, with Ashanti and Greater Accra reporting the highest rates.[78] Accra, the most populous, modern, and heterogeneous city in Ghana, has undergone extremely rapid growth, removing many people from traditional kinship, lineage, and community networks that guided social behavior.[79] An analysis of the city's murder rate shows that it remained relatively consistent between 1980 and 1996 even as petty crime increased.[80] In the Nima Police Division of Greater Accra, firearms were used in only 3% of homicides; by contrast, cutlasses, knives, hammers, and blunt cutting objects were used in 60% of homicides.[81]

73 Mensah Adinkrah, *Husbands Who Kill Their Wives: An Analysis of Uxoricides in Contemporary Ghana*, 52 Int'l J. Offender Therapy & Comp. Criminology 296, 307 (2008).

74 *Id.* at 305 (noting that nearly 22% of men who murdered their wives committed suicide afterwards, and another 3% attempted suicide).

75 Domestic murders may be easier to investigate and prosecute than random murders. As Adkinrah writes with respect to Ghana, all five cases of domestic murder reported in the newspaper resulted in a conviction for homicide and sentence of death. Adkinrah, *supra* note 73 at 306.

76 Emmanuel Akyeampong, *Diaspora and Drug Trafficking in West Africa: A Case Study of Ghana*, 104 Afr. Aff. 429, 437–38 (2005).

77 Appiahene-Gyamfi, *supra* note 71 at 312.

78 *Id.*

79 Joseph Appiahene-Gyamfi, *Urban Crime Trends and Patterns in Ghana: The Case of Accra*, 31 J. Crim. Just. 13, 15–16, 21 (2003).

80 *Id.* at 17 (table 2). In 1980, the murder rate was 43; in 1996, it was 51. This is in contrast to the much larger increases in theft, assault, and breaking and entering in this period. *Id.*

81 *Id.* at 18.

Ghana's modern court system was first installed by the British in 1844, and it remained supreme except during the period of PNDC rule between 1982 and 1993 when Public Tribunals ran parallel to it.[82] In 1993, the Public Courts Act reorganized the judiciary, creating regional, circuit, and community courts, which appeal successively to the High Court of Justice, the Court of Appeal, and the Supreme Court of Ghana.[83] Reports of judicial corruption, including bribery, plague the justice system and contribute to inconsistencies in discretionary sentencing.[84] Ghana has a Commission on Human Rights and Administrative Justice that hears human rights complaints from private citizens and possesses ombudsman functions for investigating official corruption.[85] However, the Commission lacks the power to prosecute; it can only make recommendations to the government.[86] The decline of the death penalty has gone hand-in-hand with Ghana's progress toward democratization and economic development; the country has now had five free and fair elections since the return to civilian rule, including two peaceful transfers of power between the two major parties.[87] Executions are often a sign of state weakness, not state strength, and the decline in reliance on the death penalty as a tool of statecraft is a hopeful sign of democratic traditions taking root.

4. THE CONSTITUTIONAL FRAMEWORK OF CAPITAL PUNISHMENT IN GHANA

In Ghana, the constitution is supreme and has priority over existing and subsequent laws, English common law and equity, and Ghanaian customary law.[88] The penal and criminal procedure codes predate the 1992 constitution and constitute "existing law."[89] The Constitution of the Fourth Republic protects a range of modern due process rights, among them requiring a warrant before a search or an arrest; notifying detained persons of charges against them; prohibiting detention without trial; and provisioning counsel for indigent

82 Appiahene-Gyamfi, *supra* note 71 at 313.

83 *Id. See also*, *The Republic of Ghana Judiciary*, www.judicial.gov.gh/.

84 Wisdom Akpalu & Anatu Mohammed, *Socioeconomics of Crime and Discretionary Punishment: The Case of Ghana*, 40 Int'l J. Soc. Econ. 116, 117–18 (2013).

85 Tankebe, *supra* note 23 at 81. See generally, John Hatchard, Muna Ndulo & Peter Slinn, *Comparative Constitutionalism and Good Governance in the Commonwealth: An Eastern and Southern African Perspective*, 208 *et seq*. (2004) (providing a comparative analysis of Africa's autochthonous oversight bodies).

86 Tankebe, *supra* note 23 at 81.

87 See E. Gyimah-Boadi & H. Kwasi Prempeh, *Oil, Politics, and Ghana's Democracy*, 23 J. Democracy 94, 95 (2012).

88 Appiahene-Gyamfi, *supra* note 71 at 309, citing Ghana Const. art. 11.

89 Ghana Const. art. 11(4)–(6).

defendants.[90] Ghana's criminal justice system provides for the sentences of death, imprisonment, fines, compensation, and probation. Juveniles are treated separately.[91] After arrest and interrogation, the Attorney-General's office presses criminal charges and prosecutes suspects in a court of law; however, due to understaffing, the overwhelming majority of minor criminal cases are tried by police prosecutors.[92] In this way, Ghana lacks the strict separation of police and prosecutorial functions that is traditionally a hallmark of more developed common law countries. In trials involving the death penalty or life imprisonment, a jury of seven men and women participate. Judges may preside alone or may sit with three assessors, depending on the trial court.[93]

That the right to life under Ghana's 1992 Constitution is listed as the first fundamental right underscores the importance of the dignity and worth of an individual human being.[94] The right to life at Article 13(1) contains a death penalty savings clause on the model of the ECHR, which applied briefly to Ghana during the colonial period: "No person shall be deprived of his life intentionally except in the exercise of the execution of a sentence of a court in respect of a criminal offence under the laws of Ghana of which he has been convicted."[95] In addition, the Constitution includes a human dignity provision, which states in relevant part, "[n]o person shall, whether or not he is arrested, restricted or detained, be subjected to torture or other cruel, inhuman or degrading treatment or punishment."[96] The Constitution also requires a jury trial in capital cases other than treason, and requires that the jury's decision be unanimous in order to pass a sentence of death.[97] The President of Ghana, acting in consultation with the Council of State, has the ability to pardon or reprieve a prisoner or reduce or substitute a sentence.[98] The provision also provides that in death penalty cases, a written report from the trial judge and a record of the proceedings shall be submitted to the President for mercy consideration.[99] In addition, the Constitution provides a mandatory death penalty for treason, stating that any

---

90 See Ghana Const. art. 14.

91 Appiahene-Gyamfi, *supra* note 71 at 310.

92 *Id.* at 310.

93 Cees Flinterman, *The Administration of Justice in Ghana*, 15 C.I.J.L. Bull. 26, 27 (1985).

94 Asante, *supra* note 49 at 38.

95 Ghana Const. art. 13(1). The Convention applied to European colonies upon its entry into force on September 3, 1953 on the understanding that it would lapse at independence. Ghana received independence in 1957. See European Convention for the Protection of Human Rights and Fundamental Freedoms, 213 U.N.T.S. 222, entered into force September 3, 1953; Jennifer A. Widner, *Building the Rule of Law: Francis Nyalali and the Road to Judicial Independence in Africa*, 161 (2001).

96 Ghana Const. art. 15(2).

97 Ghana Const. art. 19(2).

98 Ghana Const. art. 72(1).

99 Ghana Const. art. 72(2).

person who "commits the offence of high treason ... shall, upon conviction, be sentenced to suffer death."[100]

Ghana is a signatory to a number of international treaties that impact the application of the death penalty, including the ICCPR, the Convention Against Torture, and the African Charter.[101] Under Ghana's constitution, these treaties are not self-executing and require implementing legislation for them to be incorporated into domestic law; however, the Constitution states that courts and other officials should be guided by international human rights obligations.[102] Ghana's constitution also provides for the provision of legal aid to indigent defendants.[103] The Legal Aid Scheme Act of 1997 established the Legal Aid Board to determine the qualifications of applicants for legal aid and connect them with a practitioner, especially for serious felonies such as murder or armed robbery.[104] Nonetheless, serious shortages in legal aid remain.[105]

Under the Criminal Offences Act of 1960, the death penalty is mandatory for the crime of murder, stating that "[a] person who commits murder is liable to suffer death."[106] Murder is defined as intentionally causing "the death of another person by an unlawful harm," unless the murder is reduced to manslaughter by reason of provocation or partial excuse.[107] Infanticide by a new mother also reduced a sentence to manslaughter on the theory that she was presumed to suffer from post-partum depression.[108] In addition, the death penalty is also mandatory for genocide.[109] Besides murder and genocide, the Criminal Offences Act makes treason a capital crime, giving effect to Article 3(3) of the Constitution. According to Section 180 of the Criminal Offences Act, "[a] person who commits high treason is liable to suffer death," and high treason is defined synonymously

100 Ghana Const. art. 3(3).

101 International Covenant on Civil and Political Rights, U.N. Doc. A/6316 (1966), 999 U.N.T.S. 171, entered into force March 23, 1976 (Ghana signatory); Convention against Torture and Other Cruel, Inhuman or Degrading Treatment or Punishment, U.N. Doc. A/39/51 (1984), entered into force June 26, 1987 (Ghana signatory); African Charter on Human and Peoples' Rights, adopted June 27, 1981, OAU Doc. CAB/LEG/67/3 rev. 5, 21 I.L.M. 58 (1982), entered into force October 21, 1986 (Ghana signatory).

102 Kludze, *supra* note 45 at 682, citing Ghana Const. art. 37.

103 Ghana Const. art. 294(2)–(3).

104 See Legal Aid Scheme Act, No. 542 of 1997; Renee Aku Sitsofe Morhe, *An Overview of Legal Aid for Criminal Cases in Ghana: The History and Challenge of Providing Legal Aid*, 38 Commw. L. Bull. 105, 106 (2012).

105 Morhe, *supra* note 104 at 106–07.

106 Criminal Offences Act, 1960, No. 29, §46.

107 *Id.* at §47. Provocation is defined at §53. Insults alone are not enough. Oduro v. State, [1967] G.L.R. 36 (C.A.). Provocation ordinarily requires that one acted from terror of immediate death or grievous bodily harm. Criminal Offences Act, 1960, No. 29, §52(b). However, where a person is physically assaulted, provocation may be found even without fear of immediate death or grievous harm. State v. Ayi Grunshie, [1961] G.L.R. (II) 633 (S.C.). Adultery may also be grounds of provocation if committed in view of the defendant. Criminal Offences Act, 1960, No. 29, §53(c).

108 Criminal Offences Act, 1960, No. 29, §52(d).

109 *Id.* at §49, 49A.

with the meaning assigned to it by Article 3(3) of the Constitution.[110] Two other crimes also merit discretionary death sentences: piracy, when combined with assault with intent to murder, and attempted murder by a person serving a sentence of imprisonment of three years or longer.[111]

The Criminal and Other Offences (Procedure) Act of 1960, the country's criminal procedure code, provides the procedure for death sentences.[112] The Act forbids the death penalty for juveniles under the age of seventeen.[113] A death sentence may be carried out by hanging, lethal injection, electrocution, gas chamber, or "any other method determined by the Court," and upon sentencing, the accused must be informed of his or her right to appeal.[114] The presiding judge must forward to the Minister of Justice a copy of the minutes, the notes of evidence taken, and the full record of trial, with a report signed by the presiding judge containing his or her recommendations or observations.[115] The Minister of Justice determines the time, place, and manner of the execution, and issues a death warrant (including instructions for burial) or an order of commutation or pardon on behalf of the president.[116] Where a woman is sentenced to death, the Court must order her to be tested for pregnancy unless she is post-menopausal; the death penalty may not be carried out on a pregnant woman, and her sentence will be commuted to a period of imprisonment.[117]

The president possesses the constitutional pardon power in Ghana. As in other British colonies, the Governor-General possessed a prerogative of mercy that allowed him to commute a sentence or grant clemency to a condemned prisoner.[118] Ghanaian presidents have used this power extensively. In 2000, President Rawlings granted clemency to 1,000 prisoners, including two on death row.[119] Unlike other common law African countries, the constitution does not establish a specially-created advisory mercy committee, but rather requires consultation with the Council of State in exercising the clemency power.[120] The Council of State, akin to a traditional council of elders, is a large body that

---

110 *Id.* at §180(1)–(2). Treason is also defined extraterritorially and is applicable to Ghanaians living abroad. *Id.* at §180(3).

111 *Id.* at §194(2), amended by Act No. 646 of 2003; Death Penalty Worldwide, *Ghana*, www.deathpenaltyworldwide.org/country-search-post.cfm?country=Ghana (current as of October 14, 2012).

112 Criminal and Other Offences (Procedure) Act, Act 30 of 1960 (Ghana). See also, Henrietta J.A.N. Mensa-Bonsu, *The Annotated Criminal Procedure and Juvenile Justice Act of Ghana* (2009).

113 Criminal and Other Offences (Procedure) Act, Act 30 of 1960 at §295 (Ghana).

114 *Id.* at §§304–05.

115 *Id.* at §307.

116 *Id.* at §308–09.

117 *Id.* at §312 (also providing that arrangements for her health needs and the raising of the child will be made by the Prison Service and the social welfare department of the district).

118 Richard Rathbone, *A Murder in the Colonial Gold Coast: Law and Politics in the 1940s*, 30 J. Afr. Hist. 445, 450, 455 (1989). *See also* Ghana Const. art. 72 (1992) (pardon power).

119 Hans Goran Franck, *The Barbaric Punishment: Abolishing the Death Penalty*, 98 (2003).

120 Ghana Const. art. 72(1).

advises the president on many different executive powers. It currently comprises 24 members, including one member elected from each region; prominent citizens appointed by the president; and a host of *ex officio* members, including the chief of defense staff, inspector-general of police, and the president of the House of Chiefs, the upper house of parliament.[121] The President's constitutional pardon power specifically extends to any conviction, punishment, or forfeiture imposed by a court-martial or military tribunal, as a result of the historical abuses of Ghana's military regimes.[122] The exercise of the President's pardon power is not reviewable by Ghana's institutional ombudsman, the Commission on Human Rights and Administrative Justice.[123] As is typical of the majority rule in the English-speaking world, pardons may only be granted after conviction.[124]

The Supreme Court of Ghana has rejected a constitutional challenge to the mandatory nature of the death penalty in *Dexter Johnson v. Republic*, a four to one decision in March 2010. The lengthy opinions by Justices Rose Constance Owusu and Jones Dotse held that the mandatory death penalty was consistent with the constitution and the establishment of a discretionary death penalty was a policy decision properly left to the legislature.[125] This decision, however, did not provide a comprehensive philosophical alternative to the trend in the common law world toward discretionary capital sentencing regimes. According to the majority, the ability of a defendant to seek clemency after sentencing provided a sufficient mechanism to pass an appropriate sentence based on mitigating factors, a holding that contradicts the consensus of other Commonwealth courts and the UNHRC.[126] The majority decision also brushed off a statutory interpretation argument. Because the Criminal Offences Act states that upon conviction, "[a] person who commits murder is liable to suffer death" instead of "shall suffer death," the Supreme Court neglected an opportunity read such provision as non-mandatory as other Commonwealth courts have done.[127]

The majority opinions by Justices Owusu and Dotse engaged in a purely textual analysis of the penal code and the constitution and used the cloak of judicial restraint to avoid reconciling this analysis with contrary persuasive authority from other Commonwealth jurisdictions. Justice Owusu wrote that the death penalty was not overly rigid, because it exempted juveniles, pregnant women, and persons found to be insane, though these cases do not greatly narrow the spectrum of moral culpability inherent in the definition of murder.

---

121 Government of Ghana, *Council of State*, www.ghana.gov.gh/index.php/2012-02-08-08-18-09/council-of-state.

122 Ghana Const. art. 72(3).

123 Ghana Const. art. 219(2)(c).

124 Ghana Const. art. 72(1)(a).

125 Dexter Johnson v. Republic, (2011) 2 S.C.G.L.R. 601.

126 *Id.* at 655, 658 (Owusu, J., concurring).

127 *Id.* at 658. See also Van Der Jhultes v. Attorney General, (1989) 1 Sri L.R. 204 (1 June 1988) (Sri Lanka); Ume v. State, (2006) PGSC 9, S.C. 836 (May 19, 2006) (Papua N.G.).

Justice Owusu explained that "nothing short of death shall be the appropriate sentence" in light of the appellant's gruesome murder, a judicially activist holding that conflicts with her professed desire to leave policy decisions to the legislature.[128] Justice Dotse, in his opinion, acknowledged comparative precedent from other jurisdictions but ultimately determined that the Constitution of Ghana was clear and unambiguous. His decision, however, confused the division of murder into degrees with judicial sentencing guidelines. His argument that sentencing guidelines would be required without a mandatory death penalty did not necessarily mean this constitutional decision was a policy judgment best left to the legislature. His argument created a straw man, predicting chaos that would result if judges had to weigh mitigating and aggravating factors, an argument amply refuted by the experience of judges from throughout the English-speaking world. He did, however, advocate that the Parliament of Ghana should "seriously consider whether to have a policy shift in the mandatory death penalty regime imposed on those convicted of murder."[129]

By contrast, a strong dissenting opinion by Justice Samuel Date-Bah intensively analyzed the jurisprudence of other Commonwealth jurisdictions, which are based on constitutional frameworks similar to Ghana's. Justice Date-Bah found persuasive authority from other common law jurisdictions in the Commonwealth Caribbean and Kenya, Uganda, and Malawi, noting that these countries had constitutions that were similar to with Ghana's constitution. According to Justice Date-Bah, "when interpreting Ghanaian constitutional provisions in pari materia with other Commonwealth jurisdictions and international human rights instruments," the Court should depart from their holdings "only for tangible policy reasons."[130] Here there were none. He explained that the argument "that all murders are murders and should be treated equally is an unreasonably inflexible ideological position, belied by actual human experience."[131] He also accepted the argument that the mandatory death penalty was inherently arbitrary because it did not distinguish between the gravity of particular cases.[132] Justice Date-Bah also found that "[t]he inability of trial judges to exercise ... discretion infringes the right of the accused to a fair trial," contained at Article 19(1) of the Constitution of Ghana. He added that the mandatory death penalty infringed the separation of powers, noting that the judicial branch exercises the power to determine what sentence is appropriate on the facts of individual cases.[133] In addition, Justice Date-Bah acknowledged that the Constitution authorized the mandatory death penalty for high treason

128 *Johnson*, (2011) 2 S.C.G.L.R. at 601, 658 (Owusu, J.S.C., concurring).
129 *Id.* at 692–93, 699, 702 (Dotse, J.S.C., concurring).
130 *Id.*
131 *Johnson*, 2 S.C.G.L.R. at 622 (Date-Bah, J., dissenting).
132 *Id.* at 634.
133 *Id.* at 638.

at Article 3(3), but he explained that treason was a specific intent crime with a more limited range of moral culpability compared to murder.[134]

Although the Supreme Court upheld the constitutionality of the mandatory death penalty, the appellant Dexter Johnson filed a petition with the UNHRC in Geneva, a treaty body composed of experts who hear individual complaints under the ICCPR, of which Ghana is a state party. On March 27, 2014, the UNHRC ruled that Johnson's mandatory death sentence violated Article 6(1) of the ICCPR, which prohibits the arbitrary deprivation of life.[135] Because a mandatory death sentence did not allow judicial discretion to substitute a lesser sentence based on mitigating factors, Johnson argued that his death sentence violated the prohibition on cruel and degrading treatment under Article 7 of the ICCPR. The UNHRC rejected Ghana's arguments that a clemency procedure was sufficient to protect the right to life in death penalty cases.[136] The UNHRC added, "[t]he existence of a de facto moratorium on the death penalty is not sufficient to make a mandatory death sentence consistent with the Covenant."[137] The UNHRC confirmed its prior precedent that individualized sentencing discretion is required in capital cases.

5. APPLICATION OF THE DEATH PENALTY FOR MURDER

In general, Ghanaian courts have followed English precedent on the definition of murder and manslaughter. A murder conviction is deemed to be inappropriate where the accused did not intend to kill.[138] Similarly, where a defendant has only intention to commit bodily injury, a manslaughter conviction is appropriate.[139] English common law is also the foundation for defenses such as provocation, self-defense, and insanity. A divided Supreme Court has upheld a conviction for murder where the defendant was the aggressor in a fight and was the first to resort to deadly force, making him unable to raise defenses of self-defense or provocation.[140] However, the Court of Appeal reversed a murder conviction in favor of manslaughter where the defendant was provoked to the point where he lost self-control.[141] The burden of raising an affirmative defense

134 *Id.* at 633.

135 Johnson v. Ghana, Comm. No. 2177/2012, UN Doc. CCPR/C/110/D/2177/2012 (March 27, 2014) (UNHRC).

136 *Id.* at §7.3.

137 *Id.*

138 Quartey v. Republic, [1999–2000] 2 G.L.R. 201, 218 (Ghana C.A. 2000).

139 Idrisu Gonja v. State, [1964] G.L.R. 573, 579 (S.C.). This case is also mentioned in Henrietta J.A.N. Mensa-Bonsu, *The Annotated Criminal Offences Act of Ghana*, 70 (5th ed. 2008).

140 Boakye v. Republic, [1999–2000] 1 G.L.R. 740, 747–48 (Ghana S.C. 1999).

141 Republic v. Zinitege, [1993–94] 1 G.L.R. 1, 5–6 (Ghana C.A. 1993).

is on the defendant.[142] The Supreme Court upheld a murder conviction where the defendant's use of force was grossly disproportionate to any possible provocation.[143] Provocation must be extreme enough "to be likely to deprive a person of ordinary character of the power of self-control" and not based on "any peculiar temperament or excitability of a person."[144] A confession of adultery is not sufficient to amount to extreme provocation.[145] The Court of Appeal reduced a murder conviction to "guilty but insane" where a trial judge rejected an insanity defense in his jury instructions, rather than allowing the jury to make a finding of fact on the question of insanity.[146] The defendant has the burden of proving beyond a preponderance of the evidence that he or she did not know the nature of the criminal act or was mentally ill at the time of the offense.[147] Intoxication to the degree of temporary insanity may also reduce a murder conviction to manslaughter.[148]

Death sentences passed prior to the enactment of the 1992 constitution are heavily scrutinized by courts, especially where the sentence was passed by the Public Tribunals under the PNDC regime. In 2001, the Court of Appeal invalidated a death sentence by firing squad for an appellant convicted of robbery and conspiracy to commit robbery.[149] The appellant argued that the sentence was too harsh and excessive, as nobody was killed or hurt; as a consequence, death was a disproportionate punishment as a matter of law. The Court invalidated the death sentence without pronouncing on the appellant's argument that the death penalty was unconstitutional for armed robbery. According to the Court, the sentence was passed in 1988 by the National Public Tribunal while Ghana was still under military rule, and therefore predated the 1992 Constitution. According to the law in place in 1988, the death penalty could only be dispensed if the PNDC had specified in writing that the offence attracted the death penalty, or that very grave circumstances existed that merited such a penalty. Because neither of those conditions could be shown in the present case, the Court of Appeal found the death sentence to be unlawful as passed.[150] In 2010, the Supreme Court reversed a murder conviction and released a defendant who had been on death row for twenty years due to insufficient evidence and faulty eyewitness testimony. The Court substituted the murder conviction for manslaughter and sentenced the defendant to time served.[151]

---

142 Agyemang v. Republic, [1995–96] 1 G.L.R. 118, 121 (Ghana C.A. 1993). Also mentioned in Mensa-Bonsu, *supra* note 139 at 78.

143 Aidoo v. State, [1963] 2 G.L.R. 84, 90–91 (S.C.).

144 State v. Nimoh, [1960] G.L.R. 203, 204 (S.C.).

145 Gyeke v. State, [1964] G.L.R. 656, 660 (S.C.).

146 Collins v. Republic, [1987–88] 2 G.L.R. 521, 530–32 (Ghana C.A. 1988).

147 Dabla v. State, [1963] 2 G.L.R. 14, 18–19 (Ghana S.C.).

148 Ketsiawah v. State, [1965] G.L.R. 483, 489 (S.C.).

149 Sulemana v. Republic, [2001–02] 2 G.L.R. 243 (Ghana C.A. 2001).

150 *Id.* at 246–47.

151 Bernard Nii Okai Tagoe v. Republic, Crim. App. No. 1/2002 (June 3, 2010) (Ghana S.C.).

Except in cases involving a mandatory death sentence, Ghanaian judges routinely weigh mitigating and aggravating factors within a matrix of mandatory minimums. The Supreme Court rejected mitigating factors in an armed robbery case, including the youthfulness of the offender and prospects for rehabilitation, but found that a trial judge's sentence of 65 years was excessive, given the mandatory minimum of only ten years for robbery. In that case, the Court issued a plea for criminal justice reform, noting that more lenient criminal sentence and alternatives to incarceration would help conserve state resources and promote rehabilitation.[152] In another armed robbery case, the Ghana Court of Appeal referenced the "modern trend in correctional practices" toward shorter sentences "so as to reform the prisoner."[153] Such decisions may signify a tentative trend toward a more lenient sentencing approach to reflect the importance of rehabilitation as a sentencing goal.

6. PROSPECTS FOR ABOLITION OF THE DEATH PENALTY

Although Ghana is considered to be *de facto* abolitionist, since it has not carried out an execution in more than ten years, death sentences are still handed down. As of April 2013, 146 people were under sentence of death in Ghana.[154] In August 2015, this number was reduced to 129.[155] President Kufour, who held office from 2001 to 2009, regularly commuted death sentences and used his clemency power to commute all death sentences to life imprisonment on his last day in office.[156] Similarly, in June 2015, President Mahama freed 900 prisoners and commuted fourteen death sentences to life imprisonment.[157] In 2010, Ghana declared that it was considering abolishing the death penalty in its criminal law and that it had a *de facto* moratorium on executions.[158] Ghana's Commission on Human Rights and Administrative Justice finally advocated abolition when the media turned to it as the "conscience of the nation," helping to facilitate debate on the death penalty issue.[159]

---

152 Kwaku Frimpong v. Republic, Crim. App. No. J3/5/2010 (January 18, 2012) (Ghana S.C.).

153 Prosper Ameshinu v. Republic, Civil App. Suit No. H2/18/2010 (July 22, 2010) (Ghana C.A.).

154 Roger Hood & Carolyn Hoyle, *The Death Penalty: A Worldwide Perspective*, 203 (5th ed. 2015).

155 Justice Tankebe, Kofi E. Boakye & Atudiwe P. Atupare, *Public Opinion on the Death Penalty in Ghana: Final Report*, 1 (2015).

156 Hood & Hoyle, *supra* note 154 at 90.

157 *Mahama Frees 900 Prisoners; 14 on Death Row Sentence Reduced*, GhanaWeb, June 30, 2015, www.ghanaweb.com/GhanaHomePage/NewsArchive/Mahama-frees-900-prisoners-14-on-death-row-sentence-reduced-365493.

158 Karimunda, *supra* note 8 at 188.

159 John Hatchard, Muna Ndulo & Peter Slinn, *Comparative Constitutionalism and Good Governance in the Commonwealth: An Eastern and Southern African Perspective*, 230 (2003).

Ghana's international posture toward the death penalty has also changed. In 1998, Ghana joined a letter to the president of the UN Human Rights Commission asserting that there was no international consensus calling for abolition of the death penalty and citing religious and legal differences. A year later, Ghana opposed a UN General Assembly resolution proffered by Finland and the European Union delegation to apply international safeguards in application of death sentences, progressively restrict the death penalty, and impose a moratorium with a view to complete abolition.[160] By contrast, in 2012 Ghana improved its status by abstaining on a resolution calling for a global moratorium.[161]

Support for the death penalty in Ghana appears to be tepid. According to the Gallup International 2000 Millennium Survey Poll of 59 countries, 44.71% of Ghanaian respondents supported the death penalty, significantly lower than Nigeria (62.62%) and even several European countries.[162] In 2015, these public opinion results were confirmed in a comprehensive study performed by the Centre for Criminology and Criminal Justice in Accra, in partnership with the University of Cambridge Institute of Criminology. The large plurality of respondents (48.3%) were strongly opposed to the death penalty, and only a small minority (8.6%) were strongly in favor.[163] About seven in ten expressed support for a discretionary death penalty in place of a mandatory one, and about 71% of respondents approved of life imprisonment without the possibility of parole as an alternative to the death penalty.[164] These results are very different from public opinion surveys in other developing retentionist nations. In Trinidad and Tobago, for instance, 89% of respondents favored the death penalty, though only 26% favored a mandatory death penalty.[165] In Malaysia, 80% favored the death penalty, including 56% for the mandatory death penalty for murder.[166] In Ghana, support for abolition was highest among university graduates compared to secondary school graduates; upper class residents compared to middle- and lower-classes; women compared to men; and religious persons (especially Catholics) compared to non-religious persons.[167] Interestingly, the Ghanaian survey also revealed that international trends toward death penalty abolition

160 William A. Schabas, *The United Nations and Abolition of the Death Penalty*, in *Against the Death Penalty: International Initiatives and Implications*, 9, 29–30 (Jon Yorke ed., 2008).

161 UN Third Committee, *Moratorium on the Use of the Death Penalty*, A/C.3/67/L.44/Rev.1 (November 19, 2012), www.un.org/en/ga/third/67/docs/voting_sheets/l.44.Rev.1.pdf.

162 James Unnever, *Global Support for the Death Penalty*, 12 Punishment & Soc. 463, 473 (2010).

163 Tankebe, Boakye & Atupare, *supra* note 155 at ix.

164 *Id.*

165 Roger Hood & Florence Seemungal, *Public Opinion on the Mandatory Death Penalty in Trinidad*, vii-viii (2011).

166 Roger Hood, *The Death Penalty in Malaysia: Public Opinion on the Mandatory Death Penalty for Drug Trafficking, Murder, and Arms Offenses* (2013).

167 Tankebe, Boakye & Atupare, *supra* note 155 at 8–9.

made relatively little impact on the views of respondents, suggesting that the domestic experience was a weightier consideration.[168]

Most interestingly, the 2015 public opinion survey revealed that Ghanaian respondents who practiced African traditional religions supported capital punishment at significantly higher rates than those who did not hold similar beliefs. In particular, the survey found that among respondents who believed that ancestral spirits visit punishment on criminals, 43.5% opposed the death penalty, compared to 63.6% who did not have such beliefs. In addition, death penalty support was expressed by 64.2% of respondents who believed that traditional deities were more effective in punishing offenders (versus 41.3% who did not hold these beliefs) and 63.9% of those who stated crime victims should consult traditional deities (versus 40.6% of those who did not hold such beliefs).[169] Support for the death penalty among people who practiced traditional religions may have been statistically higher because these traditional beliefs tend to favor collective responsibility for a crime, including that misfortune could befall the family or community rather than the individual offender alone. As a result, these respondents may have endorsed more punitive sanctions for crime than persons not holding such beliefs.[170]

Political and legal elites, including the judicial profession, show these same cleavages about the propriety of capital punishment. Court of Appeal nominees were reported to disagree about whether to abolish the death penalty during their appearances before the Appointments Committee in Parliament.[171] Supreme Court Justice Rose Constance Owusu, a staunch Presbyterian, has forcefully and publicly advocated for death penalty retention.[172] By contrast, Supreme Court Justice-designate Yaw Apau indicated that he opposed the death penalty due to the fear that an innocent person could be executed.[173]

Ghana is currently poised to abolish the death penalty pending a constitutional referendum. In June 2012, the government released a White Paper formally accepting a recommendation by its Constitutional Review Commission to abandon the death penalty, stating that the "sanctity of life is a value so much engrained in the Ghanaian social psyche that it cannot be gambled away with judicial uncertainties."[174] The proposed constitutional changes required a constitutional referendum. In March 2014, the Constitutional Review Commission submitted a draft bill to abolish the death penalty and

---

168 *Id.* at 28.
169 *Id.* at 11–12.
170 *Id.* at 10.
171 Seneadza, *supra* note 71 at 125.
172 *Id.* at 126.
173 Nathan Gadugah, *I'm a Christian; I Am Against the Death Penalty – Justice Apau*, MyJoyOnline.com, June 2, 2015, https://www.modernghana.com/news/620992/1/im-a-christian-i-am-against-the-death-penalty-just.html.
174 Republic of Ghana, White Paper on the Report of the Constitutional Review Commission of Inquiry 44 (June 2012), cited in Hood & Hoyle, *supra* note 154 at 90.

substitute it with life imprisonment.[175] The narrow but decisive reelection of President Mahama preserved the White Paper, though both major candidates supported abolition.[176] Ghanaian voters will need to approve the constitutional amendments proposed by the Review Commission, including abolition of the death penalty, in a public referendum. However, this process stalled because of a constitutional challenge to the referendum process, which was finally dismissed by the Supreme Court in October 2015.[177] It is likely that the referendum will take place during 2016.[178] Abolition would require resentencing the persons on Ghana's death row.

7. CONCLUSION

Of the countries in common law Sub-Saharan Africa, death penalty abolition appears most promising in Ghana. Although the death penalty has precolonial antecedents, it was primarily used for spiritual crimes and was enforced by the community at large. A recent public opinion survey showed that Ghanaians with traditional African religious beliefs were more likely to support capital punishment than Ghanaians who identified as Catholic, Protestant, Muslim, or non-religious.[179] However, the modern death penalty regime is a product of British colonialism. Although British colonizers used capital punishment infrequently for ordinary crimes, the death penalty infamously fell on African nationalists in the late colonial period. With eroding democracy in the first years after independence, the Ghanaian government learned these lessons all too well, and the scope of the death penalty expanded to non-violent and political offenses under PNDC rule in the 1980s. However, the country has refrained from carrying out executions since 1993, shortly after the return to civilian rule. Ghana's domestic and international posture toward the death penalty has shifted since the late 1990s, growing increasingly receptive toward death penalty abolition. A public referendum on a number of constitutional amendments, including abolition, will likely take place in 2016. Recent opinion polls show that public approval is likely.

---

175 Hood & Hoyle, *supra* note 154 at 91.

176 The opposition candidate, Nana Akufo-Addo of the NPP, is on record opposing the death penalty. See Richard Asah-Asante, *I Won't Push For Death Sentences For Armed Robbers – Akufo-Addo*, The Chronicle, February 27, 2001, http://allafrica.com/stories/200102270254.html. Akufo-Addo was President Kufour's Minister of Justice at the time.

177 Tankebe, Boakye & Atupare, *supra* note 155 at 37.

178 Electoral Institute for Sustainable Democracy in Africa, *2016 African Election Calendar*, https://eisa.org.za/index.php/election-calendar (indicating that the constitutional referendum will likely take place before April 2016).

179 Tankebe, Boakye & Atupare, *supra* note 155 at 9–11.

CHAPTER 4
BOTSWANA

1. INTRODUCTION

Botswana is the only country in Africa south of the equator to regularly execute prisoners, most recently in 2013. This is in marked contrast to the country's otherwise prominent history of free and fair elections, high economic growth, and low levels of corruption, especially as a near-neighbor to countries with a history of instability.[1] In contrast to Zimbabwe, Botswana has a precolonial tradition of capital punishment without a significant history of political executions. Nonetheless, use of the death penalty since the country's independence in 1966 has waxed, waned, and waxed again. Although the country only carried out three executions between 1987 and 1996, since then it has carried out at least one every year except 2011 (though it carried out two in 2012), for a total of 47 since independence.[2] However, Botswana has not carried out an execution in 2014 or 2015. These executions typically occur without prior notice. Despite a promising commitment to government transparency, unparalleled in Sub-Saharan Africa, the capital punishment regime's opaqueness has made it vulnerable to criticism on the international level.[3]

Though limited by the scourge of HIV/AIDS, Botswana, a large and sparsely populated country, retains a strong democratic tradition and independent judiciary.[4] Unsurprisingly, Botswana has a comparatively low crime rate. The sparseness of executions creates few opportunities for challenge, with little incentive to create firm guidelines for judges.[5] The irony is that Botswana is a victim

1 See Amelia Cook & Jeremy Sarkin, *Is Botswana the Miracle of Africa? Democracy, the Rule of Law, and Human Rights Versus Economic Development*, 19 Trans. L. & Contemp. Problems 453, 455 (2010) (providing a critical view of Botswana's democracy, despite its rapid economic development).

2 Roger Hood & Carolyn Hoyle, *The Death Penalty: A Worldwide Perspective*, 96 (5th ed., 2015); Tebogo Kgalemang, *Botswana Hangs 47 Since Independence*, Botswana Gazette, June 13, 2013, www.gazettebw.com/?p=3350.

3 For the link between good governance and Botswana's economic success, see David Sebudubudu & Patrick Molutsi, *Botswana's Democracy: Explanations for Success?*, 27 Politeia 47, 56–57 (2008).

4 James Denbow & Phenyo C. Thebe, *Culture and Customs of Botswana*, 1–2, 26 (2006).

5 Alice Mogwe, *Will Basic Human Rights and Individual Freedoms Continue to be Protected, Promoted and Respected?* in *Botswana in the 21st Century*, 49, 60 (Sue Brothers, et al. eds., 1994).

of its own success: unlike other countries in Sub-Saharan Africa, including those analyzed in this volume, Botswana has never had a clean break with its past that would reduce trust in government or reflect a desire to change course. The death penalty survives because of, not in spite of, the success of the postcolonial state.

An unusual aspect defines the death penalty in Botswana: the doctrine of extenuating circumstances, which it shares with Lesotho and Zambia and, in earlier times, with South Africa, Namibia, Swaziland, and Zimbabwe. In Southern Africa, the doctrine of extenuating circumstances served as a regional mechanism for reducing the harshness of the common law mandatory death penalty after it first originated in South Africa in 1935.[6] The doctrine turns the mandatory death penalty into a rebuttable presumption in favor of death, requiring that the defendant show, beyond a fair preponderance of the evidence, that circumstances existed at the time of the offense that reduced the defendant's moral blameworthiness.[7] The doctrine works in practice like a discretionary death penalty, greatly helping to reduce the number of death sentences. However, because the death penalty is presumed, the defendant must show why he or she should *not* die by offering mitigating factors in the case. The doctrine lacks the analytical clarity of a true discretionary death sentence in which the prosecution must prove aggravating factors and may not conform to international law's discouragement of capital punishment for all but the most serious crimes.

2. THE DEATH PENALTY IN COLONIAL AND PRECOLONIAL TIMES

Botswana's legal system is an amalgamation of a European-derived hybrid regime of South African Roman-Dutch and English common law with an indigenous legal system of customary law traditionally administered by tribal chiefs.[8] The British applied the criminal law in force at the Cape of Good Hope to the recently-created Bechuanaland Protectorate in 1891.[9] The Cape did not then have a penal code, so Botswana's criminal law was initially uncodified common law.[10] Under the Order-in-Council of June 10, 1891, the Resident

6 Criminal Procedure and Evidence (Amendment) Act 46 of 1935 §61 (S. Afr.); Ellison Kahn, *How Did We Get Our Lopsided Law on the Imposition of the Death Penalty for Common-Law Crimes? And What Should We Do About It?*, 2 S. Afr. J. Crim. Just. 137, 146–50 (1989).

7 This descends from South African law. In 1947, the South African Appellate Division determined that the onus of showing extenuating circumstances on the balance of probabilities rested with the accused. R. v. Lembete, 1947 (2) S.A. 603, 609 (A.D.).

8 See Bojosi Otlhogile, *Criminal Justice and the Problems of a Dual Legal System in Botswana*, 4 Crim. L.F. 521, 521–22 (1993) (describing the interaction between received European-derived law and indigenous customary law).

9 Daniel T. Ntanda Nsereko, *Extenuating Circumstances in Capital Offences in Botswana*, 2 Crim. L.F. 235, 236 (1991).

10 *Id.*

Commissioner had the power to interfere in death penalty cases before native chiefs, though it seems this power was only rarely used.[11] A "dual" system of colonial courts largely survives intact. While an estimated eighty-five percent of criminal cases are still tried in the customary courts, serious crimes such as murder are tried exclusively in the European-derived law courts.[12] In death penalty cases, a judge typically sat with assessors, but the judge could impose the death sentence even when the assessors disagreed.[13] In Botswana, the death penalty is carried out by hanging and has been since colonial times.[14]

In 1964, shortly before independence, Botswana promulgated its first statutory penal code.[15] This penal code, similar to the ones enacted in British East Africa, is largely derived from English common law rather than from South African law.[16] English precedent rather than South African precedent governs in the event of uncertainty, a provision that British authorities intended to protect Botswana from the influence of the apartheid regime. However, since the majority of Botswana's legal professionals were trained in South Africa, and since Roman-Dutch common law governs much of the legal sphere outside the criminal law, Batswana[17] judges frequently cite and apply South African legal authorities.[18] For instance, Botswana courts have ruled that the concept of "culpable homicide" in Roman-Dutch law was in material respects the same as "manslaughter" in English common law, and therefore South African decisions dealing with the boundary between culpable homicide and murder could apply in Botswana.[19]

The doctrine of extenuating circumstances, which originally developed in South African law, survived the transplantation of English criminal law in the 1964 penal code. As the Botswana Court of Appeal has written, "on the question of extenuating circumstances the decisions of the courts of South Africa have ... [strong] persuasive force because the concept of 'extenuating circumstances' in sentences for murder as introduced into the Penal Code was plainly derived ... from and based on legislation in South Africa."[20] Courts in Botswana often take care to explain why reference is made to South African law in this regard, as

---

11 Aimé Muyoboke Karimunda, *The Death Penalty in Africa: The Path Towards Abolition*, 103 (2014).

12 Elizabeth Maxwell & Alice Mogwe, *In the Shadow of the Noose*, 20 (2006).

13 Karimunda, *supra* note 11 at 104.

14 Hood & Hoyle, *supra* note 2 at 178.

15 See I.G. Brewer, *Sources of the Criminal Law of Botswana*, 18 J. Afr. L. 24, 28 (1974).

16 *Id.*

17 "Batswana" (singular Motswana) is the demonym for nationals of Botswana and members of the Tswana-speaking peoples.

18 See Nsereko, *supra* note 9 at 237 ("No wonder, then, that decisions of the South African courts have had such an impact on Botswana's jurisprudence in matters relating to the death penalty").

19 Gardiol J. van Niekerk, *The Application of South African Law in the Courts of Botswana*, 37 Comp. & Int'l L.J. Southern Afr. 312, 317 (2004).

20 Gofhamodimo v. State, [1984] B.L.R. 119, 41 (Bots. Ct. App.).

the two legal systems have diverged considerably in the realm of criminal law.[21] Today, Botswana has two High Courts (in Gaborone and Francistown) with original jurisdiction over capital cases and other serious civil and criminal legal matters, and appellate jurisdiction from the magistrates' courts over less serious legal disputes.[22] The Court of Appeal reviews cases from the two High Courts.[23] While the Court of Appeal generally overturns High Court criminal sentences only if they are "so manifestly disproportionate to the offence committed that no reasonable trial court would have imposed" them,[24] in practice, the Court of Appeal's review of death penalty decisions is much more searching than this deferential standard of review implies.[25] An accused can appeal as of right, but the state can only appeal questions of law, not fact.[26] As a result, the state cannot appeal if the High Court decides not to impose the death penalty.[27]

The death penalty existed at Tswana customary law, particularly for conspiracy against a chief, and executions were often secret and sudden without trial.[28] The offender's property was also typically confiscated. Other punishments that existed in precolonial times included thrashing, bodily mutilation, or banishment, though after the introduction of colonial rule customary courts could only use lashing and fines as punishments.[29] Witchcraft murder was known at Tswana customary law. In cases of suspected *dipheko* (ritual murder), the public enforced collective justice, attacking and attempting to kill the alleged murderer. Suspected witches were ordered to undo their magic so a patient could recover; if the accused refused or if the victim died, a suspected witch could be tortured or killed.[30]

3. THE CONSTITUTIONAL AND LEGAL FRAMEWORK OF THE DEATH PENALTY IN BOTSWANA

Authorized by Botswana Penal Code Section 26, "any person sentenced to death was ordered to be hanged by the neck until dead."[31] Under the penal

21 Van Niekerk, *supra* note 19 at 317.
22 E.K. Quansah, *Introduction to the Botswana Legal System*, 91 (2nd ed. 1998).
23 *Id.* at 82.
24 Mudangule v. State, [1986] B.L.R. 265, 3 (Bots. Ct. App.), quoted in Nsereko, *supra* note 9 at 239 n. 7.
25 "[M]any convicts sentenced to death by the High Court have had their sentences reduced to custodial ones by the Court of Appeal." Nsereko, *supra* note 9 at 266.
26 *Id.* at 238.
27 *Id.*
28 I. Schapera, *A Handbook of Tswana Law and Custom*, 260–61 (1970).
29 *Id.*
30 Charlanne Burke, *Witchcraft Tswana Style*, in *Conformity and Conflict: Readings in Cultural Anthropology*, 358, 364 (11th ed., James Spradley & David W. McCurdy eds., 2003).
31 Nsereko, *supra* note 9 at 241.

code, the death penalty may be imposed for murder, treason, and piracy with intent to murder, although the latter two offenses have never been tried.[32] The death penalty is mandatory for treason and murder, except where extenuating circumstances exist.[33] According to the penal code, "[w]here a Court in convicting a person of murder is of the opinion that there are extenuating circumstances, the Court may impose any sentence other than death."[34] If the court does not find that extenuating circumstances exist, the death penalty is mandatory. Despite the text of the code, it is settled law that the sentencing court *must* impose a sentence other than death in the presence of extenuating circumstances.[35]

In determining whether extenuating circumstances exist, a court must inquire as to any factors that might have influenced an accused's state of mind at the time he committed the offense; whether those factors did in fact influence the accused; and whether the influence on the accused's mind was such that the act could be considered less morally reprehensible.[36] A court must consider the defendant's social background, the standards of behavior of an ordinary person in the defendant's community, and the accused's behavior according to his or her own peculiar circumstances – his or her weaknesses, foibles, defects, and beliefs. The Court of Appeal has clearly thwarted attempts to use an objective "reasonable man" standard.[37] In weighing whether extenuating circumstances exist, Botswana courts must consider the totality of all factors, both mitigating and aggravating.[38] Courts find extenuating circumstances very frequently in capital cases. Former President Festus Mogae lamented that courts were reluctant to impose death sentences even when they had the discretion to do so.[39]

---

32 Bots. Penal Code §34(1) (treason); §63(1) (piracy with intent to murder). See also Nsereko, *supra* note 9 at 241, 267 ("To date the death penalty has been imposed in murder cases only"). Two people, both South Africans, have been tried for treason, but they were never convicted. *Id.*

33 The doctrine of extenuating circumstances also applies to treason. If extenuating circumstances are found in a case of treason, the court can impose a prison sentence of between fifteen and 25 years, generally a more serious punishment than for murder. For piracy with intent to murder, however, the penal code makes no mention of extenuating circumstances. Kealeboga N. Bojosi, *A Commentary on Recent Constitutional Challenges to the Death Penalty in Botswana*, British Institute of International and Comparative Law (c. 2003), www.biicl.org/files/2191_bojosi_recent_constitutional_challenges.pdf.

34 See Bots. Penal Code §203(2).

35 Nsereko, *supra* note 9 at 246.

36 *Id.* at 261.

37 *Id.* at 262–63.

38 Generally, aggravating factors include premeditation, use of a weapon, excessive cruelty, murder during a rape or robbery, or peculiar vulnerability of the victim. Extenuating circumstances include belief in witchcraft, provocation, absence of actual intention to kill, intoxication, youth, and factors peculiar to the individual defendant. A court may not consider prior convictions unless it has found extenuating circumstances to exist. *Id.* at 246, 267.

39 Nico P. Swartz, *Does Capital Punishment Amount to Cruel, Inhuman and Degrading Punishment: A Reflection on Botswana and South Africa*, 5 J. Pol. & L. 100, 101 (2012).

The Botswana Court of Appeal has generously interpreted extenuating circumstances to include a wide range of factors. Absence of premeditation may be an extenuating circumstance in Botswana, which is a strong indicator that judges attempt to restrict the death penalty only to the narrowest class of intentional cases.[40] Botswana clearly permits provocation as an extenuating circumstance, having found that the proper inquiry is whether the totality of the circumstances that existed at the time the crime was committed had a bearing on the accused's state of mind.[41] By contrast, in Zimbabwe prior to the abolition of the doctrine of extenuating circumstances in 2013, a defense of provocation that failed at trial was likely to fail as an extenuating circumstance because the accused's version of events had already been rejected at the trial stage.[42] One logically troubling aspect of the doctrine of extenuating circumstances is that it could force a defendant to argue in the alternative, e.g., "I did not commit the crime, but even if I did, extenuating circumstances nonetheless existed."[43] Making such an argument could impact the credibility of the defendant and increase the risk of an arbitrary or erroneous outcome.[44]

The Constitution of Botswana grants the president the power to substitute, reduce, or lift a criminal sentence.[45] Like many other common law constitutions, Botswana's provides for an Advisory Committee on the Prerogative of Mercy, consisting of the attorney-general, an *ex officio* member, along with two others: a cabinet minister and a medical practitioner both designated by the president.[46] The committee regulates its own procedure, which must, as a constitutional minimum, review a report written by the trial judge in a capital case.[47] No such report is required in non-capital cases. This clemency power is representative of a "strong" presidential model: the president alone appoints the members of the advisory mercy committee and determines the length of the terms and the conditions of service.[48] Persons sentenced to death in Botswana need not apply for pardon or commutation, as the constitution obligates the president to consider exercising the mercy power to all capital convicts.[49]

---

40 Masono v. State, [2000] 1 Bots.L.R. 46 (C.A.).

41 Ndlovu v. State, [1995] Bots.L.R. 432, 438 (C.A.).

42 Jongwe v. State, Crim. App. No. 251/2002, Judgment No. S.C. 62/02, [2002] ZWSC 62 (August 8, 2002).

43 See D.S. Koyana, *The Demise of the Doctrine of Extenuating Circumstances in the Republics of South Africa and Transkei*, 4(2) Consultus 115, 118 (October 1991).

44 Andrew Novak, *Capital Sentencing Discretion in Southern Africa: A Human Rights Perspective on the Doctrine of Extenuating Circumstances in Death Penalty Cases*, 14 Afr. Hum. Rts. L.J. 24, 27 (2014).

45 Bots. Const. art. 53.

46 Bots. Const. art. 54.

47 Bots. Const. art. 55.

48 Bots. Const. art. 54(1)–(3).

49 Nsereko, *supra* note 9 at 266.

In Botswana, the president invokes the pardon power extremely rarely.[50] "The president is not … obliged to follow the Committee's advice," but should he not, he must personally sign the death warrant. "The exercise of the prerogative of mercy constitutes a serious interference with the judicial process, and is exercised only for good cause," and as a consequence, the president will likely intervene "only in the most exceptional and unusual situation" to reverse a judicially-imposed sentence.[51] The committee's lack of transparency has come in for harsh criticism from human rights NGOs, as its proceedings are not available to the defendant, the defense counsel, or the public.[52] Because the state does not notify family members, lawyers, or human rights monitoring organizations of pending executions, the secrecy makes appeal to regional and international tribunals more difficult.[53] In rejecting a stay in a death penalty case, the Botswana Court of Appeal found it irrelevant that a current president had never granted clemency. Calling the concern "presumptuous," the Court rejected claims that the clemency process was not genuine, even if it was "highly unlikely" that death row inmates would receive clemency."[54]

Botswana's judges strongly defend their sentencing discretion, even pushing back against legislative attempts to enact mandatory minimum sentencing laws. Between 1990 and 2008, parliament passed eight mandatory minimum penalties, including for crimes such as stock theft, theft of an automobile, rape, and robbery, among others, doubling the existing number of mandatory minimum sentences. The Court of Appeal invalidated most provisions that restricted whether a judge could order multiple sentences to run concurrently or consecutively.[55] In 2004, parliament delegated discretion to judges to depart from mandatory minimum sentences if "exceptional extenuating circumstances" warranted.[56] A year earlier, the Court of Appeal ruled that mandatory minimum sentences did not *per se* constitute degrading treatment, but could become unconstitutional if the mandatory minimum were grossly disproportionate to the offense.[57]

---

50 Maxwell & Mogwe, *supra* note 12 at 105 (2006); Nsereko, *supra* note 9 at 266.

51 Charles Manga Fombad, *The Separation of Powers and Constitutionalism in Africa: The Case of Botswana*, 25 B.C. Third World L.J. 301, 331 (2005).

52 Federation internationale des lingues des droits de l'homme (FIDH) & Ditshwanelo Botswana Centre for Human Rights, The Death Penalty in Botswana: Hasty and Secretive Hangings 26 (2007).

53 See Interights (on Behalf of Bosch) v. Botswana, Comm. No. 240/2001, 2003 A.H.R.L.R. 55 (ACHPR 2003) In that case, the defendant was executed while her case was still on appeal to the African Commission. Maxwell & Mogwe, *supra* note 12 at 106–07 (on the secrecy of executions).

54 Kgafela v. Attorney General (In re: Gabaokelwe), Crim. App. No. CLCGB-027-12 (April 27, 2012) (Bots. C.A.).

55 Ikanyeng S. Malila, *Emerging Trends and the General Framework for the Exercise of Sentencing Discretion in Botswana*, 6 Afr. J. Legal Stud. 171 (2013); Elizabeth Macharia-Mokobi, *Defining Exceptional Extenuating Circumstances: Statutory Omission or Judicial Opportunity?*, 24 S. Afr. J. Crim. Just. 113, 113–14 (2011).

56 Macharia-Mokobi, *supra* note 55 at 119, citing Penal Code Amendment Act 39 of 2004.

57 See Moatshe v. State, (2004) 1 B.L.R. 1, 11–12 (January 31, 2003).

4. THE DOCTRINE OF EXTENUATING CIRCUMSTANCES IN PRACTICE

Although the doctrine of extenuating circumstances as originally conceived in South African law placed the burden on the defendant to prove extenuating circumstances, the Botswana Court of Appeal has made an important modification, at least formally removing the evidentiary onus on the accused. The prosecutor, however, is still not required to prove an aggravating factor placing the case in a special category of seriousness warranting the death penalty. In a case under the traditional rule, the Court of Appeal noted that "the appellant's mental state during the attack on the deceased was left very much in the dark" and the judges knew "virtually nothing about [his] personality, his motive, his mentality, his past history, experiences, and upbringing," because the defendant's attorney failed to make a showing of extenuating circumstances.[58] The fault, however, was on the defendant: "The onus was on the Defence to provide the trial court with evidence from which extenuating circumstances might be inferred … Appellant did not do so and his motivation remains unexplained."[59] Over time, however, the Court has softened the rule, holding that if the defendant does not show extenuating circumstances, the judge may find them on his own, *sua sponte*, ruling a decade later that "the law has not put any onus on an accused to prove even on balance of probabilities that extenuating circumstances exist in his case."[60] Instead, the trial judge has the responsibility to examine the evidence after conviction, regardless of any showing by the defendant.

This significant change in Botswana's capital sentencing law derived from a series of constitutional challenges in 1995 that currently form the legal basis for Botswana's modern death penalty regime. In *Kelaletswe v. State*, the Court determined that the burden of showing extenuating circumstances no longer rested on the accused.[61] According to the Court, the prosecutor often had more resources at its disposal to show the severity of a crime and surrounding circumstances, but the accused was often the only person present when the crime was committed, so he or she was better placed to testify to personal factors. For these reasons, the Court determined that the judge and counsel themselves had as much responsibility as the defendant to inquire as to the existence or not of extenuating circumstances. The benefit of the doubt belonged to the accused.[62] In a simultaneous challenge, *Ntesang v. State*, the Court upheld the constitutionality of the death penalty and hanging as a method of execution

---

58 Sibanda v. State, [1984] BWCA 13 at 6.

59 *Id.* at 7.

60 Molale v. State, [1995] Bots.L.R. 146, 149 (C.A.).

61 Kelaletswe v. State, [1995] Bots.L.R. 100 (C.A.). This case was issued the same day as *Molale*.

62 *Id.* at 124.

based on a constitutional clause saving preexisting law, as death by hanging was legal at the time the constitution entered into force.[63] The Court confirmed that the law did not "cast any onus on … a person to show that such extenuating circumstances exist," and the determination "may be arrived at independently of whether or not the accused gives any evidence in that regard," so long as the trial judge provided an opportunity for the accused to present such evidence.[64] The Botswana Court of Appeal confirmed that the trial judge was to engage in only a single step, weighing aggravating and extenuating factors together to determine whether extenuating circumstances existed. A third challenge described how a judge was to weigh both mitigating factors and aggravating factors in order to determine whether extenuating circumstances existed. In that case, the Court upheld a death sentence for a murder committed with "cold calculation" despite the defendant's youth and lack of premeditation, which in other circumstances could have been extenuating circumstances.[65]

Following South African precedent, the imposition of a death sentence in Botswana is at least formally the discretion of a trial judge and may only be altered on appeal where the judge proceeded on a wrong principle of law, improperly evaluated evidence, or imposed a sentence substantially different than the appellate court would have imposed.[66] By contrast, in Lesotho the appellate court has more leeway to interfere with a death sentence imposed by a trial court and to find extenuating circumstances even when the trial judge did not.[67] In a capital case, the Court of Appeal of Lesotho has the duty to reexamine evidence and may set aside a death sentence if it finds that extenuating circumstances should have been found.[68] Despite the strictness of the legal standard, however, the Botswana Court of Appeal more liberally construes extenuating circumstances than the High Courts, and frequently reverses death sentences.[69]

One challenge of such a system is how to enforce consistency and uniformity in crafting a lesser sentence. The Court of Appeal has provided guidance to the High Courts about the length of an appropriate sentence for a murder committed with extenuating circumstances. In 2007, the Court of Appeal recommended a sentence of between fifteen and seventeen years for a heat of passion murder.[70] In a subsequent case where the defendant committed murder in the course of a

63 Ntesang v. State, [1995] Bots.L.R. 151 (C.A.).

64 *Id.* at 155–56.

65 Tshabang v. State, [1995] Bots.L.R. 132, 142 (C.A.). *Tshabang* and *Ntesang* were issued the same day as *Kelaletswe* and *Molale*, January 30, 1995.

66 Gorosang v. State, [2013] BWCA 40 (1 February 2013).

67 W.S. De Wet, *Extenuating Circumstances: Some Aspects of Practice on Appeal in South Africa and Lesotho*, 1 Comp. & Int'l L.J. Southern Afr. 121 (1968), citing Mokolo Ramone v. Rex, CRI/A/8/1966 (C.A.).

68 *Id.*

69 See State v. Mpelegang, Case No. CTHLB-000008-07 (October 26, 2007).

70 Ntesang v. State, [2007] 1 B.L.R. 387 (C.A.).

robbery, the Court of Appeal reduced a thirty-year sentence to a twenty-five-year sentence, believing the longer sentence was excessive.[71] In a subsequent decision, the Court of Appeal indicated that a sentence of imprisonment for longer than twenty-five years was "merited only in very rare and exceptional cases," and noted that a sentence of fifteen to twenty years was typical.[72]

On the other hand, where a murder case has significant extenuating factors, a judge may reduce a sentence of imprisonment significantly. At the lower end of the sentencing spectrum for murder, in 2010 the High Court sentenced a defendant to twelve years' imprisonment, noting that the defendant was a first offender; that he plead guilty at the earliest possible opportunity; that he was remorseful and lacked actual intent to kill; and that he drank a quantity of alcohol.[73] Provocation and heat of passion are also frequently-cited extenuating circumstances where they are not sufficient to reduce a murder charge to manslaughter.[74] Where a defendant was only twenty years old at the time of the offense and subsequently expressed remorse, the Court opted for a sentence of ten years.[75] In one recent case, a trial judge found extenuating circumstances where a woman killed her newborn child, convicting of murder rather than infanticide because the woman was not "disturbed of mind." She was ultimately sentenced to six years' imprisonment.[76]

A recent case from the Botswana High Court comprehensively compiled judicially-imposed murder sentences. In *State v. Mpelegang*, High Court Judge Unity Dow aggregated a long series of Court of Appeal decisions on extenuating circumstances and drew several general conclusions about the doctrine in practice. Judge Dow noted that the High Court tended to hand down longer sentences and tended to be less likely to find extenuating circumstances than the Court of Appeal.[77] After reviewing eighteen Court of Appeal decisions between 1977 and 2007, Judge Dow noted that a sentence of murder typically fell between ten and twenty years, "that is, generally, ten years for young, remorseful, first offenders who have pleaded guilty and twenty years for older offenders who have been particularly callous in the execution of their offences."[78] Between these guideposts, however, trial judges had great leeway and in most cases a sentence of about twelve years was issued. She concluded from the case law that

---

71 Ponatshego v. State, [2006] 2 B.L.R. 464 (C.A.). In 2013, the Court of Appeal reduced a thirty-year sentence to 25 years, finding that the evidence did not support the aggravating feature of a murder committed during an aggravated robbery. Mochona v. State, [2013] BWCA 44 (February 1, 2013).

72 Jackson v. State, [2007] 2 B.L.R. 725, 730 (C.A.).

73 State v. Bimbo, [2010] BWHC 315 (20 September 2010).

74 See, e.g., State v. Ben, [2007] BWHC 215 (2 March 2007) (provocation); State v. Mikirika, [2008] BWHC 306 (13 November 2008) (drinking alcohol and jealous rage).

75 State v. Ntema, [2008] BWHC 300 (22 October 2008).

76 State v. Nthoiwa, [2009] BWHC 146, 147 (10 September 2009).

77 State v. Mpelegang, Case No. CTHLB-000008–07 (October 26, 2007).

78 *Id.* at p. 34.

fifteen years was the starting point for a murder conviction, adding one year for each aggravating factor and subtracting one year for every mitigating factor. She noted that twelve years became the norm rather than the exception due to the prosecutorial practice of non-participation during the sentencing phase of the trial, which allowed the defendant to introduce evidence of mitigating factors without providing evidence of aggravating factors.[79] This policy of non-participation, she cautioned, neglected the victim's interest in providing to the court the impact of the offense on him or her or his or her family.[80]

In her decision, Judge Dow compiled a comprehensive list of extenuating circumstances upheld on appeal. First were factors unique to the offender: age, general intelligence, social class, remorsefulness, influence of alcohol, mental status, intimate or family relationship with the victim, and the character of the accused.[81] Although drinking alcohol was typically an extenuating circumstance, she acknowledged contrary precedent indicating that voluntary or habitual drunkenness could be the fault of the offender.[82] Second were factors that related to process, such as a confession or a plea of guilty, which could result in a sentencing reduction of up to five years. Third were offense-related factors, such as lack of premeditation, level of brutality, and motive of the offender, including whether the murder occurred in tandem with another felony.[83] Fourth were those that related to the victim, including defenselessness of or provocation by the deceased person. Finally, she acknowledged a public interest-related extenuating circumstance: the prevalence of an offense.[84] This "common law" of sentencing decisions serves as a kind of judicially-created sentencing guidelines to help provide consistency and predictability in the sentencing process.

5. INTERNATIONAL LAW AND THE DOCTRINE OF EXTENUATING CIRCUMSTANCES

The ICCPR, of which Botswana is a state party, limits the death penalty to only the "most serious crimes."[85] International human rights treaty bodies and domestic courts have understood this limitation to prohibit the mandatory death penalty.[86] Because the doctrine of extenuating circumstances has characteristics

79 *Id.* at 46–50.
80 *Id.* at 50.
81 *Id.* at 38–41.
82 *Id.* at 40.
83 *Id.* at 41–43.
84 *Id.* at 43–44. This factor is unusual because Judge Dow appears to have intended it to be construed as aggravating in nature rather than extenuating or mitigating.
85 International Covenant on Civil and Political Rights (ICCPR), art. 6(2), 99 U.N.T.S. 85, entered into force March 23, 1976. Botswana ratified on September 8, 2000.
86 UNHRC, CCPR Draft General Comment No. 36, ¶ 36 (September 2, 2015); Thompson v. St. Vincent, Comm. No. 806/1998, UN Doc. CCPR/C/70/D/806/1998 (2000) (UNHCR); Edwards

of both a mandatory and a discretionary death penalty regime, the doctrine has not explicitly been found to violate the ICCPR or the African Charter.[87] As noted, although the death penalty is mandatory in the absence of extenuating circumstances, this appears to provide sufficient tailoring to the circumstances of a crime to distinguish it from a mandatory death penalty for aggravated murder.[88] At the same time, however, the doctrine does not specifically require the prosecutor to prove an aggravating factor meriting the death penalty; the presumptive nature of a capital sentence would seem to contradict the ICCPR's requirement that the death penalty be limited to the worst of the worst cases, even if in practice in Botswana most cases are reduced to terms of imprisonment.

The lack of clarity in judicial sentencing proceedings and lack of transparency in the execution process have led to condemnations of the death penalty in Botswana from international tribunals, NGOs, and foreign governments. Two cases in particular illustrate the difficulty Botswana has had in defending its current death penalty regime on an international stage: the executions of Mariette Sonjaleen Bosch in 2001 and of Lehlohonolo Kobedi in 2003. On March 31, 2001, Bosch, a white South African woman, was executed for murdering the wife of a man she later married. The fact that Bosch never admitted guilt before a divided tribunal contributed to a public relations problem.[89] State officials dismissed the international protest as racially charged due to the fact that the defendant was white.[90] The case had several irregularities that attracted widespread criticism, including a misstatement of law by the trial judge that was found to be harmless on appeal.[91] The trial had a circus-like quality to it due to the sordid facts. The Court upheld the conviction of murder without extenuating circumstances, finding that her emotional jealousy could not be an extenuating circumstance when the murder was so carefully planned.[92]

The Bosch case was notable for the lack of transparency in Botswana's sentencing process and for the fact that she was executed while her case was still pending before the African Commission. Upon her conviction, she immediately

v. Bahamas, Case 12.067, Inter-Am. Comm'n H.R., Report No. 48/0, OEA/Ser.L/V/II.111, doc. 20 (2000); Woodson v. North Carolina, 428 U.S. 280 (1976); Mithu v. State of Punjab, (1983) 2 S.C.R. 690 (India).

87 See Swartz, *supra* note 39 at 105.

88 In *Carpo v. Philippines*, the UN Human Rights Committee found that the mandatory death penalty violated the ICCPR even when it was reserved solely for an aggravated form of murder, because even though an aggravating circumstance was necessary to triggering the capital punishment provision, a judge still had no ability to consider mitigating factors. Carpo v. Philippines, Comm. No. 1077/2002, UN Doc. CCPR/C/77/D/1077/2002 (2002). Botswana's capital sentencing regime avoids this defect because it *does* provide a mechanism by which a judge can consider mitigating factors.

89 Bester Gabotlale, *Death Penalty: Five Years After Bosch, Nothing Changed in Botswana*, Inter Press Service News Agency, May 17, 2006, http://ipsnews.net/africa/nota.asp?idnews=33275.

90 *Id.*

91 Bosch v. State, [2001] 1 Bots.L.R. 71 (C.A.).

92 *Id.*

made an application for clemency, but never received a response from the President.[93] In late March, Bosch's husband, her lawyer, and human rights observers tried to visit her in prison one weekend.[94] After they were turned away, she was quietly executed, writing in a final letter to her husband, "[t]hey did not want me to see you."[95] Bosch's family and lawyer learned of her execution in the Monday lunch news bulletin.[96] The failure to notify family members or counsel of a pending execution is a routine occurrence in death penalty cases in Botswana. In 2006, the mother of condemned prisoner Oteng Modisane Ping was turned away at the prison and told to visit the following Monday. Although prison officials were aware of Ping's death warrant, they failed to tell the family that Ping was scheduled to be executed the next day. The family learned of the execution by radio.[97]

In Bosch's international petition, the African Commission requested that the President of Botswana stay her execution pending consideration of her case. The government did not respond and Bosch was executed.[98] Although the African Commission upheld use of the death penalty under international law in a posthumous decision and determined that the lack of transparency and speed of execution did not create an arbitrary deprivation of life, it cautioned that the criminal justice system "must have a human face in matters of execution," including time to organize one's affairs, visit with family members, receive spiritual advice, and have a proper burial.[99] The Bosch petition also raised two additional challenges under Article 4 of the African Charter, the right to life provision. The first was whether the President arbitrarily deprived Bosch of her right to life. The Court did not find a violation, noting that clemency was discretionary and did not require an oral hearing; rather, the right to be heard could be confined to written submissions alone.[100] The second was whether Bosch's execution while her petition was still pending at the African Commission violated Article 4. However, the Commission indicated that it did not receive any proof that the President received the written letter requesting a stay of execution.[101] The Commission missed an opportunity to restrict application

93 Tim Curry, *Cutting the Hangman's Noose: African Initiatives to Abolish the Death Penalty*, 13 Hum. Rts. Brief 40, 43 (2006).

94 Gabotlale, *supra* note 89; Press Release, *Ditshwanelo* Botswana Ctr. for Human Rights, *Execution of Mariette Sonjaleen Bosch*, April 2, 2001, www.ditshwanelo.org.bw/april2pres.html.

95 Gabotlale, *supra* note 89.

96 *Id.*

97 Swartz, *supra* note 39 at 104.

98 Lilian Chenwi, *Taking the Death Penalty Debate Further: The African Commission on Human and Peoples' Rights*, in *Against the Death Penalty: International Initiatives and Implications*, 75, 88 (Jon Yorke ed., 2008).

99 Interights (on Behalf of Bosch) v. Botswana, Comm. No. 240/2001, 2003 A.H.R.L.R. 55 (ACHPR 2003).

100 *Id.* at ¶¶ 44–47.

101 Chenwi, *supra* note 98 at 91, *citing Interights*, ¶ 50.

of the death penalty, but the holding that a government must have a "human face" in death penalty matters, including by providing family notification of a pending execution, has been cited by several international human rights bodies on state obligations with respect to the death penalty. For instance, the African Commission's new General Comment No. 3 on the Right to Life (Article 4) of the African Charter states that retentionist states must give "reasonable advance notice of the timing, manner, and number of executions to those involved, including those under sentence of death, their families and lawyers, and to the public at large," rights first recognized by the African Commission in *Interights (on behalf of Bosch) v. Botswana*.[102]

An even more consequential case arose two years later when the Court of Appeal revisited the constitutionality of the death penalty in *Kobedi v. State* and considered a death row "syndrome" challenge.[103] While Bosch was executed within weeks of her appeal, Lehlohonolo Kobedi lingered for a decade. Convicted of a murder in 1993, Kobedi was sentenced to death in 1998 and not executed until 2003.[104] Kobedi was represented by four sets of lawyers and twice appealed his case to the Court of Appeal challenging irregularities in his trial. Represented by inexperienced *pro deo* counsel and lacking interpreters in his native language of Sesotho, Kobedi challenged two of the most serious problems with the operation of Botswana's death penalty. First, he argued the doctrine of extenuating circumstances was too restrictive since it barred consideration of mitigating factors before or after the offense took place, and second, that the long period of time he spent on death row made a constitutional sentence unconstitutional.[105] This is the so-called "death row phenomenon," the theory that poor prison conditions, excessive delay, and restrictions on health or spiritual care would make a routine capital case cruel and degrading punishment.[106] The Court of Appeal refused to reduce Kobedi's sentence, though it indicated he might have a strong case before the clemency committee.[107] Since the workings of the clemency committee are secret, "[w]e may never know

---

102 African Commission on Human and Peoples' Rights (ACHPR), General Comment No. 3 on the African Charter on Human and Peoples' Rights, adopted during 57th Session, November 4–18, 2015, ¶ 26. The Draft Comment on the Right to Life under the ICCPR is in accord, stating that failure to provide timely notification of an execution constitutes degrading treatment. United Nations Human Rights Committee (UNHRC), CCPR Draft General Comment No. 36, ¶ 42 (September 2, 2015).

103 Kobedi v. State, [2003] BWCA 22 (March 19, 2003).

104 *SA Man Executed in Botswana*, S. Afr. Press Ass'n, July 19, 2003, www.news24.com/News24/AnanziArticle/0,6935,2-7-1442_1389683,00.html.

105 See *Kobedi*, [2003] BWCA 22 at 3.

106 For a theoretical explanation of the so-called death penalty phenomenon, see also Kealeboga N. Bojosi, *The Death Row Phenomenon and the Prohibition Against Torture and Cruel, Inhuman or Degrading Treatment*, 4 Afr. Hum. Rts. L.J. 303 (2004) (describing how conditions on death row and delay can make an otherwise constitutional death sentence into impermissible cruel and unusual punishment).

107 *Kobedi*, [2003] BWCA 22.

whether the Clemency Committee considered the Court's recommendation, or the advocacy of Mr. Kobedi's lawyers," protested the *Ditshwanelo* Botswana Centre for Human Rights.[108]

In *Kobedi*, the Court distinguished the Privy Council's recent invalidation of the mandatory death penalty in Belize in *Reyes v. Queen*, noting that the death penalty in Botswana was not strictly mandatory and provided sufficiently individualized sentences. *Kobedi* also provided an occasion to bring a fair trial challenge against Botswana's *pro deo* system of legal representation in which criminal defendants could be assigned inadequate or inexperienced defense counsel. The Court was not persuaded: "It is not for this Court to criticise the Botswana *pro deo* system," as the "country has a large number of competent and skilled legal practitioners" who adequately represent most indigent capital defendants.[109] The Court found Kobedi's attorney provided "searching and vigorous" cross-examination and made "full and detailed" submissions. But this decision masks the shortcomings of a judicare model of indigent legal aid. The Constitution of Botswana guarantees the right of a defendant "to defend himself before the court in person or, at his own expense, by a legal representative of his own choice."[110] Standard practice for murder trials has been for the state to assign counsel at nominal cost to an indigent accused person, but "the quality of such representation mostly leaves a lot to be desired" and the average amount received for a *pro deo* case is one-tenth that made by an attorney in private practice for a single court appearance.[111] According to Swartz, *pro deo* lawyers received P300 per courtroom appearance, compared to an average fee to a lawyer in private practice of P450 per hour and P3,000 per court appearance.[112] State-appointed lawyers often received briefs only shortly before the trial date. "The result is that most *pro deo* cases are handled by inexperienced lawyers who lack the skills, resources, and commitment to handle such serious matters [affecting] the rights of the accused."[113]

Kobedi also argued that the definition of "extenuating circumstances" was unconstitutionally narrow. Mitigating factors were broader in scope than legally-defined "extenuating circumstances" and could include factors such as a lack of previous convictions, good behavior, religious conversion, medical needs, familial obligations, remorse after the fact, or others that did not bear on an accused's moral guilt at the time of the offense. In Kobedi's case, those

108 *Secret Executions in Botswana Questioned*, Africa Online News, July 18, 2003, www.afrol.com/articles/10357.

109 *Id.* at 42.

110 Bots. Const. art. 10(d).

111 Duma Gideon Boko, *Fair Trial and the Customary Courts in Botswana: Questions on Legal Representation*, 11 Crim. L.F. 445, 454 (2000). There is no constitutional right to a state-appointed attorney even in capital cases. See also FIDH and Ditshwanelo, *supra* note 52 at 21.

112 Swartz, *supra* note 39 at 103.

113 FIDH and Ditshwanelo, *supra* note 52 at 21.

factors included his good academic record and close family life. The Court dodged the argument, writing that nothing stopped the defendant from raising such arguments, though Botswana's current capital sentencing regime does not provide a formal place to consider them outside of the secretive clemency process.[114]

Finally, Kobedi also raised a death row syndrome challenge as five years had passed from his initial conviction to the final disposition of his appeal. Distinguishing favorable Zimbabwean precedent, the Court ruled that delay in Kobedi's case was caused by his own actions in dismissing and hiring new counsel and seeking extensions for court submissions. The Court did not reject the theory of a death row syndrome challenge, noting that such a circumstance could be unconstitutional, but "it is inherent in the [death] penalty that any person upon whom it is imposed is likely to experience mental strain and suffering. He is confined in prison and usually in segregated conditions. His life in prison is a lonely one. He has to cope with the uncertainty as to when his execution will occur, although he is aware that execution is a certainty."[115] The Court issued a stay of Kobedi's death sentence pending his mercy application, a meaningless gesture given that the constitution obliges the president to consider exercising his prerogative of mercy over all capital convicts.[116] The Court did nothing more than shift its responsibility for Kobedi's death sentence to the President.

Kobedi brought these same challenges to Botswana's capital sentencing regime before the African Commission. Kobedi's counsel argued that the mandatory imposition of the death sentence in the absence of extenuating circumstances violated the African Charter. In addition, the petition alleged that Kobedi lived under fear of execution for over a decade, exposing him to cruel and degrading treatment. Finally, the legal team alleged that hanging constituted a cruel form of punishment.[117] As to the doctrine of extenuating circumstances, Kobedi's counsel argued that the definition of extenuating circumstances limited the factors that could be taken into consideration during sentencing. A court could not consider rehabilitation of the prisoner, for instance.[118] The Commission did not squarely rule on this issue with respect to the right to life, but noted that it was not arbitrary or discriminatory under Articles 2 and 3 of

114 *Kobedi*, [2003] BWCA 22.

115 *Id.* at 52.

116 As Bojosi writes, the Court of Appeal's reasoning understated the amount of time that the defendant spent on death row and unfairly excluded delay caused by the prosecutor. In addition, it also penalized the defendant for exercising constitutional rights of appeal, even though whether a sentence became cruel and degrading after an undue amount of time and in certain conditions was irrelevant to the fault of the delay. Kealeboga N. Bojosi, *The Death Row Phenomenon Comes to Botswana:* Lehlohonolo Bernard Kobedi v. The State, 38 Comp. & Int'l L.J. South. Afr. 304, 310–12 (2005).

117 Spilg (In re: Kobedi) v. Botswana, (2011) A.H.R.L.R. 3, 4 (ACHPR 2011).

118 *Id.* at 21.

the African Charter.[119] In essence, the Commission agreed with the government of Botswana that the doctrine of extenuating circumstances sufficiently individualized the capital sentencing process even if a trial judge were restricted in the factors that he or she could consider in mitigation. The Commission also failed to find a violation of the right to life, noting that Kobedi's death sentence was for a "most serious crime" in accordance with international law, namely intentional murder with violence.[120]

Kobedi's petition included a challenge based on Article 5 of the African Charter, the prohibition on cruel and degrading treatment, due to the psychological effects of remaining on death row for a decade as well as a heart condition that would render his hanging torturous. The Commission rejected these challenges, noting that the clock began to run only when the death sentence was passed, not for the entire duration of time that he was detained.[121] This holding glossed over the fact that the death penalty was presumptively mandatory for murder, which could extend the mental torture of a pending death sentence to before conviction. In this case, the Commission found that most of the delay in carrying out his death sentence was the result of the defendant's own actions.[122] However, citing *Interights (on behalf of Bosch)*, the African Commission did confirm its prior holding that the failure of the government to notify the defendant's family of the pending execution constituted degrading treatment and violated the African Charter.[123] Of the two cases brought before the African Commission on Botswana's application of the death penalty, it was the lack of transparency in the actual execution process, not in judicial sentencing, where the country's death penalty practice proved most vulnerable.

6. PROSPECTS FOR ABOLITION OF THE DEATH PENALTY

Government officials in Botswana justify retention of the death penalty by relying on public opinion, noting that elected officials are democratically accountable and must represent popular will.[124] According to the Court of Appeal, the people of Botswana, through their elected representatives, promulgated a penal code that prescribed the death penalty for murder without extenuating circumstances and certain other offenses. Indeed, "the death penalty has been imposed in Botswana for murder since time immemorial, so that its abolition

119 *Id.* at 30.
120 *Id.* at 39–40.
121 *Id.* at 34.
122 *Id.* at 39.
123 *Id.* at 35.
124 Hood & Hoyle, *supra* note 2 at 426.

would be a departure from the expected norm."[125] The murder rate in Botswana is considerably lower than in South Africa, but still high by international standards, which could fuel death penalty populism.[126] The country routinely votes against a UN moratorium on executions and was one of only 39 countries to vote "no" in 2012.[127] Nonetheless, Botswana has ratified the Rome Statute of the International Criminal Court, signifying some consent to exclude the death penalty for the most serious international crimes.[128] The country has also been the site of activism by European governments and international human rights organizations. The European Union and Council of Europe delegations to Botswana have visited and held seminars on abolition of the death penalty in Botswana.[129] Following the execution of Zibane Thamo in 2012, the African Commission made a statement of regret that Botswana continued to use the death penalty through Zainabo Sylvie Kayitesi, the Special Rapporteur for the African Commission's Working Group of Experts on the Death Penalty.[130] Jonas writes that Botswana is "swimming against the tide" of abolition and "seems to be impervious to international legal efforts in this direction."[131]

One external wildcard could still influence the future of the death penalty in the country: the fact that Botswana cannot receive a fugitive from abroad, including from South Africa, if the fugitive could face the death penalty.[132] Botswana has refused to sign undertakings with the government of South Africa to promise that it would not seek capital charges against a fugitive. Consequently, those fugitives remain untried as South Africa refuses to return them to Botswana for trial and lacks jurisdiction to prosecute them.[133] The extradition agreement between South Africa and Botswana allows one of them to deny extradition to the other to avoid the death penalty, a practice also permitted in the Southern African Development Community (SADC) Protocol on Extradition.[134] The South African Constitutional Court has prominently ruled that it is unconstitutional for the South African government to extradite a prisoner to a country where he or she could be executed.[135] Recently, the

---

125 Kgafela (In re: Gabaokelwe) v. Attorney General, Crim. App. No. CLCGB-027-12 (April 27, 2012).

126 S.S. Terblanche, *Sentencing Murder and the Ideal of Equality*, 44 Comp. & Int'l L.J. Southern Afr. 7–8 (2011).

127 UN Third Committee, *Moratorium on the Use of the Death Penalty*, A/C.3/67/L.44/Rev.1 (November 19, 2012), www.un.org/en/ga/third/67/docs/voting_sheets/l.44.Rev.1.pdf.

128 Karimunda, *supra* note 11 at 191.

129 Hood & Hoyle, *supra* note 2 at 31.

130 Obonye Jonas, *Human Rights, Extradition and the Death Penalty: Reflections on the Standoff Between Botswana and South Africa*, 10 Sur: Int'l J. on Hum. Rts. 181, 184 (2013).

131 *Id.*

132 *Id.* at 181.

133 *Id.* at 181–82.

134 *Id.* at 185–86, citing SADC Protocol on Abolition, art. 5(c) (2006).

135 Mohamed v. President of the Republic of South Africa, 2001 (3) S.A. 893 (C.C.). *Mohamed* involved an extradition to the United States.

Constitutional Court confirmed that extraditing a prisoner to Botswana where he or she could face the death penalty was a violation of the right to life.[136] Such external pressure could discourage Botswana from carrying out executions in the future.

Perhaps the most active local organization campaigning against the death penalty in Botswana is the *Ditshwanelo* Botswana Centre for Human Rights. In 1997, *Ditshwanelo* began a public anti-death penalty campaign entitled "Who Has the Right to Kill?" During that campaign, opinion pages of the newspaper and calls to radio shows revealed vocal support for capital punishment.[137] In 1999, *Ditshwanelo* successfully sought a stay of execution for Gwara Motswetla and Tlhabologang Maauwe, two persons of indigenous San descent, 72 hours before their scheduled executions for murder.[138] The High Court set aside the convictions and death sentences and ordered a new trial. However, both men were still in prison as of March 2005, and the government was unwilling to proceed with a trial. *Ditshwanelo* returned to court on behalf of the two men, arguing that the right to a speedy and fair trial had been violated. The organization won a permanent stay of prosecution and the two men's release.[139] The case marked the first time a defendant was able to challenge a death sentence after exhausting appeals and the first time that a non-governmental organization was given standing to intervene as a party in a death penalty case.[140] In a later death penalty case, however, the Court of Appeal did not find that *Ditshwanelo* had standing to seek a stay of execution on behalf of a prisoner facing execution, as the prisoner was not a party to the proceedings.[141]

For the near-term future at least, Botswana's domestic and international posture suggests that executions will remain legal, regular, and rare. Nonetheless, political and legal elites in the country have always held diverse views. Famed South African human rights lawyer, the Greek-born George Bizos, was a judge of the Botswana Court of Appeals from 1985 to 1993. He served on the legal team for the South African constitutional challenge against the death penalty and has represented clients such as Nelson Mandela and Zimbabwean opposition leader Morgan Tsvangirai. He vocally demanded justice for Maauwe and Motswetla and remains a prominent opponent of capital punishment.[142] Another prominent opponent of the death penalty in Botswana is Duma Boko, the leader of Botswana's main opposition alliance, the Umbrella for Democratic

136 Minster of Home Affairs v. Tsebe, 2012 (5) S.A. 467 (C.C.).
137 Curry, *supra* note 93 at 43.
138 Maxwell & Mogwe, *supra* note 12 at 68.
139 Curry, *supra* note 93 at 43.
140 Maxwell & Mogwe, *supra* note 12 at 15.
141 Kgafela (In re: Gabaokelwe) v. Attorney General, Crim. App. No. CLCGB-027–12 (April 27, 2012).
142 George Bizos, *Preface One: The Death Penalty Should Be Abolished*, in Maxwell & Mogwe, *supra* note 12 at 7, 7–8.

Change. Boko has represented numerous capital defendants, including Brandon Sampson (removed from death row in 2011) and Gotlhalosamang Gabaokelwe (executed in 2012).[143] Boko has stated that the death penalty in Botswana "cheapens human life" and was "irrevocable." He has stated that if he became President of Botswana, he would not sign death warrants.[144]

7. CONCLUSION

Botswana is an actively retentionist country, having carried out an execution as recently as 2013. The country adheres to the doctrine of extenuating circumstances, adopted from South African law, in which a death sentence is presumptive unless certain mitigating factors existed in the defendant's case to remove it from the category of seriousness warranting death. Although courts in Botswana have resisted constitutional challenges to the capital punishment regime, judges have developed consistent sentencing patterns in capital cases. Although Botswana's sentencing model has survived scrutiny by the African Commission, the lack of transparency in carrying out executions has come in for criticism. Although the death penalty existed prior to the onset of colonial rule and was used sparingly by British colonial officials, political elites and NGOs are divided in their support for legal capital punishment. Nonetheless, public support for the death penalty appears strong and the sentence looks to remain lawful for the foreseeable future.

---

143 John Regonamanye, *Court of Appeal Endorses Death Penalty on Triple Murder Convict*, Sunday Standard, February 17, 2012, www.sundaystandard.info/court-appeal-endorses-death-penalty-triple-murder-convict; Isaiah Morewagae, *Death Conviction of Molefe and Sampson Quashed*, Mmegi, May 2, 2011, www.mmegi.bw/index.php?sid=1&aid=546&dir=2011/May/Monday2.

144 Alma Balopi, *Death Penalty: "It Cheapens Human Life,"* InterPress Service, April 13, 2011, www.ipsnews.net/2011/04/death-penalty-it-cheapens-human-life.

CHAPTER 5
LESOTHO AND SWAZILAND

Both Lesotho, a tiny landlocked nation completely surrounded by the Republic of South Africa, and Swaziland, an enclave between Mozambique and South Africa, are *de facto* abolitionist, defined as a country in which the death penalty remains a lawful sentence but no executions have occurred for ten years or more.[1] Both countries have very small death rows and international postures that are receptive toward abolition. The death penalty regimes of Lesotho and Swaziland have been profoundly influenced by their larger and more powerful neighbor, South Africa. Despite optimism that the abolition of the death penalty in South Africa would provide a model for other countries in Sub-Saharan Africa, the South African case has proven to be exceptional.[2] Nonetheless, the *de facto* extinction of capital punishment in the two countries since the late 1980s could be seen as a collateral consequence of abolition in South Africa, not least because extradition treaties with South Africa and Mozambique discourage capital punishment.[3]

Although this chapter treats Lesotho and Swaziland together, their death penalty legal regimes and domestic political contexts differ. Both countries are small traditional monarchies with significant resource constraints that resisted incorporation into South Africa during the colonial period. Lesotho has a more unstable if more democratic political system than Swaziland does, but the absolute nature of the Swazi monarchy severely limits fundamental rights.[4] Lesotho, like Botswana, adheres to the old South African doctrine of extenuating circumstances in which a death penalty is mandatory unless

---

1 Roger Hood & Carolyn Hoyle, *The Death Penalty: A Worldwide Perspective*, 19 (2015).

2 See *contra*, Sangmin Bae, *When the State No Longer Kills: International Human Rights Norms and the Abolition of Capital Punishment*, 61 (2007) (asserting that abolition in South Africa would influence the rest of the continent because of the country's economic importance and leadership role). Yet, in retrospect, abolition in South Africa was peculiar to the post-apartheid political context and the wording of the country's new constitution.

3 See Extradition Agreement Between the Government of the Republic of South Africa and the Government of the Kingdom of Swaziland, art. 6 (October 5, 1968); Southern African Development Community Protocol on Extradition, art 5(c) (October 3, 2002); Law Library of Congress, *Mozambique/CPLP: Extradition Treaty Ratified*, 2007 (4) Global Legal Monitor at 42.

4 Peter Fabricius, *A Tale of Two Kingdoms*, Institute of Security Studies Today, July 2, 2015, https://www.issafrica.org/iss-today/a-tale-of-two-kingdoms.

the judge specifically finds mitigating factors exist (though, like Botswana, Lesotho no longer places the onus of showing extenuating circumstances on the defendant).[5] By contrast, Swaziland's new 2005 constitution prohibits the mandatory death penalty, which ensures that judges always have discretion to substitute a lesser sentence, even absent extenuating circumstances.[6] In any event, trial judges in both countries issue death sentences extremely rarely, and appellate courts uphold them even less frequently still. Though these countries share a similar death penalty framework with Botswana, the influence of abolitionist South Africa is much greater. This chapter will turn first to Lesotho and then separately to Swaziland before discussing the prospects of abolition in both countries.

1. THE DEATH PENALTY IN THE PRECOLONIAL AND COLONIAL PERIOD IN LESOTHO

As was true of other Bantu-speaking linguistic groups, Karimunda writes that the Basotho people generally did not practice capital punishment for murder prior to the onset of colonialism.[7] The death penalty existed in precolonial times for sorcery, repeated thieving, and conspiring against a chief until King Moshoeshoe I (1786–1870) abolished the practice.[8] Moshoeshoe consolidated a united Basotho kingdom. He is widely remembered as an exemplary moral character with respected leadership traits. Unlike his contemporary Shaka Zulu, Moshoeshoe used the death penalty sparingly, preferring to rule by consultation and consent rather than bloodshed.[9] Since his time, criminal punishments were limited to fines, ridicule, and occasional banishment until the British introduced imprisonment. Even after independence, courts could award compensation to the victim for criminal acts, as per the traditional law. Such an award bars damages in a civil suit.[10] Unlike in other African societies, where suspected witches were executed, the Basotho could only "eat up" (confiscate) a perpetrator's property and banish him or her.[11]

5 See Letuka v. Rex, [1997–98] L.L.R.-L.B. 346 (February 4, 1998).

6 Swazi. Const. art. 15(2).

7 Aimé Muyoboke Karimunda, *The Death Penalty in Africa: The Path Towards Abolition*, 36 (2014).

8 S.M. Poulter, *The Judicial System of Lesotho (Conclusion)*, 3 Comp. & Int'l L.J. of Southern Afr. 309, 317 (1970).

9 Khali Victor Mofuoa, *The Exemplary Ethical Leadership of King Moshoeshoe of Basotho of Lesotho in the Nineteenth Century Southern Africa*, 5(3) J. Pub. Admin. & Governance 21, 22, 33 (2015).

10 *Id.*

11 Isaac Rasebate Mokotso, *A Sustainable Educational Response to the Recent Increased Witch Killing and Ritual Murder* "Liretlo" *in Lesotho: Introducing Traditional Basuto Traditional Religion in Lesotho Schools*, 3(4) Afr. Educ. Res. J. 209, 210 (2015).

Lesotho was a British protectorate from 1868 until 1871, after the death of King Moshoeshoe I, when it was transferred to the control of Cape Colony. The death penalty was established in law by Cape Colony Proclamation No. 74 of 1871, which required capital offenses to be tried before three magistrates with the most senior presiding. Serious criminal cases were transferred to the jurisdiction of the magistrates' courts, from which appeals were taken from the chiefs' courts.[12] However, following the Gun War of 1880 to 1881, in which the Basotho chiefs rebelled against Cape Colony rule over the right of Africans to bear arms, Basutoland reverted to British rule as a Crown colony, and the Cape Colony Proclamation no longer applied.[13] The British reestablished Basotho customary law as the law of the territory, and, as a result, the indigenous law survived the colonial period.[14]

Colonial rule in Lesotho was "indirect" – that is, the British relied on existing chieftainship structures to maintain law and order and collect taxes. However, although the hierarchy first consolidated by King Moshoeshoe I remained intact with the onset of colonial rule, chiefs grew less accountable to their subjects and popular participation in traditional decision-making declined. Chiefs lost their ability to impose capital punishment and other severe sanctions, but gained the ability to enrich themselves and curry favor with the British Resident Commissioner and the colonial establishment.[15] Unlike Ghana, also governed by the British policy of indirect rule, the chiefly courts in Lesotho were an integral part of the administrative state and were not subordinated to the colonial courts. While colonial Gold Coast had a hierarchical court system in which customary courts could appeal to a single British-style supreme court, Basutoland lacked a supreme court until late in the colonial period. The rules of Roman-Dutch law applied to non-Africans in Basutoland while a codified form of Basotho customary law applied strictly to the African majority.[16]

In the late colonial period during the 1950s and 1960s, Lesotho experienced a perceived epidemic of so-called "medicine murders" (*liretlo*) in which human flesh was taken from a victim and used to strengthen the user in achieving a desired goal.[17] British prosecution of the *liretlo* murders resulted in the executions of two principal chiefs. Although the historical record suggests that

---

12 J.R. Crawford, *The History and Nature of the Judicial System of Botswana, Lesotho and Swaziland: Introduction and the Superior Courts*, 86 S. Afr. L.J. 476, 477 (1969).

13 *Id.*

14 Karimunda, *supra* note 7 at 103.

15 Richard F. Weisfelder, *The Decline of Human Rights in Lesotho: An Evaluation of Domestic and External Determinants*, 6(4) Issue: J. of Opinion 22, 24 (1976).

16 Roger Gocking, *Colonial Rule and the "Legal Factor" in Ghana and Lesotho*, 67 Africa: J. Int'l Aff. Inst. 61, 63 (1997). The British absorption of the Sotho chiefly hierarchy had a tendency to favor the Paramount Chief's Koena clan at the expense of other rival Nguni peoples, not unlike the Akan dominance of customary law in colonial Ghana. *Id.* at 70.

17 *Id.* at 78.

judges strained to acquit defendants based on inconsistencies in testimony, Basotho defendants were typically tried by white South African judges sitting with Basotho assessors.[18] The "medicine murders" and the executions that followed were a byproduct of the inconsistent and incomplete reconciliation of Basotho customary law with English common law.

The death penalty continued to apply intermittently after Lesotho's independence in 1966. Executions in Lesotho occurred the late 1970s and early 1980s, with one execution in 1977, two in 1978, four in 1979, four in 1981, and two in 1983. Five reprieves of death row prisoners took place in that same time period.[19] Lesotho reported to the UN Human Rights Council that its last execution took place in 1996.[20]

2. CONSTITUTIONAL FRAMEWORK OF THE DEATH PENALTY IN LESOTHO

Lesotho's constitution states at Article 5(1): "Every human being has an inherent right to life. No one shall be arbitrarily deprived of his life."[21] However, Article 5(2) has a death penalty savings clause, noting that an arbitrary deprivation of life does not include an "execution of the sentence of death imposed by a court in respect of a criminal offence under the law of Lesotho of which he has been convicted."[22] In 2004, Lesotho's death row was reported to be empty because judges were able to find extenuating circumstances in every case, even in the presence of serious aggravating factors.[23] Death is by hanging. Lesotho does not have a regular hangman and was forced to bring one from abroad at the time of the country's last execution.[24] The country retains the death penalty for murder, treason, and rape where a rapist knows or has reasonable suspicion to believe that he is infected with the Human Immunodeficiency Virus (HIV).[25] No person has been sentenced to death for treason or rape in Lesotho, and the country has never had a constitutional

18 Richard F. Weisbender, *On the Cusp of Colonial Rule: Medicine Murder in Lesotho*, 51 Afr. Stud. Rev. 151, 152 (2008).

19 Christina Murray, *Hangings in Southern Africa: The Last Ten Years*, 2 S. Afr. J. Hum. Rts. 349, 350 (1986).

20 Death Penalty Worldwide, *Lesotho* (retrieved from DeathPenaltyWorldwide.org) (information current as of May 30, 2014).

21 Lesotho Const. art. 5(1).

22 Lesotho Const. art. 5(2).

23 Moses O.A. Owori, *The Death Penalty in Lesotho: The Law and Practice*, British Institute of International and Comparative Law (c. 2003), www.biicl.org/files/2298_country_report_lesotho_owori.pdf.

24 *Id.* at 7.

25 Lesotho Const. art. 5; Criminal Procedure & Evidence Act, Sec. 297; Sexual Offenses Act, No. 3 of 2003, Sec. 32(a)(vii).

challenge to capital punishment.[26] In addition, the death penalty by law cannot be carried out on persons under the age of eighteen or on pregnant women.[27] As in Botswana, indigent defendants may receive legal representation at state expense in death penalty cases, though representation may be by younger, more inexperienced attorneys.[28]

As per the Commonwealth template, Lesotho's constitution establishes a Pardons Committee on the Prerogative of Mercy, which consists of a chairman and two other members. The Pardons Committee is appointed by the king acting in accordance with the advice of the Judicial Services Commission, a vetting authority for judicial appointments. The king is not able to appoint public officers or members of parliament to the committee, and members serve for three years unless removed by the king on the advice of the Judicial Services Commission.[29] The Pardons Committee receives written and sometimes taped representations from the accused, his or her counsel, the District Secretary of his or her district, the trial judge and appellate judges, and the Director of Public Prosecutions. The Pardons Committee looks at a case in broader perspective than the judicially-defined extenuating circumstances. Only two cases came before the Pardons Committee during the 1990s, of which one was recommended for clemency and the other, a premeditated murder committed for robbery, was recommended for execution.[30]

In Lesotho, a court must impose a death sentence in the absence of extenuating circumstances; if such circumstances are found, the court has discretion to impose a lesser sentence. The Court of Appeal has, in the past, upheld a trial judge's determination that no extenuating circumstances existed and that the accused should be sentenced to death.[31] However, according to Maquto, judges "show a distinct reluctance to impose the death penalty[;] therefore they often find extenuating circumstances where their existence is sometimes slender."[32] Owori puts the state of the doctrine in Lesotho in even more stark terms: "Of the 915 murder charges brought before the courts in the last five years, there is at the moment not a single convict on death row, partly due to the courts always looking for and *finding* extenuating circumstances."[33] In the few cases where the High Court has imposed the death penalty, the Court of Appeal reversed on appeal. Like Swaziland, but unlike Zimbabwe, Lesotho has robust appellate review. According to the Court of Appeal, upon a finding

26 Michael Mathealira Ramodibedi, *The Right to Life and the Death Penalty*, Sunday Express (October 20, 2009), http://sundayexpress.co.ls/?p=1055.

27 Owori, *supra* note 23 at 1.

28 *Id.* at 5.

29 Lesotho Const. art. 102.

30 Owori, *supra* note 23 at 7.

31 See, e.g., Rex v Mabaso, [1980–84] L.A.C. 256, 259 (1984).

32 W.C.M. Maqutu, *Contemporary Constitutional History of Lesotho*, 55 (1990).

33 Emphasis original. Owori, *supra* note 23.

of extenuating circumstances, the imposition of a disproportionately harsh sentence of imprisonment is unconstitutional.[34] A judge can find extenuating circumstances and substitute a lesser punishment even where the assessors in the case do not agree.[35]

Where a trial judge neglects to consider specific extenuating circumstances at the trial level, the Court of Appeal is empowered to alter the sentence. The Lesotho Court of Appeal (previously the Appellate Division before the 1993 constitution) has long rejected South African precedent that held that an appellate court could not substitute its judgment for that of the trial court unless the determination was one to which no reasonable court could have come.[36] In a 1966 decision, the Lesotho Appellate Division reasoned that the trial by jury was never a prominent part of the legal system as in South Africa, and consequently an appellate court has no need to defer to the decision of a jury or a judge sitting with lay assessors.[37] The Lesotho Appellate Division ruled that it had "very wide power to correct the decisions of the High Court," including as to the existence or non-existence of extenuating circumstances.[38] As De Wet explains, the appellate court established that it could examine the reasoning of the trial judge when he or she failed to find extenuating circumstances and itself impose a new sentence rather than remitting the case back to the trial court for further development.[39]

The traditional rule in Lesotho, like that of South Africa, is that a death sentence is mandatory upon conviction for murder, unless the accused person can show that extenuating circumstances existed in his case.[40] The defendant, not the prosecution, has the burden of showing extenuating circumstances. Older cases reflect the strict application of this rule, such that if the convicted defendant did not carry the onus of showing extenuating circumstances, the judge was required to pass a sentence of death.[41] In 1981, the Appellate Division upheld a death sentence where the appellants made no argument at all as to the existence of extenuating circumstances.[42] In a later case from 1985, the Court found the defendant's version of events to be unpersuasive, stating that it was

34 Lefu v. Rex, [2012] LSCA 19 (April 27, 2012), citing Gaborekwe v. State, [2009] BWCA 67 (29 July 2009) (Botswana CA).

35 Rex v. Moratha, [2004] LSHC 56 (April 2, 2004) at 53.

36 W.S. De Wet, *Extenuating Circumstances: Some Aspects of Practice on Appeal in South Africa and Lesotho*, 1 Comp. & Int'l L.J. Southern Afr. 121 (1968).

37 *Id.*, citing Mokolo Ramone v. Rex, C. of A. CRI /A/8/1966.

38 Mokolo Ramone v. Rex, C. of A. CRI /A/8/1966.

39 De Wet, *supra* note 36 at 126, 129.

40 This rule still exists in Lesotho's revised penal code. Lesotho Penal Code Act of 2010, §40 (2012).

41 See, e.g., Rex v. Sello, [1981] LSCA 4 (January 12, 1981).

42 Rex v. Moshepi, [1981] LSCA 47 (July 3, 1981). This also occurred in Lephane v. Rex, [1980] LSCA 7 (January 10, 1980) ("The appellants did not choose to give evidence on extenuation").

"not for [the Court] to speculate in his favour when he chose to remain silent," especially when aggravating factors such as premeditation existed in the case.[43]

As noted with respect to Botswana, the traditional application of the doctrine of extenuating circumstances contains a fundamental contradiction: the defendant who argues innocence must concede guilt at the sentencing phase in order to persuade the court that his blameworthiness was reduced. Highlighting the inherent tension in the doctrine of extenuating circumstances, the Appellate Division pronounced that the defendant could "give evidence again, contradict his former evidence of innocence, and try to persuade the Court that extenuating circumstances existed," continuing:

> This would have involved admitting guilt. But this the defendant did not do. He tried to ride two horses, protesting his innocence (as his argument in this appeal shows) whilst contending in the alternative that if he was guilty his guilt was extenuated by facts that supplied the motive for the murder that he in fact committed. This is generally a difficult posture, and in this case, I think, an impossible one. He cannot have it both ways. If he had given evidence anew, admitted guilt and sought to prove extenuating circumstances, he would have been subject to cross-examination, in which his subjective state of mind, a matter of great importance, could have been tested.[44]

The traditional system was less rational than one in which a prosecutor must prove an aggravating factor beyond a reasonable doubt in order to trigger the death penalty precisely becouse it required an offender to admit guilt, and thereby may have contributed to potential wrongful convictions.

In *Letuka v. Rex*, the Court of Appeal developed a clear process for weighing extenuating circumstances, extensively citing case law from Botswana and South Africa in its decision.[45] In that case, the trial court imposed a death sentence over the dissent of an assessor, finding no extenuating circumstances.[46] According to the Court of Appeal, the accused must have an opportunity to give evidence to rebut the prima facie view that the offense fell into the category of heinous crimes deserving of death, including matters personal to him or her. The extenuating circumstances inquiry must be "conducted with diligence and with an anxiously enquiring mind" to determine whether extenuation is warranted.[47] After this evidence and any aggravating circumstances pointed out by the prosecution have been received by the judge, the Court must evaluate the evidence and testimony and weigh all features of the case.

---

43 Maseko v. Rex, [1985] LSCA 122 (July 26, 1985).
44 Lafaso v. Rex, [1990] LSCA 25 (January 26, 1990).
45 Lekuta v. Rex, [1997–98] L.L.R.-L.B. 346, 360 (February 4, 1998).
46 Rex v. Letuka, [1997] LSHC 66, CRI/T/45/92 (Lesotho HC) (August 20, 1997).
47 *Letuka*, [1997–98] L.L.R.-L.B. at 360.

While the Court of Appeal in *Letuka* did not specifically follow the Botswana case *Kelaletswe* and Swazi case law in holding that the burden of showing extenuating circumstances was not on the accused, the Court "caution[ed] against the use of the *onus* as the determining cause for holding that no extenuating circumstances exist," as this "bears the hallmark of ready recourse to a legal make-weight and can be employed to justify an overly retributive response to serious crime."[48] The Court extensively cited the holding in *Kelaletswe*, but noted, unlike Botswana, this situation was "not currently the law of the Kingdom of Lesotho," where the onus rested on the accused to prove the existence of extenuating circumstances "on a balance of probability." However, the Court warned that the ready invocation of the onus as a determining factor was "a course to be avoided by judicial officers" because it tended to "inhibit the employment of an enquiring mind directed at investigating the presence or absence of extenuating circumstances." Even though the accused did not testify in *Letuka*, the facts were such that the judge should have been able to discern extenuating circumstances.

Although the burden of showing extenuating circumstances still technically rests on the accused, Lesotho case law is settled that a judge must consider extenuating circumstances even without a showing by the defendant. In *Maliehe v. Rex*, the Court of Appeal reversed a death sentence where a judge found the accused had not discharged the onus of proving the existence of extenuating circumstances. According to the Court, "I doubt whether the learned Judge was right in finding that there was an onus on the accused but it is not necessary to decide that" because the prosecution conceded on appeal that extenuating circumstances existed.[49] In *Maliehe*, the Court found extenuating circumstances even where a person was hired to kill, a form of premeditation. This continued hedging as to whether the accused has the onus still occurs in the Court's jurisprudence. In reversing a death sentence in 2011, the Court noted that "[e]ven if there was an onus on the appellant, what he said about the bad relationship between him and the deceased was not challenged."[50] The finding that extenuating circumstances could be found even in the presence of a powerful aggravating factor, as in a premeditated murder for hire, greatly expands the scope of the doctrine in practice and dramatically reduces the number of death sentences.

The doctrine of extenuating circumstances in Lesotho follows the pattern of other countries in the region. In *Letuka*, the Court listed the extenuating circumstances recognized in Lesotho: youth, intoxication, emotional conflict, motive, provocation, sub-normal intelligence, general background, impulsiveness, minor role in crime, absence of *dolus directus* (direct intention

---

48 *Id.*, p. 364.

49 Maliehe v. Rex, [1997–98] L.L.R.-L.B. 168, 181 (February 5, 1997).

50 Kopano v. Rex, [2011] LSCA 19 (April 20, 2011).

to kill), witchcraft, absence of premeditation, "heavy confrontation," and rage of an accused. As the Court explained, "the mere presence of one or more of these features do[es] not automatically mean that they are extenuating in relation to the crime at issue," but rather each "must be weighed and assessed in light of the evidence as a whole."[51] Lesotho courts now treat youth as an extenuating factor even in the absence of other extenuating factors, which is likewise a broader application of the doctrine than that used in Zambia or Zimbabwe.[52] Where a trial judge found that youth could only be an extenuating circumstance in the presence of other factors, the Court of Appeal reversed, finding that the trial judge "failed to appreciate sufficiently that this was prima facie evidence of immaturity and that the evidence did not support the conclusion that the offence of the appellant was committed purely from 'inherent wickedness.'"[53] Where a provocation defense failed at trial, a judge of the High Court found that it succeeded in establishing an extenuating circumstance.[54] However, where provocation turned into a long-term blood feud, a finding of extenuating circumstances was no longer warranted due to premeditation.[55] The Court of Appeal has found extenuating circumstances where the accused had only "an indirect or inferred intention" (*dolus eventualis*), akin to recklessness, rather than a premeditated or "direct intention" (*dolus directus*).[56]

Medicine murder or ritual killing poses unique challenges for the doctrine of extenuating circumstances. In one case of medicine murder, *liretlo*, a High Court judge stated that his initial reaction was that extenuating circumstances did not exist, but his assessors disagreed. He wrote, "judges cannot divorce themselves from the people amongst whom they live," and the assessors' "more profound knowledge of the customs and habits of the people" prevented the judge from "living in a vacuum."[57] He noted that his assessors saw a distinction between the principal and the accomplices in murders perpetuated for spiritual reasons; because of a fear of evil, people might fall under the spell of witchdoctors and become unable to extricate themselves. According to the judge, the founder of

51 *Letuka*, [1997–98] L.L.R.-L.B. at 363.

52 Rex v. Raseotsana, [1995] LSHC 122 (October 30, 1995). See also, Rex v. Mokalanyane, [2001] LSHC 44 (May 15, 2001). In *Mokalanyane*, the Court "very reluctantly finds that youth in the instant case is a sufficient factor when looked upon as indicative of immaturity to constitute an extenuation," where the defendant was nineteen years old. *Id.* In another case, Rex v. Ramatla, [1989] LSHC 25 (March 9, 1989), the High Court found extenuating circumstances based on age alone: "I come to the view that your youth is a factor which serves as an extenuating factor albeit a very very tenuous one regard being had to the fact that you killed an innocent old lady who posed no threat to you." *Id.*

53 Thebe v. Rex, [1985–89] L.A.C. 33, 51 (1985), *reversing* Rex v. Thebe, [1984] LSHC 59 (June 4, 1984).

54 Rex v. Tsibela, [1986] LSHC 128 (November 3, 1986).

55 Rex v. Damane, [1990] LHSC 100 (December 10, 1990). In *Damane*, the Court ultimately found extenuating circumstances based on the defendant's consumption of alcohol. *Id.*

56 Rex v. Molise, [2007] LSCA 6 (April 4, 2007); see also Rex v. Raleshoai, [1993] LSHC 48 (August 16, 1993).

57 Rex v. Manamolela, [1982] LSHC 17 (April 29, 1982).

the Basotho nation, Moshoeshoe I, showed mercy even to suspected cannibals.[58] The judge accordingly found that extenuating circumstances existed as to the five accomplices in the murder, but not as to the four principals. In *These v. Rex* in 1985, the Court of Appeals dramatically divided two to one over whether extenuating circumstances existed in a witchcraft or medicine murder. The majority found that the defendant was only nineteen years old. While youth alone was generally not considered an extenuating circumstance at that time, South African courts recently showed a willingness to regard teenagers as immature unless the wickedness of the crime outweighed the defendant's immaturity.[59] According to the majority, the defendant was "an unsophisticated, semi-literate, rural youth, of below average intelligence," who was isolated from his peers and influenced by "irrational" thoughts. His crime was grisly and involved removing body parts (including genitalia), but the majority found that the crime was not committed purely out of "inherent wickedness."[60] They sentenced the defendant to twenty years. By contrast, the dissenting judge believed that the defendant performed the ritual killing to confer a benefit on himself. Youth alone was not an appropriate extenuating circumstance where the murder was premeditated and conducted for personal gain.[61]

Courts may find extenuating circumstances in the presence of strong aggravating factors, reflecting a general policy of reserving death for only the most serious crimes. In *State v. Ntobo*, the High Court determined that even though the accused was hired to kill, thereby evidencing premeditation, it was bound to conduct an extenuating circumstances analysis "with diligence and with an anxiously inquiring mind."[62] The Court found that the victim was killed for a reward, which was an aggravating factor, but noted even in the case of hired killers the death penalty was not an automatic sentence. The Court noted that Lesotho's 1993 constitution affirmed the inherent right to life, and therefore a death sentence "should only be imposed in the most exceptional cases where there are no prospects of reformation and where the objects of punishment such as deterrence, prevention, rehabilitation and retribution would not properly be achieved by any other sentence."[63] Finding that the defendant was a first offender, that he cooperated with police, that he had limited education, and that he was subject to manipulation by others, the Court found extenuating circumstances and sentenced him to 25 years' imprisonment.[64] High Court

---

58 *Id.*

59 These v. Rex, [1985] LSCA 23 (January 29, 1985).

60 *Id.*

61 *Id.*

62 State v. Ntobo, [2001] LHSC 133 (December 13, 2001), citing *Letuka*, [1997–98] L.L.R.-L.B. at 362.

63 State v. Ntobo, [2001] LHSC 133 (December 13, 2001), citing State v. Makwanyane, 1995 (3) S.A. 391 (C.C.).

64 The Court compared the case with that of *Maliehe*, which merited a punishment of twenty years, finding that the circumstances in *Ntobo* were graver.

decisions from the 1980s often provided little reasoning as to why a specific sentence of imprisonment was imposed. The Court of Appeal now requires this, and the High Court performs it as a matter of course. In Lesotho, courts often consider a broader range of factors in determining the length of a sentence of imprisonment than they do in determining the existence of extenuating circumstances. In one case, these included cooperation with investigators and an admission of guilt."[65] However, the Court has rejected serious health problems and offers to pay compensation to the victim as extenuating circumstances.[66]

Finding that sentences over 25 years are only appropriate in the most exceptional circumstances, the Court of Appeal found in *Monaleli v. Rex* that a sentence of forty years' imprisonment was "clearly excessive."[67] The Court has continued to cite *Monaleli* in murder cases where trial judges impose "excessively severe" sentences longer than 25 years except in "very exceptional circumstances," which has created some uniformity in sentencing.[68] The Court of Appeal has stridently asserted that the death penalty should only be limited to the rarest of the rare crimes: "the absence of extenuation compels the imposition of the ultimate penalty and that penalty should as a rule be reserved for the worst cases. Where there are factors, however remote or faint, bearing on the moral blameworthiness of the accused, a court should not lightly disregard them in determining the existence of extenuating circumstances."[69] Spending an excessive amount of time in prison prior to trial warrants a sentencing reduction in homicide cases.[70] In one case, the Court of Appeal halved a sentence of imprisonment for murder where seventeen years elapsed in bringing the accused to trial.[71] The High Court has determined that the six years that the accused person spent in custody awaiting trial "weighed heavily" on the decision to sentence the defendant in a homicide case to a reduced term of thirteen years. According to the court in that case, this was "a sad state of affairs which may only bring the justice system in this country into disrepute."[72]

The Court of Appeal is entitled to pass a different sentence where it believes the alternative sentence is warranted in law. The Lesotho Court of Appeal has even *increased* a sentence imposed at the trial level. In 1981, the Court raised a ten-year sentence to fifteen years because it was "manifestly inadequate and disproportionate to the gravity of the appellant's conduct," and the trial judge failed to "give sufficient weight to the aggravating features in the case."[73] In

65 Rex v. Maphobole, [1981] LSHC 2 (January 29, 1981).
66 Rex v. Mbobo, [2012] LSHC 78 (May 8, 2012).
67 Monaleli v. Rex, [2005–06] L.A.C. 24, 28 (2005).
68 See Lentso v. Rex, Crim. App. No. 3 of 2005 (Lesotho C.A.) (October 7, 2005).
69 Mothobi v. Rex, [2009] LSCA 9 (October 23, 2009).
70 Rex v. Mothobi, [1999] LSHC 101 (September 21, 1999) (defendant spent more than six years in custody).
71 Mokone v. Rex, [2012] LSCA 35 (September 3, 2012).
72 State v. Mothobi, [1999] LSHC 101 (September 21, 1999).
73 Phaloane v. Rex, [1980–84] L.A.C. 72, 88 (1981).

2008, the Court used a more modern version of the test, determining whether there was "a striking disparity between the sentence that this Court would have imposed and that actually imposed by the Court a quo. If the answer is in the affirmative this Court is entitled to interfere with the sentence."[74] In one case, the Court of Appeal found that the trial judge failed to adequately consider the accused's behavior after the offense (traditionally beyond the scope of the doctrine of extenuating circumstances), which included ensuring the deceased victim received medical care, inquiring about his health, and seeking to visit him in the hospital. The accused turned himself in once the victim died.[75] In those circumstances, the Court reduced a nine-year sentence to three years.

Fifteen years' imprisonment appears to be about the average sentence of imprisonment for an ordinary murder with extenuating circumstances in Lesotho, similar to Botswana and Swaziland.[76] Once the Court of Appeal found extenuating circumstances for a hired killer in *Maliehe*, lower courts became more liberal in their sentencing analyses. According to one trial judge, "If the Court of Appeal had not found a hit-man who was employed for gain to go and kill a person … [had] exterminating circumstances in that case, I would have found it impossible to have found extenuating circumstances in this case. But since this issue of extenuating circumstances has been made elastic … I find extenuating circumstances exist."[77] The judge continued, "I must add that, if we had chosen not to find extenuating circumstances we would be morally justified. Therefore, the accused is lucky." The High Court noted in the case of ritual murder and murder in the course of a robbery, extenuating circumstances would not traditionally have been found. However, a trial judge acknowledged that the "finding of extenuating circumstances in the *Maliehe* case has in fact moved the goal posts a little," and "extenuating circumstances are now found in cases where in the past they" would not have been.[78] On appeal, the judge wrote, "I myself would have been inclined to impose a lesser sentence notwithstanding the seriousness of the appellants' conduct and the heinousness of the offences," because sentences that are too high "leave little or no hope for the offender's rehabilitation and reintegration into society. However, there is not a striking disparity between the sentence I would have imposed and that in fact imposed."[79] The Court's rulings that a judge should clearly articulate an extenuating circumstances analysis helps improve consistency in sentencing.

---

74 Director of Public Prosecutions v Khama, [2008] LSCA 19 (October 17, 2008).

75 George v. Rex, [2000–04] L.A.C. 379, 384 (2001).

76 See, e.g., Maqeba v. Rex, [1994] LSCA 8 (January 22, 1994) (fifteen years with turbulent state of mind and no premeditation).

77 Rex v. Ramaema, [2003] LSHC 83 (August 6, 2003).

78 Rex v. Mosili, [2001] LSHC 87 (August 23, 2001).

79 Mosili v. Rex, [2000–04] L.A.C. 934, 942 (2004).

3. THE DEATH PENALTY IN PRECOLONIAL AND COLONIAL SWAZILAND

As in Lesotho, the Swazi people generally did not use capital punishment for murder before the modern era, though punishment for murder could include confiscation of the offender's property.[80] As is true elsewhere in the colonized world, however, Swazi culture was imagined, revived, and reinvented such that the cultural practices that early social anthropologists perceived to be ancient and immutable were actually of recent vintage.[81]

In 1893, Swaziland signed a convention making it a protectorate of the independent Republic of Transvaal, one of the Boer Republics in South Africa. A protocol dated October 5, 1898, extended the jurisdiction of the Transvaal Landdrost's court over Swaziland. The protocol limited the jurisdiction of native courts in criminal cases and gave the Landdrost's court jurisdiction over homicide crimes.[82] With Transvaal's defeat in the Anglo-Boer war, the Landdrost's court could no longer hear cases in the Swaziland protectorate after 1904, and jurisdiction was instead transferred to a special criminal court appointed by the governor of Transvaal. The special criminal court had jurisdiction over capital crimes, but executions required confirmation from the governor of Transvaal.[83] In 1907, Swaziland's judicial system was reorganized so that the court of the British Resident Commissioner had the power to impose capital punishment for Africans, similar to colonial Botswana. Europeans were tried before Assistant Commissioner's Courts, which appealed to the Special Court of Swaziland, for treason, murder, culpable homicide, and other serious offenses, unless they consented to the jurisdiction of the Resident Commissioner's Court. The Special Court included an advocate from the Supreme Court of Transvaal and two assistant commissioners.[84]

As Booth describes, the creation of a Western-style court system in Swaziland tended to benefit certain segments of society, such as young, educated women who sought protection against discrimination in the traditional chiefly legal

80 J.M.T. Labuschagne & J.A. van den Heever, *Liability Arising from the Killing of a Fellow Human Being in South African Indigenous Law*, 28 Comp. & Int'l L.J. Southern Africa 422, 427 (1995).

81 Hugh Macmillan, *Administrators, Anthropologists and 'Traditionalists' in Colonial Swaziland: The Case of the amaBhaca Fines*, 65 Africa: J. Int'l Afr. Inst. 545, 545–46 (1995). For instance, the British policy of "indirect rule" tended to benefit the royal family and royal elite. As a result, cultural practices involving administration and tax collection at the local level were reconstructed in a centralized manner. The cultural practice survived in a sense, but operated differently from precolonial times. See generally Eric Hobsbawm & Terence Ranger, *The Invention of Tradition* (1983).

82 Aimé Muyoboke Karimunda, *supra* note 7 at 103–04.

83 *Id.* at 104.

84 *Id. See also* J.R. Crawford, *The History and the Nature of the Judicial System of Botswana, Lesotho and Swaziland: Introduction and the Superior Courts*, 86 S. Afr. L.J. 476, 484–85 (1969).

system. At the same time, this system tended to disadvantage traditional power-brokers, such as ritual specialists, healers, and diviners, who were perceived to practice witchcraft.[85] In precolonial Swaziland, two courts represented the two rulers, who shared power in normal times: the court of the king (*Ingwenyama's*, or Lion's, court) and the court of the queen mother or wife of the king (*Indlovukazi's*, or She-Elephant's, court), of which the former was the final court of appeal in criminal and civil cases. Swazi traditional courts typically included a layer of dispute settlement by a homestead head, a headman, a local chief, and finally members of the royal class. In 1907, the British created an extra layer of appeal from the king's court to the Resident Commissioner's Court in civil cases and created exclusive criminal jurisdiction in British courts.[86] Death sentences required a warrant signed by the British High Commissioner.[87] British courts interfered in cases of forced marriage, but typically not with bride wealth, which was a cultural practice that was not repugnant to colonial law. With witchcraft, however, colonial courts aggressively tried to suppress the practice as ritual murders could result in cruel deaths for suspected offenders.[88] Colonial courts faced a significant increase in witchcraft-related murders during the droughts and economic depression of the 1930s.[89] As in Lesotho, prosecutions of chiefs and other prominent persons for ritual murder resulted in high-profile executions.

In 1950, the Native Courts Act returned most criminal jurisdiction to Swazi traditional courts rather than British-style courts. However, the colonial courts retained jurisdiction over witchcraft-related offenses and those offenses punished by death or life imprisonment until Swaziland's independence in 1968.[90] As Gumedze writes, politics in Swaziland continue to be a mixture of the traditional and the modern. The kingdom has a non-party-based political system based on a *tinkhundla* form of government, in which local representatives are selected from their communities to serve in parliament. The new constitution endorses this aversion to political parties.[91] The hereditary monarchy and powerful royal elite dominate politics and possess a distinctly traditional outlook. Unwritten Swazi law and custom serve as a prominent basis of the legal system.[92] The king and chiefs have immunity from civil and criminal suits and implicitly retain the power to manipulate the judiciary.[93]

---

85 Alan R. Booth, *'European Courts Protect Women and Witches': Colonial Law Courts As Redistributors of Power in Swaziland, 1920–1950*, 18 J. Southern Afr. Stud. 253, 253 (1992).

86 *Id.* at 256, 259.

87 *Id.* at 258.

88 *Id.* at 265.

89 *Id.* at 267.

90 *Id.* at 275 n. 93.

91 Sabelo Gumedze, *Human Rights and the Rule of Law in Swaziland*, 5 Afr. Hum. Rts. L.J. 266, 268 (2005).

92 *Id.* at 268–69.

93 *Id.* at 272.

4. THE CONSTITUTIONAL FRAMEWORK OF THE DEATH PENALTY IN SWAZILAND

Swaziland's criminal law is generally based on English common law, though some South African legal concepts survive.[94] Swaziland possessed a Bill of Rights in the original 1963 Order in Council, which ushered in self-government, and in the 1967 and 1968 constitutions, the latter of which became effective at Swaziland's independence in September 1968. However, the monarch suspended the constitution in 1973 during a constitutional crisis, leaving the country without supreme fundamental rights protections.[95] Even during the period of constitutional suspension between 1973 and 2005, courts in Swaziland occasionally relied on general legal principles to restrain the government's power. In 1998, for instance, the High Court awarded damages to a prison inmate who was forced to serve as a servant at a prison official's house.[96] The court found that such conduct constituted unlawful and degrading labor and awarded damages.[97] According to Bukurura, the decision was widely read among prison officials during a training academy and proved to be controversial because at the time working as a domestic servant for a prison official was a widespread practice and thought to be a form of privilege for prisoners.[98]

The 2005 Constitution provides a Bill of Rights, including the right to life and a prohibition on torture and other cruel, inhuman, and degrading treatment and punishment.[99] However, the Constitution fails to protect political freedoms or limit the power of the monarchy, and constrains important human rights provisions.[100] The death penalty provisions of the 2005 Constitution of Swaziland state in relevant part:

> 15. (1) A person shall not be deprived of life intentionally save in the execution of the sentence of a court in respect of a criminal offence under the law of Swaziland of which that person has been convicted.
>
> (2) The death penalty shall not be mandatory.
>
> (3) A sentence of life imprisonment shall not be less than twenty five years.[101]

---

94 See, e.g., Deogratias Mabirizi, *Reflections on the Defence of Provocation in Swaziland*, 9 Jahrbuch für afrikanisches Recht (Y.B. Afr. L.) 61, 68–69 (1995).

95 B.P. Wanda, *The Shaping of the Modern Constitution of Swaziland: A Review of Some Social and Historical Factors*, 6 Lesotho L.J. 137, 153–65.

96 Sufian Hemed Bukurura, *Emerging Trends in the Protection of Prisoners' Rights in Southern Africa*, 2 Afr. Hum. Rts. L.J. 92, 106–07 (2002).

97 Meshack Shabangu v. Attorney General, Civil Case No. 838/95 (September 15, 1998) (H.C.).

98 Bukurura, *supra* note 96 at 107.

99 S.M. Langwenya, *Recent Legal Developments: Swaziland*, 2 U. Bots. L.J. 167, 169 (2005).

100 Gumedze, *supra* note 91 at 276; Chris Maroleng, *Swaziland: The King's Constitution*, 12(3) Afr. Security Rev. 45, 47 (2003).

101 Swazi. Const. art. 15.

Swaziland's independence constitution of 1968 did not contain a right to life provision or a death penalty savings clause.

Under the Swazi constitution, the King's prerogative of mercy is solely limited to the death penalty and sentences of life imprisonment, though the constitution authorizes the legislature to enact a parole system under which sentences of imprisonment may be reduced for good behavior.[102] According to the constitution, the Committee on the Prerogative of Mercy must consider a written report from the trial judge in a capital case, but death sentences by court-martial are excluded from this requirement.[103] The committee must include a licensed medical practitioner, as in Botswana. In addition, two members must be drawn from the King's Advisory Council (*liqoqo*), a large body composed of male members of the royal family, traditional chiefs, and other persons of distinction. The committee also has as *ex officio* members the attorney general and the minister of justice.[104] The High Court of Swaziland has ruled that the King's prerogative of mercy is non-justiciable. The King commuted the death sentence of a condemned prisoner to life imprisonment with release at age 75. However, the Prisons Act of 1964 stated that a sentence of life imprisonment could not exceed twenty years. The Court dismissed the prisoner's complaint that the King's sentence was not authorized in law, stating that the prerogative of mercy was "not susceptible to judicial review" and the King had "wide discretion" to impose sentences. The Court also found that the provisions of the Prisons Act did not apply to capital defendants who had their sentences commuted.[105]

The doctrine of extenuating circumstances passed into Swaziland's criminal law via the Criminal Law and Procedure (Amendment) Act of 1959, which allowed a judge to substitute a sentence other than death upon a finding of extenuating circumstances.[106] Swaziland carried out eight executions in 1981 and eight more in 1983.[107] Swaziland has not carried out an execution since the ones in 1983 for murder, including a woman convicted of the ritual killing of a child.[108] In addition, ten death sentences were commuted in 1986 and five more in 1990.[109] By contrast, executions peaked in South Africa in 1987 when 181 people were executed.[110] The country made news when it opened a job search for a hangman in 1998, though the attorney general conceded that the country

102 Swazi. Const. arts. 78(1), 78(7).

103 Swazi. Const. art. 78(5).

104 Swazi. Const. art. 78(2).

105 Nkosi v. Attorney General, [2004] SZHC 79 (June 17, 2004).

106 Criminal Law and Procedure (Amendment) Act 47 of 1959.

107 Christina Murray, *Hangings in Southern Africa: The Last Ten Years*, 6 S. Afr. J. on Hum. Rts. 439, 440 (1990). These numbers are considerably higher than those mentioned in other sources. See Hood & Hoyle, *supra* note 1 at 93.

108 *Swaziland Executes Eight*, N.Y. Times (July 3, 1983) (retrieved from LexisNexis).

109 Raylene Keightley, *Hangings in Southern Africa: The Last Ten Years* (updated), 7 S. Afr. J. on Hum. Rts. 347, 348 (1991).

110 *Id.*

could not afford to pay a full-time salary. News reports suggested the country would begin using lethal injection as a method of execution since these only required a qualified medical practitioner.[111]

Prior to the abolition of the mandatory death penalty in the 2005 constitution, Swaziland generally recognized similar types of extenuating circumstances as in other jurisdictions in Southern Africa. Absence of direct intention to kill could be an extenuating circumstance. However, in a case where a bomb exploded prematurely and killed one of the people attempting to create the device, the absence of intention was not a sufficient extenuating circumstance since the offenders planned to use the bomb against other victims.[112] The High Court found that provocation, youth, and alcohol consumption could constitute extenuating circumstances.[113] Witchcraft-related murder also served as an extenuating circumstance. In 2002, the Court of Appeal (which became the Supreme Court under the 2005 Constitution) reversed a lower court finding of no extenuating circumstances. Making an inference in the defendants' favor, the Court substituted a sentence of eighteen years imprisonment as the defendants were motivated by witchcraft considerations in carrying out a double murder of a suspected witch and his wife.[114] One trial judge wrote that "the law cannot recognise and does not recognise that objectively speaking witchcraft exists," but the judge was constrained to view the matter from the perspective of the defendant, similar to the subjective standard used in Lesotho but unlike the objective one in Zimbabwe.[115] In 2007, the High Court sentenced three defendants to ten years' imprisonment for a witchcraft-related murder. The judge cited to prevailing beliefs that death by accident or as a result of illness are not natural phenomena, especially when the deceased person was young. According to the judge, such deaths were perceived to be attributable to charms and spells initiated by the evil designs of others, and those responsible deserved punishment.[116] The judge weighed the "triad" of competing interests: the nature of the crime, the interest of society, and the interest of the accused.[117]

Ratified in 2005, Section 15(2) of the Constitution of Swaziland prohibits the mandatory death penalty, the only constitution in Africa to do so until Zimbabwe's in 2013.[118] In practice, however, the doctrine of extenuating circumstances fell into disuse some years before this, after a series of decisions

---

111 *Swaziland Can't Afford a Full Time Hangman*, African Eye News Service (February 22, 2001) (retrieved from LexisNexis); *No Noose is Still Bad News*, The Evening Standard (London) (January 17, 2002) (retrieved from LexisNexis).

112 Rex v. Mbedzi, [2012] SZHC 218 (September 17, 2012).

113 Rex v. Ndlangamandla, [1998] SZHC 20 (June 15, 1998).

114 Rex v. Shongwe, [2002] SZSC 31 (November 1, 2002).

115 Rex v. Dlamini, [1997] SZHC 14 (November 24, 1997).

116 Rex v. Mamba, [2007] SZHC 22 (March 22, 2007), *citing* Rex v. Ndlovu, Crim. Case No. 30 of 1990.

117 *Id.*

118 Compare Swazi. Const. art. 15(2) with Zimbabwe Const. art. 48(2) (2013).

in which the Court of Appeal determined that the prosecutor maintained the burden of showing that no extenuating circumstances existed, turning the traditional doctrine into a true discretionary death penalty. The most recent case law requires judges to weigh aggravating and mitigating factors even in cases where no extenuating circumstances are found. This revolutionary change toward a discretionary regime provides a path forward for other retentionist nations in Southern Africa.

Swazi courts have formulated a two-part extenuating circumstances analysis. The High Court used such an analysis in *Rex v. Sean Blignaut*, determining in separate stages that extenuating circumstances existed, and then determining an appropriate sentence of imprisonment after weighing both mitigating and aggravating factors.[119] The Court cited *Daniel Dlamini v. Rex*, in which the judges wrote, "[w]e find ourselves in respectful agreement with the conclusion of the Botswana Court of Appeal that no onus rests on the accused person" in the extenuating circumstances analysis, citing *Kelaletswe v. State*.[120] Shortly after *Daniel Dlamini v. Rex* was decided, the High Court confirmed in a sentencing analysis that the defendant did not have the burden of showing extenuating circumstances. In that case, the judge confirmed that "there is no question of onus in this sort of enquiry" and added that judge was to take into account all evidence before the court in making the determination. "Once again, I repeat, there is no onus resting on you in this matter. Nothing can be said in your favour, which lessens your moral blameworthiness." The judge did not find extenuating circumstances and upheld a death sentence.[121]

Despite the ruling in *Dlamini v. Rex*, the case law evidences some early inconsistency in its application. In 2002, the Court of Appeal upheld a lower court's death sentence. According to the Court, "[n]o other possible extenuating circumstance was suggested and it therefore cannot be said that the trial judge erred in returning a verdict of murder without extenuating circumstances," and the trial judge had "no choice but to sentence the appellant to death."[122] However, in August 1998, a High Court judge sentenced a defendant to death with a finding that no extenuating circumstances existed in a case in which uncontradicted testimony from a doctor indicated that the defendant's "mental state is very close to that of an idiot."[123] The Court of Appeal reversed because

119 Rex v. Sean Blignaut, Crim. Case No. 130/2002, [2002] SZHC 10 (April 29, 2002). Mitigating factors included the defendant's status as a first-time offender, his youthfulness, and his lack of prior convictions, while aggravating factors included the fact that the killing was a brutal one, and from a position of trust as a family member. The defendant also lacked remorse. The final sentence was twenty years. *Id.*

120 Daniel Dlamini v. Rex, Crim. App. No. 11/1998 (Swaz. C.A.).

121 Rex v. Maphalala, [1998] SZHC 30 (October 6, 1998).

122 Rex v. Mabaso, [2004] SZSC 28 (November 26, 2004).

123 Rex v. Pikinini Simon Motsa & Anor., Crim. Case No. 72/1998, [1998] SZHC 31 (October 8, 1998).

the prosecution had not shown the absence of extenuating circumstances.[124] In May 2001, the High Court found that extenuating circumstances existed in a murder case, as conceded by both prosecution and defense. "For a long time in the past, courts in Swaziland consistently [held] that extenuating circumstances were to be proved by an accused person on the balance of probability," the judge wrote. "However, the Court of Appeal has since authoritatively set the record straight by handing down judgment on sentence where it categorically stated that 'no such onus rests on the accused person.'"[125]

During the period of the doctrine of extenuating circumstances in Swaziland, courts looked to similar factors as in other jurisdictions. Youth and intoxication could reduce moral blameworthiness for an offense. In one case, the judge considered the nature and circumstances of the offense, the characteristics of the offender and his circumstances, and the impact of the crime on the community.[126] In considering the offender, a judge was to consider age and background; level of education and position in society; family circumstances, including marriage and dependents; motive in committing the offence; whether the crime was committed for personal gain; prior convictions; the prospect of reformation; and a "perceptive understanding of the accused's human frailties."[127] In considering the crime, the court had to consider the moral and ethical nature of the offense. Finally, in considering the interests of the community, factors such as the protection of society and the maintenance of peace and tranquility, were relevant.

Because the new constitution abolishes the mandatory death penalty, courts have ruled that the extenuating circumstances analysis is no longer applicable. In 2009, the High Court of Swaziland ruled a court *always* possessed the discretion to substitute a lesser sentence regardless of whether extenuating circumstances existed.[128] According to the judge, "the question of extenuating circumstances upon conviction of murder falls away and the court should look into mitigating and aggravating factors," and the extenuating circumstances provision at Section 291(1) of the Criminal Procedure and Evidence Act was unconstitutional to the extent that it was inconsistent with the prohibition on the mandatory death penalty.[129] In a separate case, the Supreme Court of Swaziland agreed that courts possessed discretion to substitute a lesser sentence regardless of whether

124 Pikinini Simon Motsa v. Rex, Crim. App. No. 36/2000, [2000] SZSC 27 (December 1, 2000).

125 Rex v. Nhlanhla Charles Moratele & Anor., Crim. Case No. 93/1999, [2001] SZHC 16 (May 16, 2001). See also, Bongani Mkhwanazi v. Rex, Crim. App. No. 125/1998, [2001] SZCA 2 (November 27, 2001) (witchcraft as extenuating factor).

126 Rex v. Majahonkhe Major Mazibuko, Crim. Case No. 3/2002, [2003] SZHC 32 (judgment May 22, 2003; sentence June 26, 2003), citing State v. Zinn, 1969 (2) S.A. 537 (A.D.) and State v. Scheepers, 1977 (2) S.A. 154 (A.D.).

127 *Id.*, citing State v. Sigwahla, 1967 (4) S.A. 566 (A.D.).

128 Rex v. Musa Kotso Samuel Dlamini, Crim. Case No. 200/2007, [2009] SZHC 151 (May 29, 2009).

129 *Id.* at 15 (¶ 41).

extenuating circumstances existed.[130] The Supreme Court reasoned that the doctrine could still be *relevant* in determining a sentence as it could "fortify a decision to impose or not to impose the death penalty."[131] In determining sentences, the trial judges of the High Court were permitted to use either the old method of deciding whether extenuating circumstances existed and then weighing aggravating and mitigating factors, or the new method of weighing aggravating and mitigating factors in a single step.

Since the establishment of a purely discretionary death penalty in Swaziland, judges have been reluctant to dispense a death sentence even when they have discretion to do so. A judge of the High Court found that a defendant was guilty of murder with no extenuating circumstances *and* found that the aggravating factors "far outweigh[ed]" the mitigating factors, but nonetheless decided to "invoke section 15 (2) of the Constitution which provides that the death penalty shall not be mandatory in circumstances where no extenuating circumstances exist" as the defendant was a first offender.[132] He was sentenced to imprisonment. In *Rex v. Mbedzi*, a trial judge did not find extenuating circumstances in a case but invoked Section 15(2) of the constitution to sentence the defendant to 25 years of imprisonment on each count of murder, confirming that the death penalty was discretionary even in the absence of *any* extenuating circumstances.[133] However, in the particularly sensationalized case of serial killer David Simelane, who was convicted of 28 murders of women and girls over a two-year period, the court had no hesitation. In confirming the death sentence passed by the High Court, the presiding appeals judge wrote, "[t]his has been one of the most serious cases I have dealt with both in my career as a State Counsel or as a judge. The Appellant's conduct has sunk to the very depths of depraved and evil conduct..."[134] The case law suggests that death sentences in Swaziland are truly reserved for the rarest of the rare cases.

With the rise of a discretionary death penalty, the Supreme Court began strictly monitoring sentences of imprisonment from the High Court for consistency. A common law of sentencing is developing in Swaziland in lieu of legislative sentencing guidelines, and Swazi courts have even looked to courts elsewhere to determine the proper sentence length. In one case, the High Court cited a Botswana case to determine the appropriate sentence for a heat of passion murder.[135] In another, the Supreme Court cited to courts in Botswana and Lesotho in reducing a sentence from thirty years to 25 years, which Section 15(3)

130 Rex v. Ntokozo Adams, Crim. App. No. 16/2010, [2010] SZSC 10 (November 30, 2010).

131 *Id.* at 15 (¶ 33).

132 Rex v. Nhlanhla Lucky Dludlu, Crim. Case No. 202/2010, [2012] SZHC 236 (September 28, 2012).

133 Rex v. Mbedzi, [2012] SZHC 218 (September 17, 2012).

134 David Thabo Simelane v. Rex, Crim. App. No. 13/2011, [2011] SZSC 54 (November 30, 2012).

135 See, e.g., Rex v. Sandile Mbongeni Mtsetfwa, Crim. Case 81/2010, [2010] SZHC 145 (September 16, 2010).

of the Constitution considered to be "the lowest end of a life sentence."[136] Besides looking to foreign law, the Supreme Court has also attempted to impose sentence uniformity by comparing recent domestic cases and discerning an acceptable range for an offense. In *Tsela v. Rex*, the Court listed the sentences of every murder case in the prior ten years, determining that all sentences fell between five and 25 years, with fifteen years as the mean.[137] The Court held that judges should not deviate from this range without good reason. Interestingly, the Court noted "a controlled ratcheting upwards of sentences for the offence of murder" over the prior ten years, "evidently a reaction to the burgeoning prevalence of unlawful killings in this Kingdom coupled with a disturbing degree of brutality."[138] Multiple sentences should run concurrently if the charges arose out of the same sequence of events. The final way in which the Supreme Court has monitored sentences for consistency is through reasoning by analogy to earlier cases. For instance, in *Tfwala v. Rex*, the Supreme Court upheld a sentence of fifteen years for murder, citing to several earlier cases in which the defendant acted without provocation but otherwise had no prior convictions and was young at the time of the offense. According to the Court, "[t]hese cases serve to show in rough and general terms, the judicial trend in sentencing for murder. In the light of the above range of sentences for murder, I am inclined to hold that the custodial sentence of 15 years for murder in this case is not too harsh or high in the peculiar circumstances of this case."[139] The Supreme Court has suggested that an overly long sentence may violate the constitutional ban on cruel, inhuman, and degrading punishment.[140]

In 2013, the Supreme Court upheld a High Court sentence of twenty years' imprisonment for murder even where the trial judge did not specifically follow the rubric laid out in *Tsela v. Rex*. In that case, *Mbhamali v. Rex*, the trial judge considered the principles of parity and proportionality in sentencing by examining two prior cases in which a prison sentence of eighteen years was issued, and one in which 25 years was issued. The trial judge analogized the current case to the three prior cases and determined that the offender deserved a harsher punishment than eighteen years, as those were crimes of passion.[141] According to the Supreme Court, had the trial judge looked to the rubric in *Tsela v. Rex*, he would have reached a similar result, as the sentencing table provided cases that were similarly egregious to the one encountered by the trial judge. However, the Supreme Court concluded, the judge "exercised his sentencing discretion in a manner that cannot be faulted" and the appellate court "can only interfere if the trial judge had committed some serious violation of sentencing

136 Xolani Zinhle Nyandzeni v. Rex, Crim. App. No. 29/2010, [2012] SZSC 3 (May 31, 2012).

137 Samkeliso Madati Tsela v. Rex, Crim. App. No. 20/2010, [2011] SZSC 13 (May 31, 2012).

138 *Id.* at 30 (¶ 27).

139 Mandla Tfwala v. Rex, Crim. App. No. 36/2011, [2012] SZSC 15 (May 31, 2012).

140 Zwelithini Tsabedze v. Rex, Crim. App. No. 32/2012, [2012] SZSC 73 (November 30, 2012).

141 Mbhamali v. Rex, [2013] SZSC 8 (May 31, 2013).

law or principle." The Court concluded the case by cautioning that in the future witchcraft murders would be dealt with harshly and would no longer be considered a weighty mitigating factor at the stage in which a judge crafted the final sentence.[142]

5. PROSPECTS FOR ABOLITION

Although the death penalty remains a lawful sentence in Lesotho and Swaziland, both countries are *de facto* abolitionist and adhere to an international position favoring eventual abolition. Lesotho has ratified the ICCPR and the African Charter, but has not ratified the Second Optional Protocol to the ICCPR pertaining to the abolition of the death penalty.[143] In any event, ratifying the Second Optional would require implementing legislation to be effective in domestic law.[144] International pressure, particularly from South Africa, has taken its toll. Unlike Botswana, Lesotho has cooperated with South Africa to extradite fugitives back to the country by providing assurances that the fugitives would not face the death penalty.[145] As in Ghana, statements from public officials reveal a thaw over the past twenty years in the commitment to retain the death penalty. In 2014, Lesotho Prime Minister Thomas Thabane called for vigorous enforcement of the death penalty against high-profile murderers.[146] Nonetheless, signaling a shift, in 2008 Lesotho abstained on the UN General Assembly vote for a moratorium on capital punishment.[147]

Death penalty prosecutions for political crimes have contributed to the erosion of public legitimacy for capital punishment. In 2008, Lesotho faced condemnation from free speech advocates after a prominent journalist was arrested and charged with high treason, a capital crime, for reading a letter over the radio by members of the Lesotho Defence Force calling for the arrest of Prime Minister Phakalita Mosisili and his government for corruption. The charges were later dropped.[148] The journalist, later press secretary to the Prime Minister Thabane, fled to South Africa in 2014 after a suspected coup

---

142 *Id.*

143 Owori, *supra* note 23 at 1.

144 *Id.*

145 Obonye Jonas, *Human Rights, Extradition and the Death Penalty: Reflections on the Standoff Between Botswana and South Africa*, 10 Sur: Int'l J. on Hum. Rts. 181, 194 (2013).

146 Utloang Kajeno, *Death Penalty Won't Curb Brutal Murders*, Lesotho Post, November 13, 2014, www.pressreader.com/lesotho/lesotho-times/20141113/281685433147614/TextView.

147 United Nations Press Release, *General Assembly Adopts 52 Resolutions, 6 Decisions Recommended by Third Committee*, December 18, 2008, www.un.org/press/en/2008/ga10801.doc.htm.

148 *Journalist Released on Bail; Treason Charge Lifted*, Committee for the Protection of Journalists, June 28, 2007, https://cpj.org/2007/06/lesotho-journalist-released-on-bail-treason-charge.php.

attempt.[149] The prime minister subsequently fled to South Africa following his ouster in March 2015.[150] Certainly, episodes like this reflect state insecurity. At the same time, the decline in death sentences for ordinary crimes may evidence a more rehabilitative phase in criminal punishment in the country, one more reflective of local values. In 2008, the Lesotho Court of Appeal reversed a death sentence for murder without extenuating circumstances and found a defendant guilty of culpable homicide. The Court sentenced the defendant to six years imprisonment, of which two years were suspended upon payment of ten cattle to the family of the deceased.[151]

Swaziland's international and domestic posture toward the death penalty has likewise evolved. In the late 1990s, King Mswati III justified retention of the death penalty on the grounds that, if repealed, abolition would increase the threat of ritual murder and other serious crimes.[152] Although Swaziland enjoyed a death penalty moratorium by the early 2000s, the official government response was that the country was searching for a more humane method of carrying out executions, particularly as it had trouble hiring a hangman after the prior one died.[153] Due to strict appellate review of sentences, the number of persons on death row in Swaziland declined dramatically from 59 in 2001 to only three in 2004.[154] At the same time, the number of death sentences also fell from twelve in 2001 to zero in 2002, one in 2003, and zero in 2004 and 2005.[155] Despite limited use of the death penalty, Swaziland told the Universal Periodic Review in 2012 that it was not yet ready to ratify the Second Optional Protocol of the ICCPR or to abolish the death penalty.[156] Although Swaziland is a *de facto* abolitionist nation, it voted against the United Nations-sponsored death penalty moratorium in 2010. However, Swaziland improved its status by abstaining in 2012.[157] King Mswati III initiated a Constitutional Review Commission report to study the appropriate mechanism for abolishing the death penalty. The report remains pending. Meanwhile, in April 2011, Prime Minister Sibusiso Dlamini stated that Swaziland would retain the death penalty.[158]

Despite the progress at the elite level, however, the death penalty in Swaziland still has populist resonance. The death penalty was proposed for the

149 Bongiwe Zihlangu, *Thakalekoala Fears For His Life*, Sunday Express, September 7, 2014, http://sundayexpress.co.ls/thakalekoala-fears-for-his-life.

150 Keiso Mohloboli, *Thabane Blasts Thakalekoala*, Sunday Express, November 22, 2015, http://sundayexpress.co.ls/thabane-blasts-thakalekoala.

151 Chabelli v. Rex, [2008] LSCA 8 (April 11, 2008).

152 Lilian Chenwi, *Towards the Abolition of the Death Penalty in Africa: A Human Rights Perspective*, 15 (2007).

153 *Id.* at 53–54.

154 *Id.* at 54–55.

155 *Id.* at 56.

156 Hood & Hoyle, *supra* note 1 at 93.

157 Karimunda, *supra* note 7 at 189.

158 *Id.*

crime of rape where the perpetrator had HIV, similar to the enacted provision in Lesotho permitting the death penalty for aggravated HIV transmission.[159] The draft Sexual Offences Bill, at Section 2(8)(c), was unveiled in 2006 and proposed for rape "where HIV/AIDS is an aggravating factor." The aim of the bill was to address a grave situation involving rape and systematic abuse of young women and girls, but earned opposition from Amnesty International and other human rights organizations for the death penalty provision.[160] Nonetheless, NGO support for death penalty abolition is increasing. Local human rights organizations working on prisoner's rights in Swaziland have learned the value of coordination, forming the umbrella group Human Rights Association of Swaziland.[161] In addition, in 2008 the Working Group on the Death Penalty, established in 2005 by the African Commission, met in Manzini, Swaziland, to draw up a detailed plan for working with NGOs and member states toward death penalty abolition.[162]

6. CONCLUSION

Lesotho and Swaziland are *de facto* abolitionist; the most recent execution was more than twenty years ago. Their geographic position vis-à-vis South Africa, an abolitionist state, likely reduces the political will to reintroduce executions, especially with respect to extradition. Both countries have tiny death rows. Lesotho has a death penalty regime that mirrors Botswana, as it has adopted the doctrine of extenuating circumstances from apartheid-era South African law, in which the death penalty is presumed unless the defendant shows the existence of certain mitigating factors that existed at the time of the offense. By contrast, Swaziland has abolished the doctrine and has established a purely discretionary capital sentencing regime in which the prosecution must prove the existence of an aggravating factor. While both countries have an international posture that is increasingly conducive to death penalty abolition, there currently appears to be only incremental movement in this direction.

---

159 Chenwi, *supra* note 152 at 37–38.

160 Widney Brown, Johanna Hanefeld & James Welsh, *Criminalising HIV Transmission: Punishment Without Protection*, 17 Reproductive Health Matters 119, 122 (2009).

161 Bukurura, *supra* note 96 at 100 n. 41 (2002).

162 Andrew Novak, *The Death Penalty in Africa: Foundations and Future Prospects*, 67 (2014).

CHAPTER 6
ZIMBABWE

1. INTRODUCTION

Zimbabwe last carried out an execution in 2005, indicating that the country is now *de facto* abolitionist. A future execution seems unlikely, particularly after a new constitution in 2013 prohibited mandatory death sentences and greatly restricted the scope of capital punishment. Several pending constitutional challenges look likely to restrict capital punishment still further. Nonetheless, Zimbabwe's democracy has a troubled history and the last decade saw a massive economic contraction unique on the continent.[1] If death penalty abolition is correlated to wealth or democratization, then the differences between retentionist Botswana, a middle income democracy, and neighboring Zimbabwe, a low income country with an implicitly violent history of dominant-party rule, are stark and would seem to contradict such a correlation.[2]

At least part of the reason for this difference is that the death penalty in Zimbabwe has a troubled history, quite different from Botswana. In the precolonial era, the Shona people generally did not practice capital punishment, although the more centralized Ndebele kingdom did. While British colonizers enforced the death penalty infrequently, the punishment became a tool of political repression and control during the era of white settler rule from 1965 to 1980.[3] African nationalists could be subject to secret executions without fair trial guarantees during the war of liberation. At independence, Zimbabwe inherited a draconian security framework that took some time to dismantle, occasionally used against political opponents. By the time a new constitution was installed in 2013, after a decade of economic mismanagement and political

---

1 Michael Bratton & Eldred Masunungure, *Popular Reactions to State Repression: Operation* Murambatsvina *in Zimbabwe*, 106 Afr. Aff. 21, 22 (2006) (on the origins of Zimbabwe's economic crisis); Percyslage Chigora & Tobias Guzura, *The Politics of the Government of National Unity (GNU) and Power Sharing in Zimbabwe: Challenges and Prospects for Democracy*, 3 Afr. J. Hist. & Culture 20, 20–21 (2011).

2 For more on the correlation between wealth, democratization, and abolition, see Christian Boulanger & Austin Sarat, *Putting Culture Into the Picture: Toward a Comparative Analysis of State Killing*, in *The Cultural Lives of Capital Punishment: Comparative Perspectives*, 7–11 (Austin Sarat & Christian Boulanger eds., 2005).

3 Andrew Novak, *Abuse of State Power: The Mandatory Death Penalty for Political Crimes in Southern Rhodesia, 1963–1970*, 19 Fundamina: J. Legal Hist. 28 (2013).

manipulation, Zimbabwe's international posture on capital punishment opened to the possibility of abolition.

2. THE DEATH PENALTY IN PRECOLONIAL ZIMBABWE

Precolonial histories are subject to the limitations of oral histories and the reinvention of tradition, and in few places is history as contested as in Zimbabwe.[4] The Shona people did not practice the death penalty for murder, believing that taking another person's life would cause his spirit to return to torment the living.[5] In the Shona worldview, the loss of a second life in revenge for homicide was unnecessary. The Shona practiced a restorative form of compensation for homicide, in which an offender provided a goat, the meat from which was shared by both parties and the public as a sign of reconciliation.[6] The community could also choose to transfer a woman or girl from the perpetrator's clan or group to the victim's in order to compensate for the loss of a person. Ostracism and banishment were used for suspected witches, though the families of exiled witches could still be liable for compensation.[7] Shona customary law heavily emphasized compensation, distinguishing between justifiable and non-justifiable homicide (with certain forms of infanticide or spiritual killing considered "justifiable"), and did not generally invoke the death penalty.[8]

Among the more centralized Ndebele people, capital punishment was imposed for deliberate homicide, but cases of negligent homicide, infanticide, and self-defense were excluded. Lesser punishments include corporal punishment.[9] By the late nineteenth century, the Ndebele had even developed a system of criminal fines payable to the king.[10] Zimbabwean discourse on death penalty abolition frequently makes reference to precolonial attitudes and practices, including the relative disuse of the death penalty and a restorative approach to criminal justice. Chemhuru and Masaka write that the death penalty

---

4 Terence Ranger, *Nationalist Historiography, Patriotic History and the History of the Nation: The Struggle Over the Past in Zimbabwe*, 30 J. Southern Afr. Stud. 215 (2004).

5 E. Dumbutshena, *The Death Penalty in Zimbabwe*, 58 Revue Internationale de Droit Penal 521, 521 (1987).

6 Aimé Muyoboke Karimunda, *The Death Penalty in Africa: The Path Towards Abolition*, 37–38 (2014).

7 *Id.* at 40–41.

8 A. Mittlebeeler, *African Custom and Western Law: The Development of the Rhodesian Criminal Law for Africans*, 163–64 (1976).

9 J.M.T. Labuschagne & J.A. van den Heever, *Liability Arising from the Killing of a Fellow Human Being in South African Indigenous Law*, 28 Comp. & Int'l L.J. Southern Africa 422, 427 (1995).

10 Mittlebeeler, *supra* note 8 at 164.

was "incompatible with the communal approach to life found in Zimbabwe and Africa at large," as these societies emphasized restoring broken relationships and avoiding further injury to the community as a whole. Retribution, they wrote, was alien to African communities.[11] The hangings of the earliest Zimbabwean nationalists during the First Chimurenga (1896–97), an uprising against the newly-arrived white settlers from South Africa, loom large in historical memory.[12] The settler regime sentenced Mbuya Nehanda and Sekuru Kaguvi to death in order to silence African opposition and deter future challenges to white rule.[13]

3. THE DEATH PENALTY IN COLONIAL SOUTHERN RHODESIA

According to the 1890 Crown Charter to the British South African Company incorporating Southern Rhodesia, "careful regard shall always be had to the customs and laws of the class or tribe or nation to which the parties respectively belong."[14] Southern Rhodesia developed a dual legal system to apply customary law in certain family, probate, and land disputes while recognizing the supremacy of European-derived law. As in other British colonies, this structure reflected the practice of "indirect rule," which conserved resources and allowed subject populations a measure of self-governance.[15] The court system included different forums and avenues of appeal based on the parties' race and location. Common law courts governed disputes involving white settlers, while African civil disputes originated in a separate system of courts.[16] These divisions were

11 Munamato Chemhuru & Dennis Masaka, *Zimbabwe's Constitution Making Process and the Death Penalty: A Philosophical Reflection*, 5 Africana 123, 136 (2011).

12 Suzanne Dawson, *The First Chimurenga: 1896–1897 Uprising in Matabeleland and Mashonaland and Continued Conflicts in Academia*, 2(2) Constellations 144 (2011); Sabelo J. Ndlovu-Gatsheni, *Rethinking* Chimurenga *and* Gukurahundi *in Zimbabwe: A Critique of Partisan National History*, 55 Afr. Stud. Rev. 1 (2012).

13 Chemhuru & Masaka, *supra* note 11 at 126–27.

14 T.W. Bennett, *Conflict of Laws: The Application of Customary Law and the Common Law in Zimbabwe*, 30 Int'l & Comp. L.Q. 59, 68 (1981).

15 *Id.* at 59.

16 Ordinary disputes arose in a magistrate's court and appealed to the High Court and then to the Appellate Division in Salisbury. From there, the dispute could appeal to the Appellate Division in South Africa before 1955, the Federal Supreme Court of the Federation of Rhodesia and Nyasaland until 1963, and the Rhodesian Supreme Court thereafter. Certain disputes could also appeal to the Privy Council in London. Tapiwa B. Zimudzi, *African Women, Violent Crime and the Criminal Law in Zimbabwe, 1900–1952*, 30 J. Southern Afr. Stud. 499, 502 (2004); H.H. Marshall, *The Judicial Committee of the Privy Council: A Waning Jurisdiction*, 13 Int'l & Comp. L.Q. 697 (1964). In urban areas, civil disputes between Africans typically arose in a district commissioner's court, which appealed to the Native Appeal Court and later the Court of Appeal for African Civil Cases. In rural areas, headman's and

themselves a means of social control, reinforcing the racial and urban–rural divides.[17]

The criminal law of Southern Rhodesia bore the strong imprint of English common law. Magistrate's courts and the High Court had original jurisdiction in serious criminal cases, including capital offenses. British notions of arrest, detention, and trial largely replaced the traditional practice of providing compensation in livestock to the family of a victim in societies where resources were scarce and crime could have devastating economic consequences for a victim's family. The conflict between traditional law and European law was resolved through the doctrine of supremacy, in which any customary practices that offended European notions of civility were outlawed, such as forced marriage.[18] The criminal law attempted to tame the realm of the spiritual as well as the temporal. The Witchcraft Suppression Act of 1899 prohibited naming another as a "witch" or retaliating against a suspected witch.[19] Though based on the premise that "witchcraft" had no real existence, the Act prohibited religious rituals that were associated with traditional healing, rituals for the dead, and dispute resolution, removing a traditional form of social control and sparking significant resistance.[20] Both witchcraft confessions and witchcraft as a defense to a murder charge complicated the relationship between English common law and African traditional law.[21]

Criminal sentencing was "profoundly paternalistic" toward women accused of serious crimes.[22] Women were very rarely accused of murder even when premeditated, because they were characterized as having a "dullness of intellect" and only a "childish awareness" of their crimes.[23] Only six women were executed in Southern Rhodesia between 1900 and 1952. Traditionally "feminine" crimes such as infanticide were treated less harshly than ordinary murder. The criminal law also reflected racial biases as well, as evidenced in laws criminalizing "black peril," alleged sexual violence by black men on white women, which became at times "a fully hysterical obsession within colonial Zimbabwe's white settler community."[24] Rape and attempted rape were highly racialized crimes, punishing white female and black male sexual encounters far more harshly than white male and black female encounters or encounters between partners of the

chief's courts appealed to the Tribal Appeals Court. Andrew Ladley, *Changing the Courts in Zimbabwe: The Customary Law and Primary Courts Act*, 26 J. Afr. L. 95, 96–97 (1982).

17 *Id.* at 99.

18 See Repugnancy Clause of the Native Law and Courts Act (1937).

19 G.L. Chavunduka, *Witchcraft and the Law in Zimbabwe*, 8 Zambezia 129, 130 (1980).

20 T.J. Mafico, *Belief in Witchcraft*, 13 Zambezia 119, 120 (1986). Chavunduka, *supra* note 19 at 131.

21 *Id.* at 138.

22 Zimudzi, *supra* note 16 at 505–07.

23 *Id.* at 506–507.

24 John Pape, *Black and White: The 'Perils of Sex' in Colonial Zimbabwe*, 16 J. South. Afr. Stud. 699, 700 (1990).

same race.[25] At least formally, a single criminal and penal code applied to both black and white Rhodesians, but prosecutorial discretion in bringing charges, and prison regulations authorizing the amount and quality of food, clothing, and other essentials an inmate might receive produced overt patterns of racial discrimination.[26] While "black peril" laws resulted in the executions of thirty black African men, no white man was ever executed for a sexual crime against a black woman.[27]

Buoyed by postwar migration, Southern Rhodesia's white community numbered as much as 230,000 out of a total population of 4.8 million by 1969.[28] The installation of apartheid in South Africa in 1948, however, changed the calculus; to help dilute the political power of the white settlers and the influence of South Africa, Southern Rhodesia was amalgamated with British colonies in Northern Rhodesia (colonial Zambia) and Nyasaland (colonial Malawi) for ten tumultuous years between 1953 and 1963.[29] With independence coming rapidly to the colonies north of the Zambezi River, the white settler population in Southern Rhodesia moved hard to the political right. Reformist Prime Minister Garfield Todd, an advocate of racial integration, was replaced by the business-friendly moderate Edgar Whitehead in 1958. However, Whitehead's United Federal Party lost to the right-wing Rhodesian Front in 1962, first under Prime Minister Winston Field and then under Ian Smith. Beginning under Whitehead but accelerating under the Rhodesian Front government, the Rhodesian legislature passed increasingly draconian security legislation, providing for media censorship, suspension of *habeas corpus*, emergency powers, restriction on urban migration, and the infamous Law and Order (Maintenance) Act.[30] A landslide electoral victory in 1965 led Prime Minister Smith to declare Rhodesia unilaterally independent of the British Empire. The settler regime's unilateral declaration of independence (UDI) resulted in a suspension of diplomatic and trade relations and comprehensive United Nations sanctions on the rebellious settler-ruled state until a war with African nationalists led to majority rule in April 1980.[31]

---

25 Philip Mason, *The Birth of a Dilemma: The Conquest and Settlement of Rhodesia*, 246–47 (1962).

26 Christopher Zimmerli, *Human Rights and the Rule of Law in Southern Rhodesia*, 20 Int'l & Comp. L.Q. 239, 286 (1971). See also Carol Summers, *From Civilization to Segregation: Social Ideals and Social Control in Southern Rhodesia, 1890–1914*, 102 (1994).

27 Pape, *supra* note 24 at 720.

28 Peter Godwin & Ian Hancock, *'Rhodesians Never Die': The Impact of War and Political Change on White Rhodesia, c. 1970–1980*, 16 (1993).

29 Donald Denoon, *Southern Africa Since 1800*, 180 (1973); Patrick O'Meara, *Rhodesia/Zimbabwe: Guerrilla Warfare or Political Settlement?*, in *Southern Africa: The Continuing Crisis*, 18, 22 (Gwendolyn Carter & Patrick O'Meara eds., 1979).

30 Ruth Weiss, *Sir Garfield Todd and the Making of Zimbabwe*, 121 (1999); O'Meara, *supra* note 29 at 23–24, 26; J.R.T. Wood, *So Far and No Further: Rhodesia's Bid for Independence During the Retreat from Empire, 1959–65*, 17 (2004).

31 O'Meara, *supra* note 29 at 28, 36–37.

Like South Africa, but unlike most British colonial administrations, the white settler government of Rhodesia used the death penalty on a large scale for political crimes to prevent or punish political dissent. During the Rhodesian War, the government took increasingly desperate measures to punish and deter political crimes. In 1963, the legislature passed the mandatory death penalty for throwing a "petrol bomb" (Molotov cocktail) and in 1967 for possession of arms of war, without provision for mitigating or extenuating circumstances. The conservative Rhodesian Front played on white settler fears that a victorious African nationalist administration would free political prisoners, undermining the deterrent effects of imprisonment.[32] Indeed, the number of death sentences passed in Rhodesian courts jumped dramatically: 28 in 1965, 41 in 1966, and 71 in 1968 before falling to 15 in 1969 and 23 in 1970.[33] Both mandatory death penalty laws were eventually repealed in 1968, as they were widely considered unenforceable in practice.[34] In 1974, the Rhodesian legislature passed the death penalty for terrorist recruitment and training, but the bill allowed a judge to substitute life imprisonment based on consideration of several statutorily-defined "special circumstances."[35]

The mandatory death penalty for political crimes was doggedly opposed in Parliament by white liberal MPs and by the black African and South Asian MPs who were first elected under the constitution of 1962.[36] Legislative opposition was led by quixotic independent MP Ahrn Palley, best remembered as the only white MP to oppose UDI from the British Empire, which he declared as an act of treason to the Crown. Palley, long an opponent of Rhodesia's security legislation, including the Law and Order (Maintenance) Act, moved a long series of unsuccessful amendments to narrow the application of the mandatory death penalty and to allow consideration of extenuating circumstances. Until the 1970 constitution made him ineligible to run for reelection (and despite a nearly

---

32 Debates of the Legislative Assembly of Southern Rhodesia 603, 630 (February 26, 1963). The legislation on possession of arms of war contained an insidious clause that reversed the burden of proof, requiring the defendant to show absence of intent. The Rhodesian Constitutional Council determined that the provision violated the presumption of innocence under the Rhodesian Declaration of Rights contained in the new 1965 Constitution, but the Council was overruled by a two-thirds vote of the legislature. Richard Hodder-Williams, *Rhodesia's Search for a Constitution: Or, Whatever Happened to Whaley?*, 69 Afr. Aff. 217, 220 (1970).

33 Marie Chihambakwe, *Study of Zimbabwean Cases on the Death Penalty (Part 1)*, 2(1) Legal Forum (Harare) 41, 42 (1990).

34 Law and Order (Maintenance) Amendment Act 41 of 1968; Debates of the Legislative Assembly of Rhodesia1573 (September 25, 1968).

35 Debates of the Legislative Assembly of Rhodesia, November 14, 1974, at 914–15, 935, 941, 951–52.

36 Anthony Lemon, *Electoral Machinery and Voting Patterns in Rhodesia, 1962–1977*, 77 Afr. Aff. 511, 511 (1978) (on Rhodesia's electoral system). Ian Hancock, *White Liberals, Moderates, and Radicals in Rhodesia*, 98 (1984). See also, Law and Order (Maintenance) Amendment Act 12 of 1963; *"Hanging Bill" is Read*, Bulawayo Chronicle, February 15, 1963; *"Hanging Bill" Under Fire*, Bulawayo Chronicle, February 19, 1963.

successful comeback in the 1974 election against a marginal Rhodesian Front candidate in Salisbury City) Palley was the most dogged opponent of capital punishment in the white Rhodesian political establishment until Zimbabwe's independence in 1980.[37]

Opponents of the mandatory death penalty for petrol bombing brought constitutional challenges under the prohibition on cruel and degrading punishment provision of the 1961 and 1965 Rhodesian constitutions. Before Rhodesian courts and the Judicial Committee of the Privy Council in London, defendants argued that the mandatory death penalty was overly harsh because it did not consider mitigating circumstances.[38] The laws were upheld, based on the principle that the prohibition of cruel, inhuman, and degrading punishment related only to kind, type, or method of punishment and not to severity, quantum, or appropriateness of punishment. In 1968, the Appellate Division of Southern Rhodesia ruled that it had no jurisdiction to assess whether delay on death row was cruel and degrading, an early and unsuccessful death row syndrome challenge.[39] However, the 1969 Rhodesian constitution rendered the bill of rights non-justiciable, and courts could no longer "inquire into or pronounce upon the validity of any new law on the ground that it is inconsistent with the Declaration of Rights."[40]

In 1968, the Queen attempted to pardon three African nationalists sentenced to death by the Rhodesian Front government under Prime Minister Ian Smith, following the advice of the Commonwealth Secretary.[41] The Rhodesian cabinet and courts believed this was unconstitutional and that only the UDI government could pardon a condemned prisoner. The three men were executed to enormous international outrage, including a unanimous condemnation by the UN Security Council.[42] In 1970, the Rhodesian Front declared a republic and removed the Queen as head of state. Instead, the president exercised the mercy power, based on the advice of an executive council comprising the

37 For a biography of Ahrn Palley and the political debates over capital punishment in UDI-era Rhodesia, see Novak, *supra* note 3 at 38–40. Palley was not the only white MP to oppose capital punishment. The archconservative MP Robin James, expelled from the Rhodesian Front in 1969 for opposing the Front's "liberal" racial policies, was another quite unlikely ally. *Id.* at 39–40.

38 Regina v. Runyowa, 1966 R.L.R. 42 (P.C.) (appeal taken from Rhodesia & Nyasaland); Gundu v. Sheriff of Southern Rhodesia, 1965 R.L.R. 301 (Rhodesia A.D.); Regina v. Mapolisa, 1964 R.L.R. 591 (P.C.) (appeal taken from Rhodesia & Nyasaland). See also, Southern Rhodesian Const. art. 60(3) (1961).

39 Dhlamini v. Carter, 1968 R.L.R. 136 (Rhodesia A.D.).

40 Rhodesian Const. art. 84 (1969).

41 South African Democracy Education Trust, 1 The Road to Democracy in South Africa: 1960–1970 at 527 (2004). Two of the three, convicted of petrol bombing, were James Ndhlamini and Victor Mlambo. Appeals to the Rhodesian High Court and the Appellate Division focused on whether the Rhodesian Front regime had authority to sentence persons to death. Elaine Windrich, *Britain and the Politics of Rhodesian Independence*, 123 (1978).

42 *Amnesty International Briefing: Rhodesia/Zimbabwe*, 6 Issue: J. Opinion 34, 37 (1976).

prime minister and other ministers selected by the president. In a typical case, the minister of justice would refer the matter to the executive council after consulting with the full cabinet. According to Chihambakwe, the Rhodesian government carried out three executions in 1960, eight in 1965, 24 in 1973, 27 in 1974 and 36 in 1975.[43] As the execution rate increased after 1970, however, the rate of clemency dropped. The government commuted 168 death sentences between 1965 and 1970 inclusive, but only ten death sentences between 1973 and 1975 when the number of executions increased.[44] One pardon was granted in 1974 to a man serving a sentence of robbery after a fingerprint analysis showed that the convicted person was already in prison for a different crime when the incident occurred. He was found to have falsely confessed to protect his younger brother.[45] According to Amnesty International, the death penalty in Southern Rhodesia was "very widely used not only for criminal offences such as murder or rape, but also for those convicted of certain political offences under the Law and Order (Maintenance) Act," including arms possession or harboring terrorists.[46] More than sixty executions took place between 1968 and 1976, "over a storm of international protest."[47] Convictions under the Law and Order (Maintenance) Act peaked during 1977 and 1978, which was the height of guerilla activity in Rhodesia.[48]

The Rhodesian War escalated in 1972 when guerrillas infiltrated the northeastern region of the country, carrying out attacks on selected political targets and widening the field of operation.[49] While capital punishment faced legal challenges throughout the 1970s, "it is the execution of political offenders that has caused the greatest protest."[50] After 1972, the death penalty was used extensively against guerrilla fighters and alleged accomplices, often after trials performed in secret. After 1975, the government announced that the names of people sentenced to death or hanged would no longer be released.[51] As Hatchard notes, at least 152 executions took place between 1975 and 1979, not including secret executions. The Rhodesian government implemented emergency regulations in 1976, creating "special courts" to try political crimes and terrorism.[52] These extraconstitutional courts, formed outside the judicial branch, had the power to impose death without safeguards and were abolished at

43 Chihambakwe, *supra* note 33 at 42.
44 *Id.*
45 C.H. Rolph, *The Queen's Pardon*, 137–38.
46 Amnesty International Briefing, *supra* note 42 at 36.
47 *Id.* at 37.
48 Chihambakwe, *supra* note 33 at 45.
49 Tony Kirk, *Politics and Violence in Rhodesia*, 74 Afr. Aff. 3, 3(1975).
50 Amnesty International Briefing, *supra* note 42 at 37.
51 Denis Herbstein, *White Lies: Canon Collins and the Secret War Against Apartheid*, 268 (2004).
52 John Hatchard, *Individual Freedoms and State Security in the African Context: The Case of Zimbabwe*, 83 (1993).

independence. In addition, courts martial could try civilians and dispense death sentences after martial law was declared in 1978.[53]

4. THE DEATH PENALTY IN INDEPENDENT ZIMBABWE

Zimbabwe carried out a total of 76 executions between independence in April 1980 and the final execution in 2005.[54] At independence, Zimbabwe inherited the death penalty for attempted murder, conspiracy, treason, rape and attempted rape, aggravated robbery and attempt, certain political offenses under Rhodesian security legislation, and felony murder.[55] This legislation included at least four discretionary capital offenses under the Law and Order (Maintenance) Act, including terrorist training, recruitment for terrorist training, aggravated arms possession, and acts of terrorism or sabotage, as well as two offenses under the Railways Act (launching projectiles at trains and interfering with track).[56] The death sentence was restricted to cases of murder and treason in 1992.[57] Reflecting the colonial practice, the death penalty was prohibited in law for pregnant women and juveniles.[58] Zimbabwe's Criminal Procedure and Evidence Act also prohibited the death penalty for persons over age 70.[59] The capital offenses retained after independence were part of a much larger security apparatus that the new government inherited from the Rhodesian state, even to the point that most military officers and security officials were kept in place. In 1982, this security apparatus was implicated in a low-intensity conflict against "dissidents" in Matabeleland, known as *Gukurahundi*. The estimates of civilians killed by security forces in 1983 alone ranged from about 450 to 1,500 or more in a gross outbreak of extrajudicial state violence.[60]

The new government's policy was not to carry out executions, though the death penalty remained mandatory in the absence of extenuating circumstances, a doctrine of mitigation that Zimbabwe shared with Botswana, Lesotho, and, at the time, Swaziland and South Africa.[61] The deteriorating

---

53 Herbstein, *supra* note 51 at 269.

54 Musevengana Machaya, *The Death Penalty in Zimbabwe: A Human Rights Perspective*, LL.M. Thesis, University of the Western Cape 37 (2014).

55 G. Feltoe, *A Guide to Sentencing in Zimbabwe*, 26–27 (1990).

56 Hatchard, *supra* note 52 at 84–85; Feltoe, *supra* note 55 at 26–27.

57 Criminal Laws Amendment Act 2 of 1992. See Criminal Procedure and Evidence Act, 1 Statute Law of Zimbabwe, Cap. 9:07, §337 (1996 ed.).

58 Lilian Chenwi, *Towards the Abolition of the Death Penalty in Africa*, 42–42 (2007).

59 See Criminal Procedure and Evidence Act, §338, cited in Chenwi, *supra* note 58 at 43.

60 Michael Garcia Bochenek, *Compensation for Human Rights Abuses in Zimbabwe*, 26 Colum. Hum. Rts. L. Rev. 483, 488–89, 494 (1995).

61 Andrew Novak, *Capital Sentencing Discretion in Southern Africa: A Human Rights Perspective on the Doctrine of Extenuating Circumstances in Death Penalty Cases*, 14 Afr. Hum. Rts. L.J. 24 (2014).

security situation as a result of civil unrest in Matabeleland preempted a 1982 recommendation from the Advisory Committee on Law Reform to limit the number of capital offenses.[62] Once a political settlement to the unrest was attained in 1987, a moratorium on executions was in place between 1988 and 1992. A nascent abolitionist movement including such figures as Chief Justice Enoch Dumbutshena and the NGOs Legal Resources Foundation and Catholic Commission for Justice and Peace organized campaigns against the death sentence and a nationwide petition to President Robert Mugabe.[63] Reflecting on his judicial role, Chief Justice Dumbutshena wrote that it was "common practice among judges to lean towards a finding of manslaughter or finding extenuating circumstances. Judges are reluctant to sentence people to death."[64]

In 1987, the seven-year transitional provisions of Zimbabwe's independence Constitution constraining fundamental rights finally expired, which opened existing law to constitutional challenge for the first time.[65] Litigation on the basis of cruel, inhuman, and degrading punishment came almost immediately. In 1987, the full bench of the Supreme Court of Zimbabwe unanimously held that the sentence of whipping for adults constituted cruel and degrading punishment, looking both to international trends and to the decline in the penalty's use domestically.[66] Two years later, the Court found in a three to two vote that corporal punishment of juveniles also constituted cruel and degrading punishment, although this decision was later reversed by constitutional amendment.[67] One by one, challenges succeeded: against solitary confinement, reduced diet, retroactive punishments, and punishments based on mute confessions, in the so-called "golden age" of human rights litigation in Zimbabwe.[68]

The opening of Zimbabwe's 1980 constitution to human rights challenges created an opening for opponents of capital punishment. In 1990, the Supreme Court asked for full argument on the issue of whether the use of hanging constituted cruel or degrading punishment. Before the hearing could take place, however, the government rushed through a constitutional amendment to specifically save hanging as a method of execution.[69] According to the

62 John Hatchard & Simon Coldham, *Commonwealth Africa*, in *Capital Punishment: Global Issues and Prospects*, 155, 160–61 (Peter Hodgkinson & Andrew Rutherford eds., 1996).

63 *Id.* at 161.

64 Dumbutshena, *supra* note 5 at 524, 530.

65 See Zimbabwe Const. art. 26 (1980).

66 State v. Ncube, 1988 (2) S.A. 702, 721 (Zim. S.C.). See Zim. Const. art. 15(1) (1980).

67 A Juvenile v. State, SC 64/89, reversed by Constitution of Zimbabwe Amendment Act, No. 11 of 1990. However, nearly a year after the amendment, Parliament had not drafted implementing legislation. For more about corporal punishment in Zimbabwe see John Hatchard, *The Fall and Rise of the Cane in Zimbabwe*, 35 J. Afr. L. 198, 198–200, 202 (1991).

68 Adrian de Bourbon, *Human Rights Litigation in Zimbabwe: Past Present and Future*, 3 Afr. Hum. Rts. L.J. 195, 209–10 (2003).

69 Hatchard & Coldham, *supra* note 62 at 170.

Minister of Justice, finding hanging unconstitutional was "untenable" and the government "will not and cannot countenance a situation where the death penalty is *de facto* abolished through the back door."[70] The pinnacle of this period was the Supreme Court's famous decision in *Catholic Commission for Justice and Peace v. Attorney General*, in which the Court found that the dehumanizing factor of prolonged delay on death row, viewed in conjunction with the harsh and degrading conditions in the holding prison, meant that the executions of appellants would be unconstitutionally cruel and degrading.[71] The Court's decision was notable for the holding that a defendant was not penalized for seeking to exercise his or her constitutional right to appeal, as well as a broad standing ruling allowing a human rights organization to bring a suit on behalf of a group of prisoners. The Court cited a broad range of international authorities, including decisions of the United States, India, Canada, the Privy Council, and the United Nations Human Rights Committee.[72] As Chief Justice Anthony Gubbay wrote,

> Humaneness and dignity of the individual are the hallmarks of civilised laws. Justice must be done dispassionately and in accordance with constitutional mandates. The question is not whether this court condones the evils committed by the four condemned prisoners, for certainly it does not. It is whether the acute mental suffering and brooding horror of being hanged which has haunted them in their condemned cells over the long lapse of time since the passing of sentence of death is consistent with the guarantee against inhuman, or degrading punishment or treatment. For like article 21 of the Constitution of India, section 15(1) stands as sentinel over human misery, degradation and oppression. Its voice is that of justice and fairness. It can never be silenced on the grounds that the time to heed to its dictates ended with the passing of the death penalty. It echoes through all stages – the trial, the sentence, the incarceration on death row and finally, the execution.[73]

Like in the hanging and juvenile corporal punishment challenges, *Catholic Commission* was reversed by constitutional amendment, as the ruling party held a supermajority of seats in the legislature.[74] As amended, Article 15, the cruel

---

70 Quoted in *id.* See Chileya v. State, (1990) SC 64/90 (Zim. S.C.) (unreported).

71 Catholic Commission for Justice and Peace in Zimbabwe v. A.G., (1993) L.R.C. 277 (Zim. S.C.).

72 John Hatchard, *Delay and the Death Sentence: The Zimbabwean Approach*, 37 J. Afr. L. 185, 192 (1993).

73 *Catholic Commission*, *supra* note 71 at ¶¶ 23, 122.

74 John Hatchard, Muna Ndulo & Peter Slinn, *Comparative Constitutionalism and Good Governance in the Commonwealth: An Eastern and Southern African Perspective*, 45–47 (2004). "The Zimbabwean experience highlights the problem of centring the amendment procedure on the legislature for having had the first twenty years of independence dominated by one political party, the two-thirds parliamentary majority had proved of no practical value as a check against retrogressive constitutional amendments." *Id.* at 47.

and degrading punishment clause in Zimbabwe's 1980 constitution, eventually included a lengthy series of exclusions, including the following:

> (1) No person shall be subjected to torture or to inhuman or degrading punishment or other such treatment. …
> (3) No moderate corporal punishment inflicted … in execution of the judgment or order of a court, upon a male person under the age of eighteen years as a penalty for breach of any law shall be held to be in contravention of subsection (1) on the ground that it is inhuman or degrading.[75]
> (4) The execution of a person who has been sentenced to death by a competent court in respect of a criminal offence of which he has been convicted shall not be held to be in contravention of subsection (1) solely on the ground that the execution is carried out in the manner prescribed in section 315(2) of the Criminal Procedure and Evidence Act [Chapter 59] as that section existed on the 1st October, 1990.[76]
> (5) Delay in the execution of a sentence of death, imposed upon a person in respect of a criminal offence of which he has been convicted, shall not be held to be a contravention of subsection (1).[77] …

According to Section 31(I) of the 1980 constitution, the prerogative of mercy was exercised by the President, who could grant pardons, commutations, reprieves, or remissions of fines or forfeitures.[78] In 1987, the constitution was amended at Section 31(K) to state that a court could not inquire into the nature of any advice tendered to the President or the manner in which he exercised his discretion.[79] According to Magade, the President was not required to furnish reasons for the exercise of his discretion. Case law from the Zimbabwe Supreme Court indicated that the prerogative of mercy in death penalty cases was automatic regardless of whether the accused person sought it, but the constitution provided no specific procedure as to how the president was to exercise the mercy power.[80] Chenwi notes that Zimbabwe followed the Commonwealth practice of requiring a mercy report in death penalty cases for review by an advisory mercy committee, which tendered advice to the President as to the exercise of his prerogative of mercy. She also indicates that condemned prisoners could seek redress from Parliament in capital cases.[81]

---

75 This provision reversed A Juvenile v. State, SC 64/89. See Constitution of Zimbabwe Amendment Act, No. 11 of 1990, §5.

76 This provision preempted *Chileya v. State*, a constitutional challenge to hanging (or other "manner" of execution). Constitution of Zimbabwe Amendment Act, No. 11 of 1990, §5.

77 This provision reversed *Catholic Commission*. Constitution of Zimbabwe Amendment Act, No. 2 of 1993, §13.

78 Zimbabwe Const. art. 31(I) (1980).

79 Zimbabwe Const. art. 31(K) (1980).

80 Emmanuel Magade, *Country Report on Zimbabwe: The Right to Life and the Death Penalty*, British Institute for International and Comparative Law 5–6 (2004), www.biicl.org/files/2306_country_report_zimbabwe_magade.pdf.

81 Chenwi, *supra* note 58 at 185, 186.

Prison conditions in Zimbabwe have also occasioned constitutional challenges. In 1991, the Supreme Court described the conditions of Chikurubi Maximum Security Prison as deplorable in *Conjwayo v. Minister of Justice*, noting that prisoners were held in small, windowless cells with a sleeping mat on concrete, illuminated by a single electric light that was never switched off.[82] In *Catholic Commission* two years later, the Supreme Court described conditions in Harare Central Prison as cells two meters wide by three-and-a-half meters long, with a single very high window and a chamber pot. Prisoners were incarcerated naked in their cells overnight.[83] However, in 2003, the Supreme Court found that the government's failure to transfer an ill prisoner to South Africa for medical treatment did not constitute cruel and degrading treatment in violation of Section 15 of the 1980 Constitution.[84] The Court rejected the argument that the prisoner's life sentence without commutation or medical treatment necessarily condemned him to die a lingering death in prison.[85]

5. THE DOCTRINE OF EXTENUATING CIRCUMSTANCES

Colonial Rhodesia had early precedent suggesting that the death penalty was not strictly mandatory in all cases of murder. In *Rex v. Sanka*, the colonial court stated that "death is a possible but not a necessary sentence."[86] As Karimunda explains, on occasion courts excluded the death penalty even where murder was proven.[87] While the death penalty was used fairly frequently in Northern Rhodesia (where 49 people were sentenced to death and 26 executed by 1960) and Nyasaland (25 death sentences and nine executions in the same period), respectively, Southern Rhodesia appears to have had fewer in this period. The death sentence was imposed in at least two cases in 1938, but there is no record that these sentences were carried out.[88]

The Southern Rhodesian Legislative Assembly adopted South Africa's capital sentencing framework, known as the doctrine of extenuating circumstances, in the Criminal Procedure and Evidence Act of 1949.[89] "Extenuating circumstances" were defined as any fact that tended to reduce the moral blameworthiness

---

82 Conjwayo v. Minister of Justice, 1991 (1) Z.L.R. 105, 107–08 (Zim. S.C.).

83 Catholic Commission for Justice and Peace in Zimbabwe v. Attorney General, 1993 (1) Z.L.R. 242, 246–247 (Zim. S.C.); see also Chenwi, *supra* note 58 at 116.

84 Woods v. Commissioner of Prisons, [2003] ZWSC 74 (November 17, 2003).

85 *Id.*

86 Rex v. Sanka, [1923] R&N 20 (S.R.).

87 Rex v. Sales, [1936] R&N 55 (S.R.); Rex v. Sikonia, [1937] R&N 54 (S.R.). Cited in Karimunda, *supra* note 6 at 105.

88 Karimunda, *supra* note 6 at 105, citing Rex v. Chikokonya, [1938] R&N 122 (S.R.); Rex v. Longone, [1938] R&N 131 (S.R.).

89 Criminal Procedure and Evidence Amendment Act 52 of 1949.

but not the legal culpability of the accused at the moment the crime was committed.[90] These included failed defenses, absence of prior convictions, withdrawal from a conspiracy, provocation and emotional disturbance, intoxication, partial excuse, lack of actual intent to kill, duress, youth, political motives, accessory or accomplice liability, repentance, and mercy killing, among others.[91] During the legislative debate, Minister of Justice Thomas Beadle explained that "only half the death sentences which are passed in this Colony are ever carried out in fact."[92] One member noted that the doctrine provided clarity to the law since the current mandatory death penalty regime created "a tendency to strain the law against the finding of murder," and instead convict of manslaughter. Allowing a judge a measure of sentencing discretion would "enable the law to be administered more logically."[93] The doctrine operated as a rebuttable presumption in favor of death in which the convicted person had the burden to show extenuation.

The doctrine of extenuating circumstances continued to apply after independence. Zimbabwean courts adhered to the traditional rule placing the burden of proof on the accused.[94] Unlike other countries in Southern Africa, the Zimbabwean Supreme Court allowed trial judges wide discretion to weigh aggravating and mitigating factors to determine whether extenuating circumstances existed. A two-stage analysis like those used in Botswana or Lesotho was not necessary.[95] One unique aspect of Zimbabwe's doctrine of extenuating circumstances was the degree of deference given to a trial court's decision, and the Supreme Court refused to change a sentence in the absence of misdirection or irregularity, even if it would have imposed a lesser sentence.[96] Unlike neighboring jurisdictions, the Court strictly applied the onus requirement. The Supreme Court upheld a trial court's finding that no extenuating circumstances existed simply because no submissions were made against sentence.[97] The Court has also summarily dismissed an appellant's submission of extenuating circumstances where the appellant just repeated the same facts rejected in the trial phase.[98] If the Supreme Court upheld a death

---

90 G. Feltoe, *Extenuating Circumstances: A Life and Death Issue*, 4 Zimbabwe L. Rev. 60, 61 (1986).

91 *Id.* at 66. For witchcraft, see G. Feltoe, *Witch Murder and the Law*, 14 Rhodesian L.J. 40, 41–45 (1974).

92 Debates of the Legislative Assembly of Southern Rhodesia 2643 (October 18, 1949).

93 *Id.* at 2651.

94 See, e.g., Learnmore Judah Jongwe v. State, [2002] ZWSC 62 (August 8, 2002). The Court stated in that case that "[t]he onus to establish the defense of provocation and extenuating circumstances is on the appellant. Should the trial court reject his version of events the appellant will have problems establishing extenuating circumstances." *Id.*

95 Feltoe, *supra* note 90 at 63.

96 John Hatchard, *Capital Punishment in Southern Africa: Some Recent Developments*, 43 Int'l & Comp. L.Q. 923, 925 (1994).

97 State v. Sango, [2006] ZWSC 33 (September 18, 2006).

98 State v. Wairosi, [2011] ZWHHC 53 (February 15, 2011).

sentence, the evidence and rulings were transmitted to the president, who was required to confirm the death sentence before it could be carried out.[99]

Recent case law confirms the Supreme Court's overwhelming deference to trial court decisions. High Court decisions "almost always are confirmed on appeal because the Supreme Court is not empowered to arrive at its own sentence despite a finding of extenuating circumstances."[100] As a result, while Zimbabwe had an automatic right of appeal in death penalty cases, this did not translate into a right of substantive appellate review of sentences.[101] The Supreme Court could only "interfere if persuaded that the conclusion of the trial court could not reasonably have been reached; or where the court had regard to the wrong factors; or had mistakenly excluded factors proper to be taken into account, or had, in some other way, erred in principle."[102] This was a high threshold, and one that differed from Botswana and Lesotho. In another case, the Supreme Court found that a trial court had erred in finding a murder premeditated, but nonetheless upheld a death sentence without extenuating circumstances as the murder was still intentional.[103] In refusing to reduce a sentence for murder with extenuating circumstances from 25 years to twenty years, the justices wrote that it was "not for this Court to interfere with a sentence passed by a court of first instance merely because it might have imposed a different sentence."[104] This level of deference contrasts markedly with the efforts of other appellate courts in Southern Africa to seek uniformity in sentencing.

Because trial courts had wide latitude to determine the existence of extenuating circumstances, court decisions on extenuating circumstances in Zimbabwe were cursory, even conclusory, with virtually no analysis or evidentiary development, in sharp contrast to other jurisdictions in Southern Africa.[105] In the presence of possible extenuating circumstances, the Supreme Court upheld death sentences where aggravating factors outweighed mitigating ones.[106] In another case, the Supreme Court upheld a death sentence because the defendant's "moral blameworthiness was considered so high that the death penalty was found to be appropriate."[107] Such decisions entangled the extenuating circumstances analysis with the sentencing analysis in which

99 Dumbutshena, *supra* note 5 at 531.
100 Magade, *supra* note 80 at 1.
101 *Id.*
102 State v. Woods, 1993 (2) Zim.L.R. 258, 284 (S.C.).
103 Mbembe Porusingazi v. State, Crim. App. No. 119/06, Judgment No. S.C. 63/07 (June 9, 2008).
104 Pfungwa Mamvura v. State, Crim. App. No. 127/2003, Judgment no. S.C. 22/05 (June 20, 2005).
105 See, e.g., State v. Mamukwa, [2007] ZWSC 113 (September 7, 2007); State v. Matongo, [2005] ZWSC 61 (November 14, 2005); State v. Kanhumwa, [2004] ZWSC 151 (November 29, 2004); State v. Ndlovu, [2005] ZWSC 125 (May 19, 2005).
106 Irvine Kanhumwa & Others v. State, Crim. App. No. 189/2002, Judgment No. SC 71/07 (November 29, 2004) (finding that the defendant's youth and status as a first time offender were "totally eclipsed by the aggravating circumstances"). See also State v. Mpofu, [2006] ZWSC 81 (March 30, 2006).
107 State v. Murijo, [2005] ZWSC 139 (September 22, 2005).

aggravating and mitigating factors were weighed. A better example was a 2011 case in which the Bulawayo High Court summarized the appellant's and prosecutions arguments on extenuating circumstances, made a ruling in favor, and then moved to weigh mitigating and aggravating factors in a second step to craft a sentence of thirty years' imprisonment.[108]

The Zimbabwe Supreme Court upheld death sentences for felony murder and accomplice liability in which the defendant had only constructive intent to kill, so long as death was foreseeable.[109] However, lack of actual intent to kill could be an extenuating circumstance where the "foreseeability of the possibility of death … was rather remote."[110] In a later case, the Court clarified its holdings on constructive intent: "The finding of a constructive intent to kill in a murder case will not necessarily lead to an overall finding … that there are extenuating circumstances justifying a sentence other than death, but it is a factor which must be put [o]n the credit side in the accused's favour in that weighing-up process."[111] In one recent case, the Court upheld a trial court's finding that no extenuating circumstances existed in a felony murder case, indicating that the law was "clear" that a "murder committed in the course of a robbery attracts the death penalty unless there are weighty extenuating circumstances."[112] In addition, unlike Lesotho, Zimbabwe courts apply a "proverbial reasonable man" standard, unlike the subjective standard in the Lesotho Penal Code, which refers to "the standards of behaviour of an ordinary person of the class of the community to which the convicted person belongs."[113] In *State v. Sithole*, the Supreme Court ruled that the payment of compensation to the victim's family was not an extenuating circumstance; rather, this show of remorse could only be considered as a mitigating factor once the Court found extenuating circumstances and was tasked with crafting an appropriate sentence.[114] Extenuating circumstances, the Court confirmed, were circumstances that existed at the time the offense was committed, while mitigating factors were broader than this.

6. THE DEATH PENALTY IN THE 2013 CONSTITUTION

In May 2013, President Robert Mugabe signed into law a new constitution, one that was overwhelming ratified by voters in a popular referendum. The

108 State v. Elderman, [2011] ZWBHC 165 (October 27, 2011).

109 Piniel Murijo v. State, Crim. App. No. 124/04, Judgment No. SC 150/04, [2005] ZWSC 139 (September 22, 2005).

110 Robert Mugwanda v. State, Crim. App. No. 215/2001, Judgment No. SC 19/02 (June 6, 2002).

111 Siluli v. State, 2005 (2) Zim.L.R. 141, 146.

112 Morgan Matondo Matongo v. State, Crim. App. No. 108/04, Judgment No. SC 61/05 (November 14, 2005).

113 Compare State v. Governor, [2007] ZWHHC 9 (March 5, 2007) ("proverbial reasonable man") with Lesotho Penal Code Act of 2010 §40(4) (2012).

114 State v. Sithole, [2007] ZWSC 16 (July 17, 2007).

constitution went through several drafting phases before the detailed death penalty provisions were finalized. The 2001 National Constitutional Assembly draft permitted the death penalty for "the most heinous murders," but only after public debate about which types of murder should attract the death penalty, and only where aggravating circumstances were precisely defined in law.[115] The 2007 Kariba Draft exempted pregnant women and persons under eighteen years of age; it also required courts to have discretion in imposing death, and granted all defendants the right to seek pardon or commutation of sentence.[116] The proposed Law Society of Zimbabwe draft of 2010 abolished the death penalty and forbade executions from taking place in the country.[117]

The 2013 Constitution was a compromise of these competing views. Reflecting a desire to retain the death penalty but restrict its scope, Article 48 on the right to life reads in full:

1. Every person has the right to life.
2. A law may permit the death penalty to be imposed only on a person convicted of murder committed in aggravating circumstances, and.
   a. the law must permit the court a discretion whether or not to impose the penalty;
   b. the penalty may be carried out only in accordance with a final judgment of a competent court;
   c. the penalty must not be imposed on a person –
      i. who was less than twenty-one years old when the offence was committed; or
      ii. who is more than seventy years old;
   d. the penalty must not be imposed or carried out on a woman; and
   e. the person sentenced must have a right to seek pardon or commutation of the penalty from the President.[118]

Subclause 2(a) prohibits the mandatory death penalty, while subclauses 2(c) and (d) limit the categories of people who could be subject to a death sentence. Because Article 48 permits judicial sentencing discretion in all cases, it in effect abolishes the doctrine of extenuating circumstances. Subclause 2 only permits the death penalty for aggravated murder; the death penalty for treason is unconstitutional, as are military offenses under the Zimbabwe Defence Act, which include treason and mutiny.[119] As a result, the current criminal procedure code is inconsistent

115 National Constitutional Assembly, *Proposed Draft Constitution for Zimbabwe*, September 30, 2001, at Article 14, http://archive.kubatana.net/docs/demgg/ncaconst0201.pdf.

116 Constitution of Zimbabwe, Annexure B to the Power-Sharing Agreement of September 15, 2008 ("Kariba Draft Constitution").

117 Law Society of Zimbabwe, Constitution of Zimbabwe, October 29, 2010 ("Law Society of Zimbabwe Draft Constitution").

118 Zim. Const. art. 48 (2013).

119 See Machaya, *supra* note 54 at 41–42.

with the new constitution, and a bill is pending before parliament to reconcile the preexisting law with the new constitution.[120] Nonetheless, the Supreme Court performed an extenuating circumstances analysis in a case in which the crime was committed and the defendant tried prior to 2013, suggesting that the Court did not interpret Article 48 retroactively.[121]

Although the constitution permits the death penalty to be imposed only in the presence of "aggravating circumstances," it does not define the term. One High Court judge has suggested that "the introduction of aggravating circumstances in the Constitution suggests that the Constitution envisages the enactment of an Act of Parliament that defines the term aggravated circumstances or sets out the conditions that constitute aggravated circumstances."[122] In *State v. Mutsinze*, the High Court found that a murder was committed in aggravating circumstances, as it was performed during the course of a planned armed robbery. According to the judge, under the previous legal regime, the death penalty would have been mandatory as the case lacked extenuating circumstances. However, the new constitution "unfetter[ed]" a trial judge's discretion to pass an appropriate sentence. The Court noted that because the case did not define aggravating circumstances, the constitution necessarily contemplated additional legislation defining the term. Until that time, the judge noted, "I interpret the legal position to be that, in keeping with its international obligations and international best practices Zimbabwe inten[d]s to move away from the death penalty."[123] The judge found that the prosecution had the burden of showing aggravating circumstances and had not made such a showing; consequently, he could not impose a death sentence in "the spirit of the new law."[124]

Other benches of the High Court have attempted to define "aggravating circumstances" based on the old extenuating circumstances case law. In *State v. Malundu*, the Harare High Court ruled that until the legislature passes implementing legislation, the current Criminal Procedure and Evidence Act must be interpreted in conformity with the constitution. The effect of such interpretation is that an extenuating circumstances analysis is no longer necessary and a court must specifically find that a murder was committed in aggravating circumstances.[125] To define "aggravating circumstances," the High Court looked to pre-2013 decisions, in which aggravating circumstances were relevant to determining whether extenuating circumstances existed. The Court then considered all mitigating and aggravating evidence. According to the Court, the "circumstances in which the crime was committed and the nature of the crime far outweigh the mitigatory features advanced by

120 General Laws Amendment Bill of 2015, H.B. 3A (2015).
121 State v. Wairosi, [2015] ZWSC 20 (May 21, 2015).
122 Machaya, *supra* note 54 at 39.
123 State v. Mutsinze, HH 645–14 (October 14, 2014), www.veritaszim.net/node/1164.
124 *Id.*
125 State v. Malundu, [2015] ZWHHC 68 (January 23, 2015).

the accused," but the "aggravating features do not, however, call for the imposition of the death penalty."[126] Although the Court found aggravating factors outweighed mitigating ones, the death penalty was not mandatory. Some defendants have argued that because the constitution does not define aggravating circumstances, Zimbabwe no longer has an operable death penalty law. The High Court disagreed in *State v. Mlambo*, indicating that in an unprovoked murder for robbery, Zimbabwean precedent was clear that a murder committed for robbery had always been considered as committed in "aggravating circumstances." The court indicated that there was "no need to pretend" that aggravating circumstances were not defined in law prior to the 2013 constitution. According to the court, the offense was committed in a "callous manner" and "screams loudly for the imposition of the death penalty."[127] In another case, the Harare High Court reconfirmed this view that "aggravating circumstances" could be derived from case law, as a constitutional provision must be afforded "a generous and purposive interpretation" rather than rendered meaningless.[128]

Given this uncertainty over whether the death penalty remains lawful without amended legislation, Veritas, a Zimbabwean-based charity, is bringing a series of constitutional challenges on behalf of death row inmates. The attorney of record is Tendai Biti, previously Zimbabwe's finance minister and current opposition member of parliament. In *Dolosi v. Minister of Justice*, the applicant, convicted of murder, argued that his death sentence was not constitutional because Zimbabwe lacks an operative death penalty statute.[129] *Chawira v. Minister of Justice* is a pending death row syndrome challenge brought by fourteen applicants who were on death row from between four and eight years and incarcerated for as long as twenty years.[130] Finally, in *Ndlovu v. Minister of Justice*, the applicant is challenging his death sentence on the basis that the 2013 constitution applies retroactively and the law under which he was sentenced is not in conformity with the new constitution.[131] The implementation of the new constitution has also led to separate constitutional challenges to juvenile corporal punishment and to life imprisonment without the possibility of parole.[132] In December 2014, the High Court found juvenile corporal punishment unconstitutional, noting that the new constitution did not contain the same exception for juvenile corporal punishment that the prior constitution

126 *Id.*

127 State v. Mlambo, [2015] ZWHHC 351 (October 9, 2014).

128 State v. Paliza, [2015] ZWHHC 111 (January 23, 2015).

129 Dolosi v. Minister of Justice, [Case number not assigned] (Zimbabwe C.C.). Special thanks to Kuda Hove and Veritas Zimbabwe for assistance in obtaining the pending constitutional complaints.

130 Chawira v. Minister of Justice, CCZ 47/2015 (Zimbabwe C.C.).

131 Ndlovu v. Minister of Justice, CCZ 50/2015 (Zimbabwe C.C.).

132 Makoni v. Commissioner of Prisons, CCZ 48/2015 (Zimbabwe C.C.); State v. A Juvenile, CCZ 29/15 (Zimbabwe C.C.).

contained.[133] In June 2015, the Constitutional Court provisionally set aside the High Court's ruling pending appeal.[134]

The General Laws Amendment Bill of 2015 would, if passed by parliament, define "aggravating circumstances" for purposes of Article 48. The Bill lists two kinds of aggravating factors: those that are exclusive and may authorize the death penalty even in the presence of mitigating factors, and those that are non-exclusive and may be considered with other aggravating or mitigating factors.[135] The exclusive aggravating factors include murder committed during the course of another violent crime, multiple or serial murder, murder preceded by torture or mutilation of the victim, and murder in a public place that involves risk of serious injury to bystanders.[136] The non-exclusive aggravating factors, to be weighed against mitigating factors and considered with other aggravating factors, include premeditation, or murder of a law enforcement officer or vulnerable person, including a pregnant woman, child, disabled person, or elderly person.[137] According to the Bill, these factors are "not exhaustive, and ... a court may find other circumstances in which a murder is committed to be aggravating."[138] The Bill indicates that the appropriate sentence for a murder committed in aggravating circumstances is a death sentence, life imprisonment, or a defined period of imprisonment not less than twenty years. The appropriate sentence in all other murder cases would be a defined period of imprisonment.[139]

Zimbabwe's constitution includes a new clemency provision at Article 112. The clemency provision allows the president to pardon, commute sentences, issue temporary reprieves, and remit fines and forfeitures.[140] Both Zimbabwe's 1980 and 2013 constitutions require that the president consult with the cabinet in making mercy decisions.[141] Zimbabwe does not follow the majority rule in the common law world that an executive may only grant pardon after conviction; instead, the president has the power to pardon "any person *concerned in* or convicted of" an offense, which means he or she can issue a pardon after a crime has been committed but before the offender was convicted.[142]

---

133 S. v. C. (a Juvenile), [2015] ZWHHC 718 (December 31, 2015).

134 Daniel Nemukuyu, *Court Upholds Corporal Punishment*, The Herald, June 18, 2015, www.herald.co.zw/court-upholds-corporal-punishment.

135 Part XX, General Laws Amendment Bill of 2015, H.B. 3A (2015).

136 *Id.* at Part XX, Art. 3.

137 *Id.* at Part XX, Art. 4.

138 *Id.* at Part XX, Art. 6.

139 *Id.* at Part XX, Art. 5.

140 Zim. Const. art. 112 (2013).

141 Zim. Const. sched. 8, art. 20.1.3(g) (1980) ("on the advice of Cabinet); Zim. Const. art. 112(1) (2013) ("after consultation with the Cabinet").

142 Zim. Const. art. 112(1)(a) (2013). For an explanation of the majority rule, see Andrew Novak, *Comparative Executive Clemency: The Constitutional Pardon Power and the Prerogative of Mercy in Global Perspective*, 101 (2015).

7. PROSPECTS FOR ABOLITION OF THE DEATH PENALTY

Before the turn of the century, Zimbabwe expressed a commitment to legal capital punishment. In 1998, Zimbabwe joined fifty other nations in a note to the president of the UN Human Rights Commission asserting that no international consensus existed on the abolition of the death penalty.[143] The following year, Zimbabwe joined a UN General Assembly draft resolution asserting that capital punishment was primarily a criminal justice issue, not a human rights one.[144] Chemhuru and Masaka write that the death penalty has a "dirty" political history in Zimbabwe, imposed as it was by colonialism and used to suppress political activity. Before the 1996 presidential elections, Ndabaningi Sithole, first leader of the Zimbabwe African National Union (ZANU), faced capital treason charges, of which he was convicted but ultimately released due to failing health.[145] Political use of the death penalty for treason has reduced public trust. Capital charges alarmed the political opposition after the leader of the Movement for Democratic Change (MDC), Morgan Tsvangirai, was charged with treason in 2003. In 2008, Tendai Biti, who served as Secretary-General of the MDC and an elected member of parliament, was also charged with capital treason.[146]

The government has given mixed signals about its future plans. In 2012, Zimbabwe expressed its intention to ratify the Second Optional Protocol to the ICCPR during the universal periodic review process at the UN Human Rights Council.[147] However, that same year Zimbabwe voted against the resolution for a global moratorium on the death penalty.[148] Zimbabwe has not executed anyone since July 2005, though death sentences continue to be imposed. These included at least eleven in 2012 and sixteen in 2013.[149] Human rights groups were alarmed when a new hangman was appointed, filling a post left vacant since 2005.[150] At the end of 2013, Zimbabwe was estimated to have 89 persons on death row.[151] In 2007, the Zimbabwe Association for Crime Prevention and Rehabilitation of Offenders (ZACRO) has campaigned against the death penalty for treason and joined with a number of Christian churches to promote abolition.[152] Later

---

143 William A. Schabas, *The United Nations and Abolition of the Death Penalty*, in *Against the Death Penalty: International Initiatives and Implications*, 9, 29 (Jon Yorke ed., 2008).

144 *Id.* at 30.

145 Chemhuru & Masaka, *supra* note 13 at 128.

146 Norman Mlambo, *Between Civil Rights and Property Rights: Debating the Selective Application of Human Rights in Zimbabwe*, 38(4) Africa Insight 94, 99 (2009).

147 Roger Hood & Carolyn Hoyle, *The Death Penalty: A Worldwide Perspective*, 28 (5th ed. 2015).

148 *Id.* at 43.

149 *Id.* at 94.

150 *Id.*

151 *Id.* at 203.

152 Stanley Kwenda, *Zimbabwe: Death Penalty Stifling Free Speech*, InterPress Service, February 27, 2007, www.ipsnews.net/2007/02/zimbabwe-death-penalty-stifling-free-speech.

in 2013, an alliance of civil society, including human rights groups, formed an "Anti-Death Penalty Coalition" and launched a public awareness campaign.[153]

Until his death in July 2015, Chenjerai Hove, one of Zimbabwe's greatest writers, was an opponent of capital punishment: "The death sentence is abominable, as abominable as the crime itself. Our state must be based on love, not hatred and victimization. Our penal code must be based on rehabilitation rather than annihilation."[154] Other voices against capital punishment have included two former chief justices of the Supreme Court of Zimbabwe, Enoch Dumbutshena and Anthony Gubbay.[155] No Zimbabwean political figure has as much authority on the issue of death penalty abolition as Vice President Emmerson Mnangagwa, former minister of justice and one-time death row inmate in Rhodesia for his nationalist activities. He escaped hanging because he was under age 21 at the time.[156] On World Day Against the Death Penalty in October 2014, Mnangagwa spoke at an event sponsored by the local Amnesty International chapter, where he stated, "I want to pronounce myself clearly that the death penalty is the ultimate denial of human rights and a cold blooded and abhorrent killing of a human being by the state in the name of justice."[157] Though Vice President Mnangagwa was at one time considered a likely successor to President Mugabe, the government has made clear by its defense of the death penalty in the pending constitutional litigation that Mnangagwa's views do not represent those of the government.

8. CONCLUSION

The death penalty in Zimbabwe has an unusually troubled history. As the Shona people did not generally practice capital punishment, the death penalty is largely a residue of British colonial rule. With UDI in 1965, colonial Rhodesia's white settlers enacted a draconian security framework and used capital punishment as a weapon against African nationalists until Zimbabwe's inependence in 1980. Although the death penalty was intermittently used after independence, political elites remained divided. Impressive human rights decisions from the Zimbabwe Supreme Court were eventually reversed by a supermajority in parliament, and the government of President Robert Mugabe brought capital treason charges

153 Hood & Hoyle, *supra* note 147 at 94.

154 Michael Ross, *A View From Death Row*, 22(3) Hum. Rts. 20, 32 (Summer 1995).

155 Chemhuru & Masaka, *supra* note 13 at 141–42.

156 Jason Moyo, *Emmerson Mnangagwa: The Man Who Would Be King in Zimbabwe*, Mail & Guardian Africa, December 11, 2014, http://mgafrica.com/article/2014-12-11-emmerson-mnangagwa-the-man-who-would-be-king-in-zimbabwe.

157 *Amnesty International Urges Zim to Follow the Trend and Abolish the Death Penalty*, New Zimbabwe, July 22, 2015, www.newzimbabwe.com/NEWS-23855-Death+penalty+10+years+no+executions/NEWS.aspx.

against several of his political opponents. Zimbabwe retained the doctrine of extenuating circumstances in capital cases, which rendered death sentences largely discretionary, though the doctrine was never applied as rationally as in other Southern African countries. The new framework of the 2013 constitution, however, dramatically narrows the scope of capital punishment and creates new opportunities for death penalty opponents. Several major cases remain pending at the Constitutional Court to give content to the 2013 constitution's new mandate.

CHAPTER 7
KENYA

1. INTRODUCTION

Kenya is *de facto* abolitionist, having not carried out an execution since 1987. The country has a posture receptive to abolition, but the political uncertainties of a new constitutional framework, endemic corruption, and continued fallout from the 2007 election violence, including a now-concluded International Criminal Court investigation and increased ethnic mobilization, suggest that death penalty abolition is not a priority for current political elites. Nonetheless, the country's active judiciary, new Supreme Court, and membership in the East African Community have created new opportunities for opponents of capital punishment. The death penalty was known in precolonial Kenya, though the frequency of executions varied by locale. The modern death penalty, however, is overwhelmingly a product of colonial rule. The scale of political executions during the state of emergency in the 1950s was unparalleled in the history of British colonialism.[1] Eroding democracy after independence led to an overburdened and underresourced criminal justice system and politicized prosecutions. Following a 2002 transfer of power, however, Kenya has successfully moved to a relatively open and competitive political environment, punctured by ethnic and intercommunal tensions that have surrounded national elections.[2]

2. THE DEATH PENALTY IN PRECOLONIAL KENYA

As elsewhere in Sub-Saharan Africa, use of capital punishment varied widely in Kenya, especially outside the Islamic coastal zone.[3] The penalty was typically

1 David Anderson, *Histories of the Hanged: The Dirty War in Kenya and the End of Empire*, 7 (2005).

2 Nic Cheeseman, Gabrielle Lynch & Justin Willis, *Democracy and Its Discontents: Understanding Kenya's 2013 Elections*, 8 J. Eastern Afr. Stud. 2 (2014).

3 The death penalty was known in the Sultanate of Zanzibar, which governed the Kenyan coast. A. Hardinge, *Legislative Methods in the Zanzibar and East African Protectorates*, 1–2 J. Soc. Comp. Leg. 4 (1899). However, "[c]apital punishment was very rare under the *Ismaili Shi*

used when other forms of economic compensation were inadequate. Other forms of punishment in precolonial Kenya could involve banishment or ostracism for crimes of witchcraft and sorcery, as among the Abanyole people of the Luyha ethnic group in Western Province, or even beating or execution of witches, as among the Kisii in Nyanza Province.[4] The death penalty was known among the Luhya people. An offender was typically tried and, if convicted, given a life sentence or executed, although lesser sentences or acquittals were possible.[5] Even today, the Kenyan legal system continues to recognize compensation for victims of crime, although the amount is limited by law.[6]

Compensation served as the paradigmatic punishment for homicide or other serious offenses against the person in many communities. Among the Gusii, a heinous offense required a fine in the form of cattle, goats, and sheep, as well as a sacrifice to chase away evil spirits and bring about social harmony, although retaliatory killings did occur.[7] Nonetheless, the death penalty was permissible even in societies that generally did not practice capital punishment in the event that the offender did not pay compensation. The Bukusu people allowed a victim's clan to "kill a member of the opposite sex of the murderer's clan" when the latter failed to pay a blood fine.[8] The Kalenjin people did not distinguish between unintentional and intentional murder; compensation was paid in either case. The deceased's family was entitled to make a show of force if compensation was not immediate so that elders of both clans were obliged to settle the matter. The deceased's family was entitled to ask for a claim of reasonable compensation, such as a hut, goats, or a calf.[9]

The Maasai people likewise preferred compensation to execution. Compensation served as repayment to the family of the victim for the economic loss of a person. A Maasai man could only be found guilty of murder if he killed someone also of the Maasai ethnic group.[10] The practice of treating the murder of a kinsman more harshly than the murder of someone outside the group was not unusual in Sub-Saharan Africa.[11] While revenge killing could and did take

---

School [of Jurisprudence] in Zanzibar and on the coast. Even murders that involved mutilation were punished by *diyya* [compensation] provided the victim consented to receiving it." Aimé Muyoboke Karimunda, *The Death Penalty in Africa: The Path Towards Abolition*, 93 (2014).

4 Ezekiel Alembi, *Issues in the Socio-Cultural Perception of Death as Reflected in the Abanyole Dirges*, 27 Indian Folklife 15 (2007).

5 *Id.* at 19 (2007).

6 Kenya Criminal Procedure Code, sec. 175 (2009) (limiting compensation to a crime punishable by a fine and only when an amount of substantial value is at stake).

7 John S. Akama, *Social Organization and Administration of Justice*, in *Ethnography of the Gusii of Western Kenya: A Vanishing Cultural Heritage*, 93 (John S. Akama & Robert Maxon eds., 2006).

8 Karimunda, *supra* note 3 at 31.

9 *Id.* at 39–40.

10 S.S. Ole Sankan, *The Maasai*, 14 (1976).

11 See, e.g., O. Oko Elechi, *Doing Justice Without the State: The Afikpo (Ehugpo) Nigeria Model*, 183 (2006) (indicating that the Afikpo of Southeastern Nigeria treated murder against a

place among the Maasai, the family of the murderer usually engaged in peaceful negotiations with the family of the victim, most often involving a transfer of cattle or sheep.[12] A victim's clan could also raid the clan of the murderer for economic compensation, typically cattle, if compensation were not paid.[13] The Turkana peoples of Coast Province also punished murder with compensation in cattle as blood money. In contrast, execution was reserved for serious spiritual crimes of witchcraft or incest.[14] Crimes of theft typically required the restoration of the stolen value; crimes of injury required payment for the victim's care and rehabilitation.[15]

The Kikuyu people only rarely practiced capital punishment, reserving it for habitual murderers and major sexual offenses.[16] In these cases, the condemned person was bound and died of exposure.[17] In less serious cases, the Kikuyu favored a system of compensation to an injured victim or a deceased person's family. "Since the payment would be collected from a wide family group on behalf of the evil-doer they would all have an interest in deterring him for the future."[18] Even when the offender was arrested and was made to pay compensation, the family of the deceased might still be entitled to kill a member of the offender's clan if the offender escaped arrest.[19] Former President Jomo Kenyatta, himself Kikuyu, wrote that criminal cases in precolonial times were treated the same as civil ones, with compensation rather than imprisonment as the paradigmatic sanction.[20] Ostracism played a major role: the stigma attached to a criminal offense was much worse than that attached to European imprisonment.[21] As Kinyanjui explains, while the Kikuyu could conduct retaliatory raids on the homestead of a murderer, the raid was only symbolic as the Kikuyu were guided by the saying *tutingihe hiti keri* ("we wouldn't give the

---

kinsman more seriously than ordinary murder). As Ntanda-Nsereko writes with Botswana in mind, many precolonial African societies focused on the status of the victim, not the offender, in calculating punishments, a sharp cultural difference to British penal policy, which focused on the *mens rea* of the murderer. Daniel Ntanda-Nsereko, *Compensating the Victims of Crime in Botswana*, 33 J. Afr. L. 157, 158 (1989).

12 Because of the symbolic significance of the numbers eight and nine, a murderer of a man would pay a denomination of cattle ending with the number nine (such as 49) while a murderer of a woman, a much rarer event, would trigger a denomination of cattle ending with the number 8 (such as 28 or 48). Murders of non-Maasai people would result in a cleansing ceremony rather than an economic penalty. Sankan, *supra* note 10 at 14–15.

13 J.S.B. Leakey, *Notes on the Masai of Kenya Colony*, 60 J. Royal Anth. Inst. Great Britain & Ireland 185, 209 (1930).

14 J.S.S. Rowlands, *Notes on Native Law and Custom in Kenya: I*, 6 J. Afr. L. 192, 193 (1962).

15 *Id.*

16 Neil McGlashan, *Indigenous Kikuyu Education*, 63 Afr. Aff. 47, 51 (1964).

17 *Id.* Often, a guilty party would commit suicide. *Id.*

18 *Id.*

19 Karimunda, *supra* note 3 at 31–32.

20 Quoted in James Read, *Crime and punishment in East Africa: The Twilight of Customary Law*, 10 How. L.J. 164, 170 (1964).

21 *Id.*

hyenas twice"), which means that a death did not require a second death.[22] She argues that restorative justice practices such as compensation were successful means of governing conduct and maintaining order in the precolonial period.[23]

The Luo of Western Kenya had an alternate means of compensating for the economic loss caused by homicide: after murder the killer was to marry the wife of the victim in order to prevent two fatherless households by executing a killer.[24] Different ceremonial cleansing rituals applied depending on whether the murder was premeditated or unplanned. A premeditated murder could bring spiritual harm to an entire community and, therefore, required a more intensive ritual, while a heat of passion murder only brought spiritual harm on the offender.[25] In Nandi society, compensation was only payable if the person killed was of a different clan than the killer; if they were of the same clan, then the economic loss was the clan's own, though a reduced payment in cattle might be warranted to the immediate family. The death penalty was only reserved for habitual offenders.[26]

The economic impact of murder was also recognized among the Kamba people. Clan elders settled disputes involving homicide with the payment of cattle, which often would number eleven or fourteen cows, one or two bulls, and a goat.[27] More specific rules governed the disposition of the cattle: one to the senior wife or mother of the deceased, for instance; another to the father's family; and a third for a purification ceremony.[28] Even after the onset of British rule, this "blood price" was still payable, although it could be reduced according to the severity of the criminal punishment. If the murderer was put to death, no blood price was paid.[29] As the economic loss of a person was not related to the intent of the murderer, Kamba law did not distinguish among murder, manslaughter, or accidental death, nor between children and adults.[30] The full blood price would be payable in every case. Under British administration, these

---

22 Sarah Kinyanjui, *Restorative Justice in Traditional Pre-Colonial "Criminal Justice Systems" in Kenya*, 10 Tribal L.J. 1, 11 (2009).

23 *Id.* at 16.

24 Lillian Manka Chenwi, *Toward the Abolition of the Death Penalty in Africa: A Human Rights Perspective*, 19 (2007).

25 G.M. Wilson, *Homicide and Suicide Among the Joluo of Kenya*, in *African Homicide and Suicide*, 182–83 (P. Bohannan ed., 1967).

26 G.S. Snell, *Nandi Customary Law*, 63–65 (1954).

27 D.J. Penwill, *Kamba Customary Law: Notes Taken in the Machakos District of Kenya Colony*, 78–79 (1951).

28 *Id.* at 79.

29 *Id.* at 80–81. If the murderer went to prison and was released, half the price would be payable. *Id.*

30 *Id.* at 81–83. In line with the compensatory nature of the penalty for economic loss, the blood price might be reduced if the victim was elderly as the economic contribution of the deceased person was not as high. *Id.* at 83. Likewise, blood price would be payable for a stillborn child or a miscarriage, but not if a man kills his childless wife for whom he has already paid the full bride price, as the economic loss was his own. *Id.* at 83.

customary penalties were codified and enforceable by the Native Tribunal, the clan's customary court.[31] Nonetheless, the Kamba recognized a distinction akin to that between criminal law and non-criminal law. When the elders felt that a crime was too serious to be atoned for with the fine of one bull or by banishment, the offender would be brought before an assembly of male adults. The assembly was permitted to authorize execution in public.[32] Elias writes that the Kamba had a process in which elders performed a post-mortem examination of a corpse in order to find the cause of an unknown or inexplicable death, and were skilled at detecting internal injuries. A death that could not be explained could be attributed to spiritual causes.[33]

3. THE DEATH PENALTY DURING THE COLONIAL PERIOD

The British East Africa Company was chartered in 1888, shortly after the Berlin Conference of 1885 established a British sphere of influence over the region. British rule was formalized in 1895 with the company's failure.[34] British colonization of Kenya followed a familiar pattern: a Western-style penal code replaced customary law for serious crimes, including capital offenses, while a general policy of "indirect rule" allowed modified customary law structures to survive at the local level.[35] Although the British allowed customary courts to pass death sentences during the early years of colonial rule, the frequency with which they did so, including for witchcraft, led to a change of policy in 1911 that required the district commissioner to approve all death sentences.[36] In British East Africa, including Kenya, Uganda, and Tanganyika, the criminal law of India applied until it was replaced by the Colonial Office Model Code in 1930. Although India had a penal code that made concessions to local context, Kenya's new code more generally applied pure English law.[37] The 1930 penal code installed a mandatory death penalty for treason, piracy, and murder, and magistrates began to impose harsh punishments routinely. The East African Court of Appeal confirmed that the death penalty was mandatory under the new penal code in a 1941 decision.[38]

31 *Id.* at 82.
32 T. Olawale Elias, *The Nature of African Customary Law*, 113 (1956).
33 Elias, *supra* note 32 at 236.
34 Marjorie Ruth Dilley, *British Policy in Kenya Colony*, 15 (1966).
35 Katherine Luongo, *Witchcraft and Colonial Rule in Kenya, 1900–1955*, 75 (2011).
36 Karimunda, *supra* note 3 at 95.
37 *Id.* at 96–97. See also Stacey Hynd, *Murder and Mercy: Capital Punishment in Colonial Kenya, ca. 1909–1956*, 45 Int'l J. Afr. Hist. Stud. 81, 84 (2012).
38 Karimunda, *supra* note 3 at 98, citing Rex v. Kichanjele s/o Ndamungu, 8 E.A.C.A. 65 (1941).

Colonial use of the death penalty was highly contested between London and local colonial administrators. The Colonial Office discouraged public executions in the colonies, though white settlers and others in Kenya called for such as late as the 1940s.[39] After sentencing and appeal, a capital conviction was sent to the governor sitting with his executive council for clemency consideration.[40] While some grants of clemency were no doubt arbitrary and others followed familiar British precedents, a number were unique to their colonial context: interracial murders or murders of state officials, for instance, were treated harshly, as were Indian defendants, as they were perceived to be above "savagery" of the African. By contrast, murders that resulted from attacks on suspected witch killers were more complicated because executing a suspected witch killer could provoke a public outcry. In addition, the accused killer could also plead that the witchcraft practiced by the victim constituted provocation. Murders that occurred as a result of a local cultural practice, such as infanticide or retaliation for rape, also received mercy.[41]

One difference between Britain's colonies in East Africa compared to colonies in West Africa was the complicating presence of significant white and South Asian populations.[42] As the British began devolving power to majority-ruled governments in West Africa, white settler demands in East and Southern Africa led the Colonial Office to implement a new paradigm for decolonization, multiracial power-sharing, which was intended to satisfy the competing demands of this constituency.[43] The colonial East African governors, especially the governor of Kenya, Sir Phillip Mitchell, opposed the efforts to increase the numbers of black African representatives in colonial legislatures.[44] The Colonial Office's attempts to create power-sharing regimes in East and Central Africa uniformly met with failure as white settlers refused to cede power and African nationalists viewed the policy as a sham.[45]

---

39 Stacey Hynd, *Killing the Condemned: The Practice and Process of Capital Punishment in British Africa, 1900–1950s*, 49 J. Afr. Hist. 403, 409–410 (2008).

40 Hynd, *supra* note 37 at 83, 86.

41 *Id.* at 87–90. See also Stacey Hynd, *Deadlier Than the Male? Women and the Death Penalty in Colonial Kenya and Nyasaland, c. 1920–57*, 12 Wiener Zeitschrift für Kritische Afrikastudien 13, 19 (2007). This category also included deaths that occurred in retaliatory communal or tribal raids, which were a local practice among some groups but that challenged the colonial order. As with witchcraft, the colonial state attempted to suppress these practices but had to tread carefully. Clemency was used in such cases. Hynd, *supra* note 37 at 92–93.

42 Cranford Pratt, *Colonial Governments and the Transfer of Power in East Africa*, in *The Transfer of Power in Africa: Decolonization, 1940–1960*, 249, 259 (Prosser Gifford & William Roger Louis eds., 1982).

43 George Bennett, *Kenya: A Political History*, 135–37 (1963).

44 Pratt, *supra* note 42 at 260.

45 *Id.* at 261.

About 80,000 British settlers lived in Kenya, primarily inhabiting the White Highlands, a plateau area to the north of Nairobi.[46] White settlers steadfastly opposed independence, though given reliance on British market subsidies the settler agriculture industry was not competitive in the long-term. In the 1950s, it became clear that the settlers were dependent on metropolitan Britain for military and police security as well. The settlers proved unable to resist a peasant uprising by local populations, primarily the Kikuyu, which broke out in 1952.[47] This uprising became known as the Mau Mau War, after the name given to the religio-political Kikuyu movement. Although Mau Mau was defeated, the Emergency broke the strength of the white settler community as dependence on British security forces to restore order allowed colonial officials to continue the transitional process toward independence.[48]

4. THE DEATH PENALTY FOR EXTRAORDINARY CRIMES IN LATE COLONIAL KENYA

The British only very sparingly employed the death penalty for political crimes in their twentieth century Empire. There was one exception. During the Mau Mau Emergency in Kenya between 1952 and 1958, 2,509 mostly Kikuyu people were tried on capital charges; of these, 1,090 Kikuyu were executed.[49] "At no

46 Once consequence of indirect rule was that white settlers in British colonies tended to be more powerful than their counterparts in French or Portuguese Africa because of Britain's generally laissez-faire form of governance. In Kenya, the white left led by Michael Blundell eventually outmaneuvered the white right led by Ferdinand Cavendish-Bentinck, the Speaker of the Kenyan Legislative Council, to avoid a Rhodesian-style situation in which white settlers seized control of the state upon decolonization. White settler rule in Kenya was never able to stand on its own without economic and political assistance from Britain. Gary Wasserman, *Politics of Decolonization: Kenya Europeans and the Land Issue 1960–65, passim* (2009).

47 As Lonsdale writes, memory of Mau Mau generates strong feelings both in Britain and in Kenya, as a symbol of African savagery, militant nationalism, or tribalist thuggery, depending on one's perspective. John Lonsdale, *Mau Maus of the Mind: Making Mau Mau and Remaking Kenya*, 31 J. Afr. Hist. 393, 393–94 (1990). The origins of the movement seem to lay in part with the Kikuyu alienation of land to white settlers and their incorporation into a capitalist economy that forced a cycle of dependence. David W. Throup, *The Origins of Mau Mau*, 84 Afr. Aff. 399, *et seq.* (1985).

48 Pratt, *supra* note 42 at 262. See Caroline Elkins, *Imperial Reckoning: The Untold Story of Britain's Gulag in Kenya*, 38 (2005). As the power of the white settlers waned, the British colonial officials could increasingly rely on Jomo Kenyatta to mediate between the radicals and the loyalists, while a white settler left wing, led by the New Kenya Group and Michael Blundell, helped to moderate settler demands. Geoff Lamb, *Peasant Politics: Conflict and Development in Murang'a* (1974); Wasserman, *supra* note 46.

49 Anderson, *supra* note 1 at 6–7. Historians have not traditionally recognized the Mau Mau movement as a legitimate political movement because it did not fit the traditional nationalist paradigm. See, for instance, Roland Oliver & J.D. Fage, *A Short History of Africa*, 214 (1988). According to Oliver and Fage, the Mau Mau movement was "as much a psychological and magico-religious as a political reaction to alien pressures." *Id.* In the very next sentence,

other place, and at no other time in the history of British imperialism, was state execution used on such a scale as this," Oxford historian David Anderson writes of the Mau Mau Emergency.[50] This was more than double the number of executions of political criminals by the French during the Algerian War, and many times more the number carried out by the British in the other postwar emergencies in Palestine, Cyprus, and Aden.[51] Even the emergency in colonial Malaya, the nearest analogy to the Mau Mau War, involved state execution on a considerably smaller scale.[52] By contrast, excluding Mau Mau crimes, 1,080 death sentences were passed in colonial Kenya between 1908 and 1956, resulting in only 459 executions, less than half the number carried out during Mau Mau.[53]

For eight years after October 1952, Kenya was ruled under a State of Emergency that resulted in the deaths of 11,500 Mau Mau fighters and the arrest or detention of at least tens of thousands more.[54] The vast majority of the detained were never formally convicted in court; suspicion of association with Mau Mau was enough.[55] The British law and order response to the Mau Mau uprising in the 1950s involved repressive police action, an unsophisticated justice system (though the British did assign lawyers to indigent defendants who could not afford them), and an intricate series of detention camps called the "Pipeline."[56] Mau Mau detainees were circulated through a network of about

---

Oliver and Fage state that African nationalist movements, even those that were nonviolent, were "[u]ltimately much more significant." *Id.* On the other hand, early Kenyan politician Tom Mboya presented the opposing counterhistorical argument that the Mau Mau uprising led to independence. "It is also true that it was not until Mau Mau had erupted that logical changes began to take place towards improving African conditions in Kenya. The colour-bar began to disappear, racial discrimination in the civil service was ruled out ... wages improved and in many other ways Africans were given fuller recognition." He concludes, "had it not been for Mau Mau, perhaps these changes would never have taken place; at any rate, they would never have come as quickly as they did." Tom Mboya, *Freedom and After,* 51 (1963).

50 Anderson, *supra* note 1 at 7.

51 *Id* at 7, 292.

52 For more on the communist uprising in colonial Malaya, see T.N. Harper, *The End of Empire and the Making of Malaya,* 149–52 (2001) (noting that 2,890 police, 3,253 civilians, and 518 soldiers were killed by the end of the emergency).

53 See Hynd, *supra* note 37 at 85. In addition, 347 saw their sentences commuted. The rest were declared unfit to stand trial or guilty but insane, or had their death sentences reversed on appeal. *Id.* at 86.

54 By contrast, Mau Mau soldiers killed 1,800 African civilians and 32 European settlers. Daniel Branch, *Imprisonment and Colonialism in Kenya, c. 1930–1952: Escaping the Carceral Archipelago,* 38 Int'l J. Afr. Hist. Stud. 239, 262 (2005).

55 Anderson, *supra* note 1 at 314.

56 As Elkins explains, the British efforts to "rehabilitate" the Kikuyu during the Emergency led to the placement of at least 80,000 Kikuyu – and likely tens of thousands more – in about 100 detention and reeducation camps where they would pass through "the Pipeline." The Pipeline was intended to capture the "hearts and minds" of the Mau Mau adherents. It was not intended to be punitive; rather it was cast in terms of reform-minded liberal paternalism. Caroline Elkins, *The Struggle for Mau Mau Rehabilitation in Late Colonial Kenya,* 33 Int'l J. Afr. Hist. Stud. 25, 25–26 (2000). Despite this justifying myth for the brutal methods of the Emergency, the detention camps bred lawlessness and contributed to the colonial state's loss

a hundred detention camps and prisons.[57] Although the European Convention on Human Rights (ECHR) applied to Kenya beginning in 1953, the colonial government could derogate the Convention during States of Emergency at least as to detention without trial (but not as to torture or degrading punishment).[58] "As a critical component of the counterinsurgency campaign, the penal system consumed a disproportionate share of a vast influx of capital into the colony during the war against Mau Mau."[59] The prisons and camps remained staffed by inadequately trained personnel, violence was commonplace, and the institutions were extremely unhealthy.[60]

As Anderson explains, it could have been worse: more than 400 Mau Mau fighters, including all female offenders, were granted clemency because they were under the age of eighteen or had mitigating circumstances in their cases.[61] However, they were not released, and often remained in detention on lesser charges for years. Of the 1,090 Kikuyu men executed during the Emergency, 346 were convicted of murder, mostly of collaborators or "loyalists," 472 of capital possession of arms or ammunition, 62 of administering the Mau Mau oath, and 210 of consorting with terrorists.[62] During the same period 247 Kenyan subjects were convicted of ordinary capital murder, of which three out of five had their sentences reversed or commuted. By contrast, only 27 persons out of 1,499 who had been convicted of capital Mau Mau-related offenses had their sentences commuted.[63] "Mau Mau offenders were more harshly treated than others," Anderson writes. "State judicial execution, the highest form of institutional violence available under the rule of law, was ruthlessly deployed in the suppression of the rebellion."[64] Between 1950 and 1963, the rate of executions in Kenya was almost seven times higher than that of neighboring Tanganyika. Trials were notable for poor quality evidence, which did not dissuade judges from imposing death sentences. Extrajudicial depositions were approved, while inexperienced magistrates used inconsistent or unreliable testimony. Judges rarely excluded confessions allegedly obtained by coercion and torture.[65]

The abuses of British power during the Mau Mau War led to political scandal as the major newspapers and the opposition Labour Party began bringing

---

of legitimacy and control. *Id.* at 54–55. No doubt the entire process was counterproductive. Attitudes hardened in the detention camps and the underlying causes of the Mau Mau War, such as food insecurity, economic disempowerment, and especially friction over land, remained wholly unaddressed. In the end, the brutal methods of the Pipeline, discredited after the Hola Massacre in 1959, hastened the fall of British East Africa. *Id.* at 56–57.

57 Branch, *supra* note 54 at 262.

58 European Convention on Human Rights (November 4, 1950), Art. 15.

59 Branch, *supra* note 54 at 263.

60 *Id.*

61 Anderson, *supra* note 1 at 7.

62 *Id.* at 291.

63 *Id.*

64 *Id.*

65 Karimunda, *supra* note 3 at 101.

atrocities to light back in London.[66] The deterioration of Kenya's criminal justice regime during the 1950s contrasted sharply with the modernization of Britain's own system of punishment during this time. Kenya and other British African colonies rejected the British government's advances to abolish the death penalty between 1947 and 1956, believing that violence was increasing in a number of colonial territories and nationalist movements would interpret abolition as a sign of weakness.[67] The Kenyan colony and coastal protectorate received independence and were united on December 12, 1963, with Jomo Kenyatta as the first president. Kenyatta, a hero of the Mau Mau guerrillas but not one of them, did not perpetuate Mau Mau divisions after independence, given the country's heterogeneity and the frailty of the ruling regime.[68] Kenyatta was Muigwithania, Kikuyu for "the reconciler."[69]

5. THE CRIMINAL JUSTICE SYSTEM AND ERODING DEMOCRACY AFTER INDEPENDENCE

At independence, Kenya adopted a constitution that provided for a multiparty democracy, a freely elected bicameral parliament, and judicial independence.[70] Despite this progressive framework, "the post-colonial state was autocratic at its inception because it wholly inherited the laws, culture, and practices of the colonial state."[71] The independence constitution contained numerous exceptions that qualified or limited many fundamental rights.[72] In addition, the constitution allowed derogation of fundamental rights during states of emergency.[73] The rigid 1962 Lancaster House constitution in place at the time of Kenya's independence in 1963 was amended in December 1964 to make important changes to the structure of Kenya's government, including an effective

66 Elkins, *supra* note 48 at 344, 350–51.

67 Hynd, *supra* note 37 at 97.

68 *Id.* at 360–63.

69 Bruce J. Berman & John M. Lonsdale, *The Labors of* Muigwithania*: Jomo Kenyatta as Author, 1928–45*, 29 Res. Afr. Literatures 16, 17 (1998). *Muigwithania* is an authoritative elder who resolves disputes. The word was also the title of a Kikuyu civil society newspaper that Kenyatta edited in the late 1920s. *Id.*

70 Makau Mutua, *Justice Under Siege: The Rule of Law and Judicial Subservience in Kenya*, 23 Hum. Rts. Q. 96, 97 (2001).

71 *Id.*

72 Anthony Wambugu Munene, *The Bill of Rights and Constitutional Order: A Kenyan Perspective*, 2 Afr. Hum. Rts. L.J. 135, 154 (2002), citing Kenya Const. art. 70 (general limitation clause). "Apart from the protection from slavery, servitude and torture, all other rights are accompanied by a claw-back clause." *Id.*

73 *Id.* at 154–55, citing Kenya Const. art. 83(1) (former constitution). Implicit in Article 83(1) is that some fundamental human rights are non-derogable. *Id.* at 155.

ban on opposition parties.[74] Amendments also favored a more centralized state, benefiting the ruling Kenyan African National Union (KANU).[75]

Although the constitution, replaced again in 1969, gave the executive branch more power over the judiciary, the original constitution's extensive fundamental human rights provisions remained intact.[76] The Kenyan bill of rights closely tracked the ECHR and other international instruments protecting civil and political rights, including an explicit right to life provision with a death penalty savings clause.[77] Other protected rights included due process and fair trial rights, protections on forced labor and slavery, the freedom of movement, freedoms of conscience and expression, and property rights. However, the bill of rights was "reduced to a mere declaration" and rendered non-enforceable during the Kenyatta and Moi eras, although a series of constitutional amendments in 1991 allowed for a formal multiparty political system.[78] In 1963, the restlessness of the Somali people of northeastern Kenya brought repression from President Kenyatta, who declared a state of emergency allowing detention without trial, confiscation of assets, and restrictions on the freedom of movement. The death penalty was made mandatory for unauthorized possession of firearms, and special courts were created to prosecute violations without due process safeguards.[79]

President Kenyatta died in 1978 and power peacefully passed to Daniel arap Moi, the vice president, in an effectively one-party election.[80] During the reign of President Moi, from 1978 to 2002, the independence of the judiciary and the legal profession eroded. Moi politicized the office of the attorney general and oversaw the passage of a constitutional amendment allowing for easier impeachment and removal of judges.[81] In 1986 and 1987, Moi initiated a series

---

74 Amending the constitution required a 90% vote in the Senate and 75% in the House of Representatives, and KANU, the ruling party, could not muster the 90% in the Senate. Consequently, the law as passed was wonky, and enjoyed enough defectors in the Senate to pass. Chanan Singh, *The Republican Constitution of Kenya: Historical Background and Analysis*, 14 Int'l & Comp. L.Q. 878, 926–28 (1965). "The Independence Constitution was a manifestation of a mistrust of power with the result that a weak form of government was established, in contrast with the previous colonial government which was premised on the consolidation of power in the executive. Three broad themes characterised this Constitution: regionalism to safeguard KADU [opposition Kenyan African Democratic Union], safeguards for minorities and the control of the exercise of political power." Munene, *supra* note 72 at 141.

75 H.W.O. Okoth-Ogendo, *The Politics of Constitutional Change in Kenya Since Independence, 1963–98*, 71 Afr. Aff. 9, 18 (1972).

76 Stephen B. Pfeiffer, *Notes on the Role of the Judiciary in the Constitutional Systems of East Africa Since Independence*, 10 Case W. Res. J. Int'l L. 11, 30 (1978).

77 *Id.* at 144.

78 *Id.* at 136.

79 Alex De Waal, *Famine Crimes: Politics and the Disaster Relief Industry in Africa*, 40 (2002).

80 M. Tamarkin, *From Kenyatta to Moi – The Anatomy of a Peaceful Transition of Power*, 26 Afr. Today 21, 22, 30–31 (1979). Moi entered office immensely popular. *Id.* at 35. Kenya became a *de jure* one-party state via a constitutional amendment in 1982.

81 Mutua, *supra* note 70 at 101–02.

of arrests of prominent attorneys for representing detainees and filing habeas petitions.[82] Both Kenyatta and Moi frequently appointed expatriate contract judges to the national courts, who were more supportive of the positions of government to ensure their reappointment but were also potentially more resistant to corruption.[83] Judges who expressed a desire for more independence were greeted with hostility. The reputation of the judiciary and the legal profession was further tarnished with the failure to investigate and prosecute those responsible for the Goldenberg Scandal, the longest-running scheme of massive corruption in Kenya's history.[84] Judicial corruption and political manipulation of the legal profession continue in modern Kenyan politics. "Due to allegations of abuse of power and corruption, significant segments of the citizenry perceive the judiciary as having lost its legitimacy as a dispute resolution forum." This is one cause of the 2007 election violence, as the public did not trust the judiciary to resolve electoral irregularities.[85] Major scandals, such as the Anglo-Leasing procurement scandal during the Mwai Kibaki administration, continue to plague Kenyan politics.[86]

Constitutional protections for prisoners and criminal defendants eroded during the Moi era. Although Kenya enjoyed a Bill of Rights, the High Court held that it had no jurisdiction to hear certain cases, rendering several provisions non-justiciable.[87] The Moi regime was particularly fond of abusing the prosecution of the crime of robbery with violence, which carried the mandatory death penalty but, unlike other capital offenses, did not entitle an indigent defendant to free legal aid.[88] Such charges were brought against human rights

---

82 *Id.* at 102.

83 *Id.* at 107–10.

84 *Id.* at 116–18. The Goldenberg scandal involved an $800 million scam involving government rebates for fake diamond exports during the Moi administration. In 2004, the Kibaki government appointed a judicial commission to investigate the scandal, releasing its findings in February 2006, implicating high level government officials both in the ruling party and in the opposition. Despite high-level prosecutions, no one was ever convicted in conjunction with the scandal. Michael Chege, *Kenya: Back from the Brink?*, 19 J. Democracy 125, 129 (2008).

85 Migai Akech, *Abuse of Power and Corruption in Kenya: Will the New Constitution Enhance Government Accountability?*, 18 Ind. J. Global Legal Stud. 341, 342–43 (2011).

86 For more on the Anglo-Leasing scandal and its whistleblower John Githongo, see Michela Wrong, *It's Our Turn to Eat: The Story of a Kenyan Whistleblower* (2009). More recently, a scandal involving bribery of Supreme Court Justice Philip Tunoi and another into the misuse of funds in the National Youth Service have rocked Kenyan politics. Peter Leftie, *Uhuru Kenyatta Appoints Tribunal to Probe Justice Tunoi*, Daily Nation, February 23, 2016; Caroline Wafula, *21 Govt Officials Named in NYS Scandal Report*, Daily Nation, September 11, 2015. These developments suggest that corruption in Kenya is a deep institutional problem and not one that can be laid at the feet of Moi. Akech, *supra* note 85 at 343.

87 This was in direct conflict with the Kenyan constitution, Kenya Const. art. 84, which grants redress before the High Court for any violation of its provisions. Stanley D. Ross, *The Rule of Law and Lawyers in Kenya*, 30 J. Mod. Afr. Stud. 421, 424 (1992).

88 David Bryan Sullivan, *The Trial of Koigi wa Wamwere et al.*, 22 Rev. Afr. Pol. Econ. 262, 266 (1995).

attorney and former Member of Parliament Koigi wa Wamwere in November 1993 in a public trial that enflamed Kenya's ethnic rivalries.[89] Previously, Wamwere was imprisoned in Block G of Kamiti Prison with other death row inmates. The government of Norway protested the arrest and suspended foreign aid; the Moi regime broke relations in response. Protestors called for a hunger strike, and Amnesty International advocated Wamwere's release. In September 1993, Wamwere was charged with the crime of capital robbery with violence, in what he called a "trial by hyena" in which exculpatory evidence was irrelevant.[90] Public opinion on the trial tended to follow ethnic lines; Wamwere and his co-defendants were Kikuyu while the trial magistrate and Moi himself were Kalenjin. "By accusing political opponents of common criminal offences rather than detaining them without trial or charging them with 'political' offences … the Kenyan government can declare domestic and international attention to their trial inappropriate."[91] Wamwere was convicted in October 1995 and sentenced to four years in prison and six strokes of a cane; he was released on bond in December 1996.[92] According to Amnesty International's report for 1995, at least eight other political opponents of the Moi regime were charged with robbery with violence and were considered prisoners of conscience.[93] Amnesty also noted "widespread reports of torture and ill-treatment of prisoners," and added that a total of 568 people were under sentence of death at the end of 1995.[94]

Penal policy fared no better than criminal justice policy. In 1992, Attorney General Amos Wako reported that the prisons had a total population of 28,914 inmates, exceeding capacity by more than 56%.[95] In addition to overcrowding, food rations were inadequate and nutritionally poor; toilet facilities were strained; insects infested the facilities; uniforms could not be replaced; and disease was rampant.[96] Beatings and hard labor were routine and often inflicted permanent psychological damage; several inmates died of torture.[97] This strain existed despite the existence of a number of alternative punishments to incarceration authorized by the Kenyan Penal Code, including a parole mechanism.[98] In Kenya's sentencing regime, "gross sentencing disparities exist[ed] among similarly situated individuals convicted of the same offense," an

---

89 *Id.* at 265–66 (1995).

90 Koigi wa Wamwere, *I Refuse to Die: My Journey for Freedom*, 305–08, 312–15, 316, 330–31 (2002).

91 Sullivan, *supra* note 88 at 265.

92 Wamwere, *supra* note 90 at 338–51, 357.

93 Amnesty International, *Amnesty International Report 1995: Kenya*, www.unhcr.org/refworld/docid/3ae6a9fb4c.html.

94 *Id.*

95 Yash Vyas, *Alternatives to Imprisonment in Kenya*, 6 Crim. L.F. 73, 76 (1995).

96 *Id.*

97 *Id.* at 76, 80.

98 *Id.* at 79–95.

issue that continues to plague Kenya's criminal justice system.[99] Appellate courts only irregularly corrected the most egregious abuses.

6. CONSTITUTIONAL REFORM AND THE DEATH PENALTY AFTER 1987

Since independence on December 12, 1963, a total of 280 prisoners were executed.[100] Between 1963 and 2000, 3,584 people were sentenced to death and 135 received clemency.[101] The last to die, Hezekiah Ochuka, was condemned in 1982 for treason after leading a nearly-successful coup against the Moi regime; he was executed in 1987.[102] Ochuka's coup attempt was triggered by Kenya's conversion to a *de jure* one-party state.[103] Agitation for a replacement to Kenya's heavily-modified independence constitution began in the early 1990s.[104] Although President Moi ushered in multiparty rule, he preserved the dominance of the party in power since independence, KANU.[105] Moi won two irregular election campaigns, marred by inconsistencies and targeted violence, the first with only 36% of the vote against a divided opposition in 1992 and the second against another splintered field in 1997.[106] "Since 1992, the state periodically has engineered and orchestrated inter-ethnic violence," particularly those who supported opposition candidates.[107] As Mutua wrote at the time, "police and security force constantly invoke colonial era legislation to restrict the activities of the press and civic and human rights groups," while the judiciary, lacking independence, "continues to be a captive instrument of repression."[108]

The first major voices in favor of constitutional reform came forward in 1995 by a group of reformist lawyers who sought to reduce the president's

---

99 Rachel Muthoga & Robert Bowman, *A Brief Survey of Sentencing Law and Its Practice in Kenya*, 22 Fed. Sent'g Rep. 249, 249 (2010).

100 Lisa Weighton, *Death Row Inmates Living in Anxiety, Unsure of Last Say*, Daily Nation (January 19, 2011) (retrieved from AllAfrica.com).

101 Robert Odoul, *Capital Punishment: Texas to Kenya*, Generator 21: The World's Magazine (2000).

102 Weighton, *supra* note 100.

103 See Singh, *supra* note 74 at 926–27; Mutua, *supra* note 70 at 98.

104 Diane Ciekawy, *Constitutional and Legal Reform in the Postcolony of Kenya*, 25 Issue: J. of Opinion 16 (1997) (noting the rise of a "demand for constitutional and legal reform" following the 1992 elections, led by "lawyers, academics, clergy members and politicians").

105 Martin Meredith, *The Fate of Africa: A History of Fifty Years of Independence*, 403–04 (2005).

106 Joel D. Barkan & Njuguna Ng'ethe, *Kenya Tries Again*, 9(2) J. Democracy 32, 32–33, 40–41 (1998); Stephen Brown, *Authoritarian Leaders and Multiparty Elections in Africa: How Foreign Donors Help to Keep Kenya's Daniel arap Moi in Power*, 22 Third World Q. 725, 730 (2001).

107 Mutua, *supra* note 70 at 98.

108 *Id.*

executive power and create a comprehensive and enforceable bill of rights.[109] The legal profession had long been under siege in Kenya. Important members of the Law Society of Kenya were opposition leaders who faced continual threat of prosecution under the Public Order Act.[110] Detention, torture, arbitrary arrest, police brutality and even assassination were carried out against political opponents during the Moi era, and a number of prominent human rights lawyers fled the country.[111] Civil society became mobilized in Kenya during the mid-1990s, led by organizations such as the Kenyan Human Rights Commission and Mwangaza Trust.[112] Moi's efforts to eliminate security of tenure for judges aroused considerable criticism even in the ruling party, and his most sweeping proposals were not implemented.[113] Lawyers were frequently arrested for political activities, and the bar association became a site of contested political control between Moi loyalists and opposition members.[114] An internationally famous court battle between a widow and her late husband's family over burial rites revealed the depth of the contradiction between English common law and local customary practices.[115]

Under civil society pressure, a constitutional review process was initiated in 1997 during the twilight of the Moi regime, to comprise a period of initial consultation and drafting, revisions by a constitutional convention, and ratification by Parliament.[116] Moi left office in 2002 without a new constitution in place, as he dissolved Parliament in order to prevent it from ratifying a new

109 Barkan and Ng'ethe, *supra* note 106 at 35 (describing how a group of reformist lawyers published a proposal for reduced presidential power in *Nairobi Law Monthly*).

110 Makau wa Mutua, *Human Rights and State Despotism in Kenya: Institutional Problems*, 41 Afr. Today 50, 53 (1994).

111 Korwa G. Adar & Issac M. Munyae, *Human Rights Abuse in Kenya Under Daniel arap Moi, 1978–2001*, 5 Afr. Stud. Q. [online] (2001), http://web.africa.ufl.edu/asq/v5/v5i1a1.htm.

112 *Id.* at 54–55.

113 Stanley D. Ross, *The Rule of Law and Lawyers in Kenya*, 30 J. Mod. Afr. Stud. 421, 429 (1992).

114 *Id.* at 437–38.

115 *Id.* at 430. Probably no single court case during the Moi regime in Kenya has produced as much scholarly commentary as that which arose over the burial dispute of S.M. Otieno, a prominent criminal lawyer who died intestate in 1986. Otieno's widow, Wambui Otieno, was a member of the Kikuyu tribe and sought to bury her husband in Nairobi; Otieno himself was Luo, and his clan demanded that he be buried in western Kenya, the Luo homeland. Wambui's attorneys argued that given Otieno's Christian religion, lifestyle, and residence, Kenyan common law should apply and not Luo customary law. In May 1987, the Kenya Court of Appeal ruled in favor of Otieno's Luo clansmen and his body returned to western Kenya. The decision inflamed ethnic tensions and set back women's rights, according to some observers. The funeral was treated as a major vindication of the Luo ethnic group; Wambui refused to attend, as required of widows under Luo customary law, and Otieno was buried as a single man. Wambui herself was subjected to intensely personal attacks from prominent political and legal figures, and was vilified in the national press. The court case has faced particularly intense scrutiny from feminist scholars. Patricia Stamp, *Burying Otieno: The Politics of Gender and Ethnicity in Kenya*, 16 Signs 808, 808–09 (1991).

116 Alicia L. Bannon, Note, *Designing a Constitution-Drafting Process: Lessons from Kenya*, 116 Yale L.J. 1824, 1832 (2007).

constitutional draft.[117] Moi's handpicked successor, Uhuru Kenyatta, lost a hotly contested election to opposition coalition leader Mwai Kibaki of the National Rainbow Coalition (NARC).[118] In 2003, the newly-elected President Kibaki released 27 prisoners who had been on death row for between fifteen and twenty years and commuted to life the sentences of 195 others. Shortly before this, Minister of Justice Kiraitu Murungi declared that he was personally opposed to the death penalty.[119] Although Murungi urged the National Constitutional Conference to abolish the death penalty, the Conference eventually proposed a draft constitution that permitted it for the most serious crimes.[120]

The pending draft constitution, known as the Bomas Draft after the location of the talks, was never enacted by Parliament or presented for a referendum because Kibaki reneged on commitments to his coalition partner Raila Odinga to share power.[121] Kibaki's government went on to present a watered down draft constitution, known as the Wako or Kilifi Draft, to the Kenyan electorate.[122] Fifty-seven percent of the population, and seven of eight provinces, voted the draft down in November 2005.[123] The failure of the constitutional referendum proved to be a serious point of contention between Odinga and Kibaki in the 2007 general election, the outcome of which was extremely close and shrouded in controversy; more than 1,000 people died in the violence that followed. Kibaki pronounced himself the winner of an election he well may not have won.[124] "Although sparked by the controversial election results, the violence grew out of long-standing economic and political tensions among various groups, and thus took on an ethnic dimension," including attacks on Kikuyu in the Rift Valley and reprisal attacks on Luo and Kalenjin in the west.[125]

---

117 Stephen Brown, *Theorising Kenya's Protracted Transition to Democracy*, 22 J. Contemp. Afr. Stud. 325, 329 (2004); Bannon, *supra* note 116 at 1834.

118 Brown, *supra* note 117 at 334; David Throup, *The Kenya General Election: December 27, 2002*, 14 Africa Notes 1 (2003). See also, Joel D. Barkan, *Kenya After Moi*, 83 Foreign Aff. 87, 90 (2004).

119 Margaret A. Burnham, *The Death Penalty in East Africa: Law and Transnational Advocacy*, in *Human Rights NGOs in East Africa: Political and Normative Tensions*, 263, 268 (Makau Mutua ed., 2009).

120 *Id.*

121 Bannon, *supra* note 116 at 1838.

122 *Id.* at 1838–39.

123 *Id.* at 1839–41.

124 Stephen Brown, *Donor Responses to the 2008 Kenyan Crisis: Finally Getting it Right?*, 27 J. Contemp. Afr. Stud. 389 (2009). "Initial tallies gathered from polling stations showed Odinga in the lead, but the results reported by the Electoral Commission of Kenya from Kibaki's strongholds seemed to shift totals in his favor." On December 30, the Commission had stopped reporting results and hastily declared Kibaki the winner. Within hours, protests erupted. In addition to the 1,000 killed around the country, 500,000 Kenyans were displaced by the violence. Beth Elise Whitaker & Jason Giersch, *Voting on a Constitution: Implications for Democracy in Kenya*, 27 J. Contemp. Afr. Stud. 1, 14–15 (2009).

125 Whitaker & Giersch, *supra* note 124 at 14–15. Kibaki lost support for his failure to address corruption and for his political miscalculations. Polling before the 2007 election showed him in third place. Godwin R. Murunga & Shadrack W. Nasong'o, *Bent on Self-Destruction: The Kibaki Regime in Kenya*, 24 J. Contemp. Afr. Stud. 1, 5–6, 23 (2006).

The violence following the 2007 elections produced an interim power-sharing agreement, the National Accord and Reconciliation Act, which governed until a new constitution went into effect. The agreement created the post of prime minister for Raila Odinga, and the posts of deputy prime minister for each party in the interim coalition and balanced cabinet portfolios between the two major parties.[126] The death penalty looked to be a controversial topic during the period before the constitutional referendum, particularly as President Kibaki commuted more than 4,000 death sentences in August 2009.[127] Kibaki's commutation, made to relieve the "undue mental anguish and suffering, psychological trauma and anxiety" that resulted from extended periods of time on death row, is the largest known to Amnesty International. By 2013, however, more than 1,600 people were again under sentence of death.[128] The commutation of death sentences sparked calls by victims' rights groups for restitution to taxpayers and compensation to victims.[129]

Kenyan voters approved a new constitution in August 2010. Public debate over the status of the death penalty was eclipsed by two constitutional issues in particular, with churches leading the opposition: the legal status of abortion, and the existence of separate customary courts, so-called Kadhis' Courts, that would apply Islamic law to certain property, family, and probate disputes.[130] During the colonial period, the majority-Muslim coastal region was governed separately from the interior of Kenya colony, but the Islamic court system in this protectorate was abolished at independence.[131] Despite these challenges, the Constitution passed with 67% in favor and 31% opposed. It won in seven of the eight provinces, losing only in Rift Valley Province, a sharp change from the 2005 referendum results.[132] The base of President Kibaki, the Kikuyu regions in central Kenya, voted overwhelmingly for the 2005 and 2010 constitutional drafts, while the base of former President Moi, the Kalenjin regions in west central Kenya, voted heavily against both. Moi had been the most powerful voice opposed to ratification in 2010.[133] The majority-Muslim zones in the north and

---

126 *Text of Kenya's Power-Sharing Deal*, Christian Science Monitor, February 29, 2008, www.csmonitor.com/World/Africa/2008/0229/p25s01-woaf.html.

127 See UN Department of Public Information, *General Assembly Will Reaffirm Resolution on Death Penalty Moratorium*, November 20, 2008, GA/SHC/3939; "Kenyan President Praised for Commuting 4,000 Death Sentences," Catholic News Agency, August 5, 2009.

128 Roger Hood & Carolyn Hoyle, *The Death Penalty: A Worldwide Perspective*, 94 (5th ed. 2015).

129 Ken Opala, "Kibaki's Mercy on Death Row Prisoners Sparks Calls for Compensation to Victims," Daily Nation (August 15, 2009).

130 See, e.g., *Church Position: No to Unamended Draft*, Catholic Information Service for Africa, April 13, 2010 (listing abortion and the Khadis' Courts as the primary issues in the referendum).

131 Anne Cussac, *Muslims and Politics in Kenya: The Issue of the Kadhis' Courts in the Constitutional Review Process*, 28 J. Muslim Minority Aff. 289, 291–92 (2008).

132 Interim Independent Electoral Commission, August 4, 2010 Referendum Results, www.iiec.or.ke/sites/default/files/Final%20Referendum%20Results%20announced%20on%20 06_08_10.pdf.

133 Robin Dixon, *Kenya's Vote on Constitution May Renew Tribal Conflicts*, L.A. Times, August 3, 2010.

east and the Luo region in the southwest supported the 2010 draft even though the 2005 constitution lost in these areas.[134] The constitutional referendum played into the ethnic mobilization of Kenyan politics after the 2007 elections.[135]

The new constitution entered into force on August 27, 2010. It generally sets up a system of checks and balances by creating a bicameral legislature and a new Supreme Court, headed by a president, who is both head of state and head of government.[136] Greater powers are devolved to local governments. A number of other provisions are intended to increase transparency of the national treasury, reduce corruption, and allow independent electoral oversight. The document provides strict independence of the judiciary as bulwarks against corruption.[137] The interim post of prime minister, held by Raila Odinga, was abolished, and a second house of parliament created as an additional check on presidential power.[138]

The new constitution includes an elaborate clemency provision that is designed to reduce politicization of a traditionally expansive executive power. Among other limitations, the new constitution prohibits interim or transitional pardons: a president is not entitled to exercise the clemency power beginning on the first day of the vote in a presidential election and continuing through the remainder of the term until a newly-elected president assumes office. The provision also prohibits exercise of the clemency power while the president is incapacitated.[139] The president cannot grant pardons to a person before conviction.[140] The constitution establishes an Advisory Committee on the Prerogative of Mercy, but the president no longer has unfettered control over the appointments. The Committee now comprises the attorney general, the cabinet secretary responsible for corrections, and "at least five other members … none of whom may be a State officer or in public service," another new provision.[141] The new constitution requires the legislature to regulate the membership and proceedings of the advisory committee and mandates that the president consult with the committee.[142] In addition, the constitution provides that the committee "may take into account the views of the victims of the offense" during its deliberations, reflecting restorative justice goals.[143]

---

134 Whitaker & Giersch, *supra* note 124 at 1–2.

135 *Id.*

136 See generally Kenya Const. Ch. 8–10 (2010).

137 *Kenya's New Constitution Sparks Hopes of Rebirth*, BBC News, August 27, 2010, www.bbc.co.uk/news/world-africa-11103008.

138 *Q&A: Kenya's Constitutional Referendum*, BBC News, July 26, 2010, www.bbc.co.uk/news/world-africa-10729860.

139 Kenya Const. art. 134(1) (2010).

140 Kenya Const. art. 133(1)(a) (2010).

141 Kenya Const. art. 133(2) (2010).

142 Patricia Kameri Mbote & Migai Akech, *Kenya: Justice Sector and the Rule of Law*, 69 (2011).

143 Kenya Const. art. 133(4) (2010).

Kenya's pardon power in the new constitution has moved to a model in which the president is less central to the process. By contrast, the independence constitution established an advisory committee on the prerogative of mercy, consisting of the attorney general and up to five other members appointed by the president. The president was not bound by the committee's advice.[144] Successive presidents routinely granted amnesties to groups of prisoners as part of annual independence day celebrations. However, the mercy power "has typically been exercised in a subjective manner" and presidents faced criticism for abusing it.[145] In particular, Moi granted a pardon to a former attorney general in 1984, shortly after the minister had been found guilty of abusing his office. Kibaki pardoned the former president of the National AIDS Control Council in 2004 after she had been in prison only twelve months for a corruption conviction.[146] Such pardons "reinforce[d] public perceptions that there are different sets of laws for the rich and the poor."[147] If an execution is ever carried out, the president must sign a death warrant or commute the sentence. The death warrant shall state the time and place of the execution and provide directions as to the burial or cremation of the body.[148]

7. THE ABOLITION AND REVIVAL OF THE MANDATORY DEATH PENALTY

In July 2010, a three-judge panel of the Kenyan Court of Appeal invalidated the mandatory death sentence for murder in *Mutiso v. Republic*.[149] In that case, the defendant was convicted of a premeditated murder and sentenced to death, although his sentence was reduced to life imprisonment in the August 2009 mass commutation.[150] The Court accepted jurisdiction notwithstanding the commutation or the attorney general's concession that the mandatory death penalty was unconstitutional. Ultimately, the Court invalidated the mandatory death penalty for murder on the grounds that the sentence violated the right to life, that it constituted cruel, inhuman, and degrading punishment, and that it violated the right to a fair trial.[151] The August 2010 constitutional referendum followed the *Mutiso* decision by one week.[152]

---

144 Kenya Const. art. 89 (1963).

145 Mbote & Akech, *supra* note 142 at 68.

146 *Id.*

147 *Id.*

148 Joy K. Asiema & Ongoya Z. Elisha, *The Application of the Death Penalty in Kenya: A Case of Torturous* De Facto *Abstinence*, British Institute of International and Comparative Law (c. 2003), www.biicl.org/files/2196_country_report_kenya_asiema.pdf.

149 Mutiso v. Republic, [2011] 1 E.A.L.R. 342 (Kenya C.A.).

150 Republic v. Mutiso, Crim. Case No 55/2004 (February 29, 2008) (Kenya H.C.).

151 *Mutiso*, [2011] 1 E.A.L.R. at 354–355 (Kenya C.A.).

152 See Jeffrey Gettleman, *Kenyan Constitution Opens New Front in Culture Wars*, N.Y. Times, May 14, 2010), at A6.

In *Mutiso*, the Court of Appeal noted that where the mandatory death penalty fell on defendants who did not deserve a death sentence, a right to life violation occurred.[153] Constitutional litigation over the right to life is particularly prolific in Kenya, and legal debates implicating the right to life clause have concerned abortion access, domestic violence, and environmental rights, among others.[154] *Mutiso* was similar to judgments from courts in Malawi and Uganda, which also found the mandatory death penalty unconstitutional. Like those courts, the Kenyan Court of Appeal found that because the death penalty did not distinguish among accused persons, the result "may be wholly disproportionate to the accused's criminal responsibility," and therefore cruel, inhuman, and degrading punishment. The Court also found that because the mandatory death penalty did not permit a sentencing hearing, it violated the right to a fair trial. Although the Court did not explicitly find that the mandatory death penalty violated the separation of powers because of legislative constraints on judicial sentencing discretion, it quoted this holding from the Ugandan Supreme Court in *Attorney General v. Kigula*.[155] The Court's caution was warranted because Kenya's new constitution altered the separation of powers. The Court dismissed the argument that sentencing discretion was unnecessary because of the existence of a mechanism for executive clemency.[156] The Court noted it was "satisfied" that foreign case law was "persuasive in our jurisdiction and we make no apology for applying" it.[157] The Court issued strong dicta indicating that the mandatory death penalty for crimes other than murder was also unconstitutional, which included treason, robbery with violence, and attempted robbery with violence.[158] The Court indicated a future willingness to entertain a death row syndrome challenge to the extensive delays that death row prisoners in Kenya faced.[159]

Finally, the Court successfully bridged the gap between Kenya's independence constitution and the 2010 constitution. Kenya's original constitution possessed a partial savings clause immunizing from constitutional challenge any form of punishment in existence at independence on the grounds that it was cruel and degrading.[160] The Court interpreted the clause to hold that the mandatory death penalty was a manner of sentencing, not a judicial punishment, and thus was not saved.[161] Like the Ugandan Supreme Court, the Kenyan court looked to drafters'

---

153 *Mutiso*, [2011] 1 E.A.L.R. at 353.

154 See, e.g., Waweru v. Republic, (2006) 1 K.L.R. 677, 677, 681, 684 (Kenya H.C.); Eunice Brookman Amissah & Josephine Banda Moyo, *Abortion Law Reform in Sub-Saharan Africa: No Turning Back*, 12 Reproductive Health Matters 227, 231 (2004).

155 *Mutiso*, [2011] 1 E.A.L.R. at 356–37.

156 *Id.* at 350.

157 *Id.* at 355.

158 *Id.* at 357–58.

159 *Id.* at 350.

160 Kenya Const. art. 74(2) (1969) (there is no equivalent in the 2010 constitution).

161 *Mutiso*, [2011] 1 E.A.L.R. at 353.

intent, noting that the new constitution "was arrived at through a consultative and public process," and consequently one could assume "that the people of Kenya, owing to their own philosophy and circumstances, have resolved to qualify the right to life and retain the death penalty in the statute books."[162] The Court appeared to close the door on a direct challenge to the constitutionality of the death penalty.[163]

The death penalty under the independence-era constitution was clearly saved at Article 71(1), modeled on that of the ECHR: "No person shall be deprived of his life intentionally save in execution of the sentence of a court in respect of a criminal offence under the law of Kenya of which he has been convicted."[164] In comparison, however, the new constitution is less clearly worded:

> 26(1) Every person has the right to life.
> 26(2) The life of a person begins at conception.
> 26(3) A person shall not be deprived of life intentionally, except to the extent authorized by this constitution or other written law.
> 26(4) Abortion is not permitted [with exceptions].[165]

The new right to life provision at Article 26 contains two ambiguities. First, the clause that could be construed as "saving" the death penalty is a separate clause from, and not a modifying subclause of, the grammatically absolute right to life. Second, 26(3) appears to be circular, because it states that a person shall not be deprived of life except where constitutionally authorized, and provides no constitutional authorization except for abortion exceptions. According to one of the experts on the Constitutional Review Commission, this ambiguity was intentional, to reconcile Kenyan popular opinion with global trends toward the death penalty. While it is possible to interpret "other written law" as inclusive of a penal code or other implementing legislation that prescribes capital punishment, as an interpretive matter the exception would swallow the rule by allowing any deprivation of life so long as it is written in law. For this reason, a narrower reading of the clause may be preferred over a broader one.

In June 2011, High Court Judge John Matthew Anyara Emukule found the death penalty unconstitutional, highlighting both of the ambiguities in Article 26.[166] In accepting the mitigating factors of the case, including the defendant's young age and the ethnic and political dimension of the murder, Judge Emukule held "that Article 26(2) (on deprivation of life) is inconsistent with

162 *Id.* at 352.

163 However, the High Court has extended *Mutiso*'s mandatory death penalty holding to the crime of robbery with violence. Evanson Muiruri Gichane v. Republic, Crim. App. No. 277 of 2007 (December 10, 2010) (Kenya H.C.).

164 Kenya Const. art. 71(1) (1969).

165 Kenya Const. art. 26 (2010).

166 Republic v. John Kimita Mwaniki, Crim. Case No. 116 of 2007 (June 10, 2011) (Kenya H.C.).

the right to life preserved under Article 26(1) of the Constitution."[167] However, in December 2011, High Court Judge M. Warsame came to the opposite conclusion, not only upholding the constitutionality of the death penalty, but also rejecting *Mutiso* and finding that the new constitution authorized a mandatory death penalty.[168] Judge Warsame compared the wording of the old constitution to the new constitution and found that the new constitution actually expanded the application of the death penalty because the phrase "the extent authorized by this constitution or other written law" in Article 26(3) of the new constitution was broader than "save in execution of the sentence of a court" in Article 71(1) of the former constitution. He rejected the belief that the death penalty was cruel and inhuman punishment. He made his disagreement with Judge Emukule explicit, believing that murder itself was a form of inhuman treatment and that a perpetrator "must pay for it in equal measure."[169]

Despite this conflict in High Court opinions, most capital sentencing cases at the High Court after *Mutiso* treated the death penalty as constitutional, but discretionary, allowing the accused was permitted to offer mitigating evidence.[170] In March 2012, the Court of Appeal also upheld two discretionary death sentences imposed on the defendants after they had the opportunity to present mitigating evidence.[171] However, in October 2013, a five-judge panel of the Court of Appeal, including former High Court Judge Warsame, issued a decision that purported to overturn the three-judge bench in *Mutiso*. In this decision, *Mwaura v. Republic*, the Court of Appeal upheld the constitutionality of capital punishment under the new constitution.[172] The Court concluded that the authorization of the death penalty in the penal code constituted "other

167 *Mwaniki*, Crim. Case No. 116 of 2007 at 26. Judge Emukule again reiterated his opposition to the death penalty under the new constitution in dicta in Republic v. Milton Kabulit, Crim. Case No. 115/2008 (January 26, 2012) (Kenya H.C.).

168 Republic v. Dickson Mwangi Munene, Crim. Case No. 11 of 2009 (December 10, 2011) (Kenya H.C.).

169 *Id.*

170 Note that the High Court sits as the trial court with original jurisdiction in murder cases, but as an appellate court in robbery with violence cases. See, e.g., Vincent Jared Ogutu v. Republic, Crim. App. No. 89/2010 (November 1, 2011) (Kenya H.C.); Boaz Onyango v. Republic, Crim. App. 53 & 55/2010 (September 23, 2011) (Kenya H.C.). For homicide, see Republic v. Jacob Juma Msituni, Crim. Case No. 10/2008 (March 12, 2012) (Kenya H.C.) and Republic v. Mbaruk Mwangeti, Crim. Case No. 15/2008 (March 16, 2012) (Kenya H.C.). In both cases, the High Court judges weighed the evidence in the first instance and then proceeded to a sentencing phase where the defendant was permitted to offer mitigating evidence.

171 Benard Mutua Matheka v. Republic, Crim. App. No. 155/2009 (March 15, 2012) (Kenya C.A.); James Maina Magare et al. v. Republic, Crim. App. No. 224/2009 (March 16, 2012) (Kenya C.A.). Interestingly, the Court of Appeal noted at the end of the *Magare* judgment that one of the judges on the three judge panel refused to sign the decision. The Court of Appeal also expressed some skepticism of the death penalty for armed robbery in David Njoroge Macharia v. Republic, Crim. App. 497/2007 (March 18, 2011) (Kenya C.A.).

172 Mwaura v. Republic, Crim. App. 5/2008 (October 18, 2013) (Kenya C.A.).

written law" as required by Article 26 of the new constitution. The Court noted that it had "the power to depart from [prior] decisions where we consider that in the circumstances, it is correct to do so."[173] The Court held that *Mutiso* was "per incuriam in so far as it purports to grant discretion in sentencing with regard to capital offences."[174] *Mwaura* does not square with the intent of the constitution's drafters and fails to interpret an ambiguous constitutional right to life provision in a manner consistent with Kenya's international human rights obligations and its internal political culture. Following *Mwaura*, however, High Court judges have turned away constitutional challenges to the abolition of the mandatory death penalty.[175]

In the end, the Supreme Court of Kenya will need to resolve the split among the High Court and Court of Appeal panels.[176] The 2010 constitution established the Supreme Court as the final court of last resort, adding an additional level of appeal.[177] There are some indicators for optimism: a number of pending judicial candidates have told the Judicial Services Commission during the vetting process that they believe the death penalty is unconstitutional under Article 26, hints of jurisprudence yet to be written.[178] In the interim, however, the Court of Appeal's vindicating decision in *Mutiso* remains in constitutional limbo. In January 2016, the Kenyan Supreme Court issued new policy guidelines for criminal sentencing to the country's judiciary, confirming that the death penalty remains mandatory for capital offenses, including murder, treason, aggravated robbery, and attempted robbery with violence. A committee composed of judges and local advoctes at the Judicial Training Institute, led by Justice Msagha Mboghli, pronounced the guidelines, which were launched by Chief Justice Willy Mutunga.[179]

The strategy of human rights groups that brought the *Mutiso* challenge has faced criticism for the fact that it did not address the problems of resentencing such a large number of prisoners, as many as 6,000, who have been sentenced

---

173 *Id.* at 23.

174 *Id.* at 25.

175 See Ngugi v. Republic, Petition No. 14 of 2012 (September 28, 2015) (Kenya H.C.). Rejecting *Mutiso* and relying on *Mwaura*, the High Court has also refused to find unconstitutional a mandatory sentence of twenty years' imprisonment for defilement of a minor. Ochoo v. Republic, Crim. App. No. 48 of 2014 (April 30, 2015) (Kenya H.C.).

176 Sam Kiplagat, *Death Row Convict Goes to Supreme Court to Overturn Sentence*, The Star, November 5, 2013 (retrieved from AllAfrica.com).

177 John Harrington & Ambreena Manji, *Restoring Leviathan? The Kenyan Supreme Court, Constitutional Transformation, and the Presidential Election of 2013*, 9 J. Eastern Afr. Stud. 175, 175–76 (2015).

178 *Death Penalty Cruel, JSC Told*, Daily Nation, July 6, 2011; *Magistrates Push for Repeal of Death Penalty*, Daily Nation, August 4, 2011.

179 Paul Ogemba, *Judiciary's New Policy Spells Doom for Death Row Convicts*, Daily Nation, January 26, 2016, http://allafrica.com/stories/201601260105.html. A member of the committee clarified with the present author that the new guidelines only restate the existing state of the law and do not purport to pronounce on the constitutionality of the mandatory death penalty.

to death or commuted to life imprisonment without the opportunity to present mitigating evidence in their cases. Hodgkinson and Akers write that the *Mutiso* challenge "could be more aptly comprehended as a token political gesture" considering that shortly before all death row prisoners had their sentences commuted to life without parole.[180] By commuting the death sentences to life imprisonment without the possibility of parole or remission, President Kibaki denied these prisoners the opportunity to mitigate their sentences in a resentencing hearing.[181] However, according to advocates involved with the *Mutiso* litigation, Kibaki's mass clemency was deliberately made in anticipation of the pending ruling in *Mutiso* finding the mandatory death penalty unconstitutional, which would suggest that the constitutional litigation was more than simply a token gesture.

8. PROSPECTS FOR ABOLITION OF THE DEATH PENALTY

Kenya's penal code has never undergone a comprehensive review to ensure proportionality of punishment. Corporal punishment in the form of caning was abolished in 2003. Many of the more recently enacted provisions of the penal code provide for mandatory minimum and maximum sentences, and non-capital trials include a sentencing hearing as a matter of practice. Courts may consider the period of time spent in detention, victim impact statements, and any restitution paid to the victim in determining sentence length. Nonetheless, the criminal justice system suffers from notable resource shortages, including irregular publication of decisions and loss of case files.[182]

In 1999, Kenya joined the draft amendments by Egypt and Singapore that declared no global consensus on capital punishment existed in international law and that abolition was not suitable for all members.[183] Nonetheless, the end of the Moi regime in Kenya improved prospects for death penalty abolition. In 2005, Justice Minister Kiraitu Murungi renewed his calls that the death penalty was a violation of the right to life and stated that the government was committed to its abolition.[184] A motion to abolish the death penalty was heavily defeated

180 Kerry Ann Akers & Peter Hodgkinson, *A Critique of Litigation and Abolition Strategies: A Glass Half Empty*, in *Capital Punishment: New Perspectives*, 29, 49 (Peter Hodgkinson ed., 2013).

181 *Id.*

182 Muthoga & Bowman, *supra* note 99 at 250–52.

183 William A. Schabas, *The United Nations and Abolition of the Death Penalty*, in *Against the Death Penalty: International Initiatives and Implications*, 9, 30 (Jon Yorke ed., 2008).

184 *Kenya Committed to Abolishing Capital Punishment*, The Nation, June 7, 2005, www.deathpenaltyinfo.org/node/1471.

in the Kenyan Parliament in July 2007.[185] However, new legislation to abolish the death penalty was introduced in June 2015 and remains pending.[186] In 2007, the Kenyan National Commission on Human Rights released a position paper calling for death penalty abolition, noting that the punishment "violates international human rights standards and norms to which Kenya is a state party and has pledged to uphold."[187] The rewriting of Kenya's Constitution following the election crisis provided an occasion to reassess public opinion on the death penalty. Civil society organizations and newspaper editorial boards called for the abolition of the death penalty in light of Kenya's vote to abstain on a UN General Assembly resolution in December 2007 calling for a worldwide moratorium on executions.[188]

In February 2010, Kenya notified the United Nations Human Rights Council that a *de facto* moratorium, in place since 1987, would remain in place, although it rejected calls to abolish the death penalty.[189] Kenya also alerted the Council that an exhaustive review was underway to assess empirical evidence as to whether the death penalty had any impact in the fight against crime.[190] In May 2010, the Human Rights Council recommended death penalty abolition, which Kenya rejected despite the support of the Kenyan member of the Council.[191] Despite commendation from the Council members that the country had made progress toward death penalty abolition, the Kenyan government noted the "widespread public support for its retention, as had been observed during the constitutional review," but stated that the government was working to create public awareness about death penalty abolition.[192] From time to time, penal

185 Hood & Hoyle, *supra* note 128 at 94.

186 *MP Proposes Bill to Abolish Death Penalty in Kenya*, Mwakilish.com, June 19, 2015, www.mwakilishi.com/content/articles/2015/06/19/mp-proposes-bill-to-abolish-death-penalty-in-kenya.html.

187 Kenya National Commission on Human Rights, *Abolition of the Death Penalty in Kenya*, Position Paper No. 2 of 2007, www.knchr.org.

188 The vote was 104 in favor, 54 against, with 29 abstentions. General Assembly Resolution, Moratorium on the Death Penalty, UN Doc. A/RES/62/149 (December 18, 2007). See also, Kenya National Commission on Human Rights, Position Paper No. 2 on the Abolition of the Death Penalty 15–17 (2007), www.knchr.org/dmdocuments/PositionPaperonDeath.pdf.

189 National Report of Kenya Submitted in Accordance with Paragraph 15(a) of the Annex to the Human Rights Council Resolution 5/1, A/HRC/WG.6/8/KEN/1 (UN Human Rights Council) (February 22, 2010).

190 *Id.*; *Death Penalty and Ban on Gay Unions to Stay*, Daily Nation on the Web (May 11, 2010).

191 United Nations Office at Geneva, "Human Rights Council Adopts Outcomes of Universal Periodic Review of Kenya and Armenia," September 22, 2010, www.unog.ch (click on News & Media, Press Releases & Meeting Summaries, Human Rights Council).

192 Human Rights Council, Draft Report of the Working Group on the Universal Periodic Review, Eighth Session, A/HRC/WG.6/8/L.7 (May 10, 2010). The Holy See delegation objected to the use of the death penalty for crimes other than the most serious crimes. *Id.* at ¶ 86. Although Kenya accepted the Holy See's recommendation to review its death penalty legislation, it did not accept the recommendation to abolish the death penalty or declare a formal moratorium, as suggested by Argentina, Australia, Austria, Belgium, Germany, Ireland, Spain, and Uruguay during the Council review. *Id.* at ¶¶ 101.42, 103.2–103.3.

populism has triggered legislative proposals to broaden the scope of capital punishment.[193]

In the election violence that followed the elections of December 27, 2007, the country suffered ethnic-based violence that resulted in the deaths of 1,133 people, as well as significant property destruction and internal displacement. In October 2008, a Commission of Inquiry headed by Chief Justice Philip Waki determined that crimes against humanity may have been committed and recommended either the establishment of a special tribunal to try the perpetrators or submission of the case to the International Criminal Court for prosecution.[194] Kenya has ratified the Rome Statute of the International Criminal Court, which does not provide for the death penalty for serious crimes such as genocide or crimes against humanity. In addition, the Kenyan parliament debated and then voted down the Special Tribunal for Kenya Bill to try perpetrators of election violence. This proposal included life imprisonment as the most serious punishment, creating an awkward contradiction with the Kenyan penal code, which authorized the death penalty for crimes that were significantly less serious than crimes against humanity.[195] Ultimately, the case was forwarded for prosecution to the International Criminal Court. Subsequent to the Court's prosecution, the indicted defendants Uhuru Kenyatta and William Ruto were elected president and vice-president, respectively, having delayed prosecution until after the 2013 elections. The Kenyan government refused to hand over vital evidence and witnesses were bribed and intimidated to prevent their testimony. In late 2014, the ICC Prosecutor withdrew the case against Kenyatta; in early 2016 she withdrew the case against Ruto.[196]

Despite a moratorium, Kenya extended capital punishment to a variety of non-lethal military offenses, including treason, desertion, and cowardice, in the Defence Forces Act of 2012.[197] In 2010, based on recommendation of the Advisory Committee, President Kibaki issued a blanket pardon for 2,850 prisoners, including those who were terminally ill, those over age 65, and those guilty of petty offenses who had served their time or had six months or less remaining on their sentences. He also released another 1,227 prisoners who had nine months remaining on their sentences in order to help ease prison

---

193 In 2009, law enforcement agencies pushed to make owning an illegal weapon a capital offense. Kenneth Ogosia, *Owning AK-47 Soon to Be a Hanging Offence*, Daily Nation, October 6, 2009. An editorial by the paper slammed the proposal. *Death Penalty Over Guns Misplaced*, Daily Nation, October 7, 2009.

194 Antonina Okuta, *National Legislation for Prosecution of International Crimes in Kenya*, 7 J. Int'l Crim. Just. 1063, 1064–65 (2009).

195 *Id.* at 1066–67.

196 BBC News, *ICC Drops Uhuru Kenyatta Charges for Kenya Election Violence*, December 5, 2014; Susanne D. Mueller, *Kenya and the International Criminal Court (ICC): Politics, the Election and the Law*, 8 J. East Afr. Stud. 29, 37–38.

197 Karimunda, *supra* note 8 at 189.

overcrowding.[198] "Working closely with international legal organizations, NGOs in East Africa are developing litigation strategies to break the logjam on the death penalty."[199] Organizations such as the Katiba Institute and the Kenyan branch of Christian Lawyers for Justice (CLEAR) have participated in constitutional litigation in death penalty cases, in conjunction with the London-based Death Penalty Project and others.

9. CONCLUSION

Kenya's current posture on the death penalty is receptive to abolition following a thirty-year moratorium on executions. However, eventual abolition is complicated by the country's fragile political circumstances due to the fallout from the 2007 election violence and the creation of a new constitutional framework in 2010. Like Zimbabwe, Kenya had only a spotty tradition of capital punishment prior to the colonial era, but suffered significant abuse of state-sanctioned execution in the late colonial period. Although the death penalty was politicized in the post-independence period of one-party rule, the last fifteen years have ushered in a period of democratic consolidation. The best prospects for death penalty abolition in Kenya likely rest on the judiciary: a future constitutional challenge would be premised on the failure of Article 26 of the 2010 constitution to provide clear authorization for capital punishment. Short of total abolition, the newly-created Supreme Court of Kenya will face pressure in coming years to resolve conflicting High Court and Court of Appeal decisions on the constitutionality of the mandatory death penalty.

---

198 *Kenyan President Pardons Dying Prisoners, Reformed Inmates*, PanaPress, December 23, 2012.

199 Burnham, *supra* note 119 at 281.

CHAPTER 8
UGANDA

1. INTRODUCTION

Uganda last carried out an execution in 2003, though some reports suggest that military executions may have occurred as late as 2006. However, the country remains steadfastly supportive of the death penalty and has a posture less receptive of eventual abolition than neighboring Kenya.[1] Unlike Kenya, which has abstained on UN General Assembly resolutions calling for a global moratorium on executions, Uganda routinely voted against until 2014, when it abstained for the first time.[2] Statements from senior political leaders, including President Yoweri Museveni, advocate capital punishment for its deterrent value and public support.[3] As in Kenya, the death penalty was known in the precolonial period, though most communities tended to prefer compensation to the victim in lieu of executions. The death penalty as it currently exists, however, is overwhelmingly the product of colonial rule, which persisted after independence and into the ruinous administrations of Milton Obote and Idi Amin. The reconstruction of the state after the rise of Museveni and the National Resistance Movement (NRM) led to the establishment of a new constitutional order and emerging judicial independence.

Proposals to expand the scope of capital punishment have occurred in recent years, potentially adding to an already overbroad list of capital offenses. The most infamous example was the Anti-Homosexuality Bill of 2009, which would have authorized the death penalty for "aggravated homosexuality" and certain forms of HIV/AIDS transmission.[4] Although the law no longer included the death penalty by the time it passed in 2014 and has subsequently been found unconstitutional, the episode created significant resistance from civil society, the public health community, and Uganda's aid donors. Despite episodes of penal populism in a political environment best characterized as softly authoritarian,

---

1 See Graeme L. Hall, *Successful Capital Litigation in Uganda: A Counterintuitive Approach?*, in *Capital Punishment: New Perspectives*, 297, 297 (Peter Hodgkinson ed., 2013).

2 *Id.* at 300. United Nations Third Committee, *Moratorium on the Use of the Death Penalty*, A/C.3/69/L.51/Rev.1 (November 24, 2014).

3 *Museveni Wants Death Penalty for Murderers*, New Vision, February 24, 2015, www.newvision.co.ug/new_vision/news/1321330/museveni-death-penalty-murderers.

4 The Anti-Homosexuality Bill of 2009, Uganda Gazette, No. 47 Vol. CII, September 25, 2009.

Uganda has made progress in restricting the scope of the death penalty. In 2009, the Ugandan Supreme Court invalidated the mandatory death penalty on the grounds that it overpunished and unconstitutionally constrained judicial discretion.[5] Despite the lack of clarity in derivative challenges about application of life imprisonment in lieu of the death penalty, the case led to a revolution in capital sentencing and significantly reduced the country's death row population.

2. THE DEATH PENALTY IN PRECOLONIAL UGANDA

Although the death penalty has precolonial antecedents, the modern construction of capital punishment descends from English rule. According to Fernandez, it is "almost undeniable that the death penalty did exist in pre-colonial Uganda," but "it would be erroneous to assume that executions were prevalent, uniformly practiced, or in any way culturally entrenched among the diverse communities that form the territory of modern-day Uganda."[6] As elsewhere, historical traditions were not static, and evolved and reinvented themselves over time. Uganda is "an arbitrarily delimited, culturally heterogeneous, historically shallow collection of peoples," similar to other African states. Individual ethnic identities and languages are of relatively recent vintage, categorized and crystallized during the colonial period.[7] According to anthropological writings, local communities in Uganda tended to prefer compensation, particularly in less centralized societies. Wrongs concerned only the individuals affected, with homicide normally settled by a payment of blood-money comprising seven head of cattle to the next of kin. Only in the case of intra-family homicide was the death penalty exacted, since it was considered inappropriate to allow family cattle to be forfeited by one member to another.[8]

In some places, the death penalty was one of a range of punishments. For the Gisu and Alur peoples, compensation was one way to restore harmony, while retaliatory killing or warfare between clans could do so as well. Which method was preferred depended on the social distance between the groups of the offender and the victim. Compensation was preferred among close relations, while retaliation was more likely with strangers.[9] The Teso people of eastern Uganda exacted blood money when the murderer was apprehended, but if he

5 Attorney General v. Kigula, [2009] 2 E.A.L.R. 1 (Uganda S.C.).

6 Orlando Fernandez, *Towards Abolition of the Death Penalty in Uganda*, 3 (2008).

7 Christopher Wrigley, *Four Steps Towards Disaster*, in *Uganda Now: Between Decay and Development*, 27, 28 (Holger Bernt Hansen & Michael Twaddle eds., 1988).

8 T. Olawale Elias, *The Nature of African Customary Law*, 135 (1956).

9 J. La Fontaine, *Homicide and Suicide Among the Gisu*, in *African Homicide and Suicide*, 96–97 (Paul Bohannan ed., 1967); A.W. Southall, *Homicide and Suicide Among the Alur*, in *African Homicide and Suicide*, 216 (Paul Bohannan ed., 1967).

escaped, he was outlawed and the members of the deceased's clan were entitled to kill a member of the murderer's clan. The Basoga people employed capital punishment as the penalty for murder, while most other offenses were paid by fines supplemented by flogging.[10] For the Basoga, the death penalty was a divine sanction for which the murderer must be killed to appease the deceased person's ghost.[11]

By the middle of the nineteenth century, many communities in Uganda had reached a stage of development in which they differentiated between deliberate killing and any less culpable form of homicide. The former was generally dealt with by infliction of the death penalty and the latter by compensation. While liability for compensation typically rested on the individual, the family or kin group could be liable for compensation if the offender could not pay.[12] The Banyoro and Bagishu peoples were among those who distinguished between accidental homicide and intentional homicide. In the case of accidental homicide, the offender was to provide a feast for the surviving relatives on both sides as an act of reconciliation. If a killer was a member of the same clan as the victim, he was required to pay a fine equal in value to the marriage payment for a wife, and this was payable to the victim's father who might raise another child to replace the victim. The Baganda sometimes executed murderers, but generally compensation was preferred.[13] According to Karimunda, the Baganda typically applied the death penalty for murder in the rare event that the deceased's relatives demanded it.[14] As for the Banyoro, death was required for murder, and the escape of an offender could trigger a lengthy blood feud.[15]

In the late precolonial period, a new distinction developed: between civil and criminal law. Even by the late nineteenth century, some wrongs were already recognized as injuring society at large and therefore required a penalty that stamped the disapproval of the state beyond simply a penalty commensurate with the wrong done to an individual. The use of the death penalty among the Lango in cases of fratricide or patricide may have been the result of the inefficiency of compensation among close families, but also reflected an emerging distinction in traditional law between the civil and the criminal. Certainly, among more centralized societies, offenses such as witchcraft, incest, and certain sexual offenses were treated as crimes against the community or group and not just against another individual.[16] A Ganda proverb from Uganda summed up the

10 Elias, *supra* note 8 at 135.

11 Aimé Muyoboke Karimunda, *The Death Penalty in Africa: The Path Towards Abolition*, 32 (2014).

12 Elias, *supra* note 8 at 136–37.

13 *Id.* at 135–36.

14 Karimunda, *supra* note 11 at 22.

15 H.R. Hone, *The Native of Uganda and the Criminal Law*, 21 J. Comp. Leg. & Int'l L. 179, 183 (1939).

16 *Id.* at 117.

philosophy of collective law enforcement and justice: *omula mmamba aba omu n'avumaganya ekika* ("the whole clan is shamed by the clansman's offense").[17] The treatment of adultery was less uniform than spiritual offenses. Adultery was punished harshly among the Baganda and Banyoro, particularly where it occurred across class lines or between a master and slave, typically involving capital punishment or bodily mutilation.[18] Not all societies used punishments of the body for adultery, however; among the Teso, a sentence of between three goats to three heads of cattle was imposed for confessed adultery.[19]

Theft could be punished by mutilation or the payment of compensation among some groups in precolonial Uganda, though amputation and disfigurement appear to have been unusual in Sub-Saharan Africa.[20] The Baganda people had a particular aversion to theft and a person caught red-handed could be killed on the spot with the body displayed after death. Such a harsh punishment of summary execution for theft was unusual among precolonial African societies, many of which did not criminalize theft at all.[21] Torture was known for the purpose of extracting information or a confession.[22] Imprisonment was not widespread in precolonial Africa generally, but in Uganda a convicted person could be confined in a stock created by boring a hole through a heavy log attached to a rope and attaching the log to an offender's foot or arm.[23] Methods of execution reflected prevailing attitudes toward death and authority. Among the Toro people, death by amputation of the arms and legs was used for robbery. Crucifixion was common among the Banyoro and Bahima.[24]

More than Uganda's other precolonial political structures, the highly-centralized Buganda monarchy had advanced judicial organization, with a well-graded hierarchy of courts comprising those of a village *miruka* chiefs, higher district *gombolola* chiefs, higher county *zaza* chiefs, to the central court of the great Lukiko, the final court of appeal except in cases of the greatest public importance that were presided over by the *kabaka* (king) himself. The judicial organization included a series of fees and court dues paid by the parties.[25] The judicial organization in Buganda was in a stable and advanced state at the time of the European arrival, while systems of justice among the Nilotic peoples were much less clearly defined.[26] However, owing to the

17 J.W. Sempebwa, *The Ontological and Normative Structure in the Social Reality of a Bantu Society: A Systematic Study of Ganda Ontology and Ethics*, Ph.D. Thesis, Rurprecht-Karl-Universität Heidelberg at 285 (1978).
18 Karimunda, *supra* note 11 at 23.
19 *Id.* at 38.
20 Elias, *supra* note 8 at 262–63.
21 Karimunda, *supra* note 11 at 25.
22 Elias, *supra* note 8 at 237.
23 *Id.* at 262.
24 Karimunda, *supra* note 11 at 35–36.
25 Elias, *supra* note 8 at 242.
26 Hone, *supra* note 15 at 180.

kabaka's semi-divine status, the Baganda also practiced ritual murder in which humans could be killed to commemorate important royal events or to benefit the king's strength or health.[27]

3. THE DEATH PENALTY DURING THE COLONIAL ERA

The original British concern in East Africa was suppression of the slave trade based in the Zanzibar sultanate, where slavery was not abolished until 1897. At the Berlin Conference of 1885, the territory that is now Kenya was designated a British "sphere of influence," while the status of Uganda was left undecided until 1890 when it was likewise awarded to Britain.

A year later, the British government and the Imperial British East Africa Company jointly began a railroad through to Uganda, but the failure of the Company in 1893 led the British to declare a protectorate over the territory. Skilled labor from British India was used to build the railroad, though it did not reach Kampala until 1931.[28] The source of considerable political instability in the postcolonial period was the decision to amalgamate the Buganda kingdom with a host of considerably smaller and dissimilar ethnic groups, such that Buganda was large enough to retain a sense of privilege but not large enough to control the state.[29]

In 1926, joint British administration united Kenya, Uganda, and Tanganyika, though the three territories' criminal justice policies were interlinked before this through the East African Court of Appeal, which heard appeals from all three territories. The British attempted to modify indigenous law and procedure in East Africa to reflect British preferences as to the elements of the offenses and to eliminate other offenses from the law.[30] The same tensions over land that plagued the African communities in the White Highlands of Kenya and the Rhodesian plateau were largely absent from Uganda, though tensions arose over the kingdom of Buganda's status in the colonial polity and over the subordinate political status of Uganda's sizable South Asian population.[31] The far northeast region of Uganda remained underdeveloped with only a skeletal administration until late in the colonial period.[32]

In general, British administration in Uganda was centered on a governor-general, who administered through district commissioners. Below the district commissioners were the Native Authorities, who governed through chiefly

27 Karimunda, *supra* note 11 at 34.
28 H.S. Morris, *The Indians of Uganda: A Study of Caste and Sect in a Plural Society*, 5–9 (1968).
29 Wright, *supra* note 7 at 29–30.
30 Karimunda, *supra* note 11 at 94–95.
31 Kenneth Ingham, *A History of East Africa*, 288–90 (1967).
32 *Id.* at 308.

hierarchies that the British incorporated into the colonial state (and that the British created in communities that were egalitarian in political structure). The British used violence to suppress local resistance to their rule, even to attack a village when several local chiefs murdered an agent of the government in the early 1900s.[33] As in other British African colonies, colonial Uganda had a penal code based on English common law principles, with only a minor role for customary criminal law. A dual system of laws (English and customary) was reflected in a dual court system. A Western-style court system with magistrate's courts that followed British criminal procedure with provision to appeal to higher courts. On the other hand were customary courts presided over by chiefs and "traditional" authorities, which generally did not follow formal rules of evidence and procedure. These courts could try minor criminal offenses, but typically serious crimes were tried in Western-style courts.[34] The Native Authority divided the country into counties, sub-counties, and parishes, which reflected the hierarchical organization of the court system. Customary law played some role in lower-level courts, but the body of law was controlled by the chiefs, who served as both judge and local administrator.[35]

Capital punishment was introduced by the British in Uganda under the Reception Clause of 1902. Until independence in 1962, all death sentences were subject to the approval of the governor-general in Uganda, although this fact in itself did not reduce the application of capital punishment.[36] Looking at homicide cases in Western Uganda between 1955 and 1966, Mushanga found that young adults and males committed a disproportionate number of the 484 homicides in that time. In addition, Mushanga reported that certain subcultural norms affected the incidence of homicide, including traditions of carrying spears or other weapons or of cattle raids or other forms of collective violence.[37] Uganda's penal code remains substantially similar to the one imposed during the colonial period. "The penal policies of independent African governments show a remarkable continuity with those of their colonial predecessors," Coldham writes.[38] Despite political emphasis on African traditions and socialism, few countries made efforts to incorporate these into colonial penal codes. Penal policy continued to be characterized by its harshness and its emphasis on retribution and general deterrence, rather than on individualization of a penalty or rehabilitation.[39]

33 Tarsis B. Kabwegyere, *The Dynamics of Colonial Violence: The Inductive System in Uganda*, 9 J. Peace Res. 303, 304, 306 (1972).

34 Simon Coldham, *Criminal Justice Policies in Commonwealth Africa: Trends and Prospects*, 44 J. Afr. L. 218, 219–20 (2000).

35 Kabwegyere, *supra* note 33 at 311.

36 Fernandez, *supra* note 6 at 4.

37 Tibamanya Mwena Mushanga, *Criminal Homicide in Uganda: A Sociological Study of Violent Deaths*, in *Ankole, Kigezi and Toro Districts of Western Uganda*, 3 (2011).

38 Coldham, *supra* note 34 at 223.

39 *Id.*

4. THE DEATH PENALTY AFTER INDEPENDENCE

Uganda achieved independence in October 1962. While constitutionalism may have existed in the precolonial and colonial eras, especially in the Kingdom of Buganda around 1900 when constraints were first placed on the *kabaka*'s power, the first modern constitutional order began with Uganda's independence in 1962 and the first written constitution promulgated that year.[40] African representatives, including those from the Buganda polity, became members of the Legislative Council beginning in 1950s. In 1961, the British introduced universal suffrage to the overwhelming majority of African representatives, which caused consternation in Buganda due to the dilution of the traditional kingdom's influence in the state.[41] An alliance between the Uganda Peoples Congress and the Buganda-based Kabaka Yekka party elected Milton Obote to be Uganda's first president in the 1962 elections.[42] The first constitution and the two that followed in 1966 and 1967 failed to properly balance the interests of the state with the interests of the Buganda monarchy, which represented the largest national ethnic group.[43] Constitutional revisions in 1966 drastically centralized the state and reduced the power of kingdoms, and the 1967 constitution abolished kingdoms outright.[44]

The independence constitution was the culmination of a long negotiation to balance the interests of the large Buganda kingdom with the array of other communities in Uganda, the result of which was a delicate compromise between a federal and unitary system. Within three years, the constitutional structure had been heavily amended and the 1962 constitution suspended altogether in 1966. The 1967 constitution that replaced the independence one emphasized a "unitary" state over a federal one and removed any special protections of the status of the Buganda kingdom within the greater Ugandan state.[45] In effect, the constitution abolished the kingdoms and the Buganda polity and replaced it with organs of district and local administration, a clear shift of power to Kampala. The constitution also augmented the power of the president and gave the government greater control over law and order, limiting the scope of the bill of rights.[46]

---

40 David Mukholi, *A Complete Guide to Uganda's Fourth Constitution*, 1–5 (1995).
41 Ingham, *supra* note 31 at 403, 419–21.
42 *Id.* at 421.
43 *Id.* at 10–18.
44 D.A. Low, *The dislocated polity*, in *Uganda Now: Between Decay and Development*, 36, 40 (Holger Bernt Hansen & Michael Twaddle eds., 1988) (describing how, at independence, Baganda were elite and economically well-endowed and held positions of great national prestige, but a majority of the Ugandan population viewed the Baganda as collaborators with the colonial state and resented their status).
45 H.F. Morris, *The Uganda Constitution, April 1966*, 10 J. Afr. L. 112, 112, 114–15 (1966).
46 A.W. Bradley, *Constitution-Making in Uganda*, 32 Transition (Kampala) 25, 26–28 (1967).

Over decades of misrule following independence, Uganda experienced the arbitrary and political application of the death penalty. Upon overthrowing the ruinous administration of Milton Obote in 1971, Idi Amin made enemies through his erratic and destructive policies, persecution of political opponents and the middle class, and massacres of the Acholi and Lango peoples. Amin carried out public executions of alleged guerillas after an abortive coup attempt in 1972 to deter political opposition.[47] After independence, the increasing incidence of crimes against property prompted a draconian response from the Ugandan government. In 1968, Uganda introduced a mandatory death sentence for robbery where the accused used or threatened to use a deadly weapon or where the offender caused death or grievous harm. A similar shift occurred with economic instability brought on by structural adjustment and economic contraction during the 1980s. In 1987, Uganda made armed smuggling a capital offense.[48] By January 1986, following a guerrilla war, the National Resistance Army under Yoweri Museveni captured power and began to stabilize the country.[49] Uganda's Fourth Constitution, which entered into force in 1995, was prepared in a much more open and democratic manner than the three that preceded it, and attempted to strike a new federalism balance between the central state and the kingdoms, and among the three branches of government.[50]

5. THE CONSTITUTION AND THE DEATH PENALTY IN UGANDA

The right to life provision at Article 22 of the Ugandan constitution states in relevant part:

> No person shall be deprived of life intentionally except in execution of a sentence passed in a fair trial by a court of competent jurisdiction in respect of a criminal offence under the laws of Uganda and the conviction and sentence have been confirmed by the highest appellate court.[51]

---

47 Andrew Novak, *The Death Penalty in Africa: Foundations and Future Prospects*, 44–45 (2014).

48 John Hatchard & Simon Coldham, *Commonwealth Africa*, in *Capital Punishment: Global Issues and Prospects*, 155, 158–59 (Peter Hodgkinson & Andrew Rutherford eds., 1996).

49 Muhumuza William, *Money and Power in Uganda's 1996 Elections*, 2 Afr. J. Political Sci. 168, 169 (1997) (describing origins of Museveni administration).

50 George Mugwanya, *The Legitimisation of the Constitution-Making Process in Uganda*, in *Constitution-Making and Democratisation in Africa*, 162, 166 (Goran Hyden & Denis Venter, eds., 2001) (describing popular participation in the making of the 1995 constitution). *Cf.*, Benjamin Odoki, *The Challenges of Constitution-Making and Implementation in Uganda*, in *Constitutionalism in Africa: Creating Opportunities, Facing Challenges*, 263, 264 (J. Oloka-Onyango ed., 2001) (describing the lack of popular participation in the earlier constitutions).

51 Uganda Const. art. 22.

This provision includes a death penalty savings clause, though it is more elaborate than one on the model of Article 2 of the European Convention on Human Rights (ECHR), as it includes a fair trial requirement and mandatory review by a court of final appeal. Uganda's 1962 independence constitution contained a death penalty savings clause closer to the ECHR model, respecting the right to life "save in execution of the sentence of a court in respect of a criminal offence under the law of Uganda of which he has been convicted."[52]

Retention of the death penalty was one of the most contentious issues facing the Constitutional Draft Commission following its extensive public consultation campaign. A large majority of the commissioners and the public supported retention, but an abolitionist minority was vocal in opposition. Under the leadership of Chief Justice Benjamin Odoki, the public's views on the death penalty were statistically analyzed along with a series of other contentious issues.[53] The Commission's final report, while praising civil society's abolitionist efforts and acknowledging abolition in other jurisdictions, concluded that it had not found "sufficient reasons to justify going against the majority views" and recommended retention for serious crimes until a later shift in public opinion. However, the Commission expressly recommended replacing all mandatory death statutes with discretionary ones.[54] The constitutional draft presented to the Constituent Assembly for final ratification did not include the clause enshrining a right to final appeal; this clause was added by the Assembly during a subsequent debate on the death penalty.[55] In addition, although the Constituent Assembly confirmed a death penalty savings clause, it did not include any limitations on the right to be free from torture and other cruel or degrading punishment, unlike the constitutions of 1962 and 1967.[56]

Uganda has a broad list of capital crimes, including non-violent and political offenses. Capital offenses include murder, kidnapping with intent to murder, armed robbery, defilement, and rape.[57] Treason also carries a mandatory death penalty, but incitement to commit mutinous or treacherous acts provides only a maximum discretionary death sentence.[58] However, as Makubuya explains, defilement and rape were only recently made capital offenses in a bid to curb the spread of HIV/AIDS, though the legislation does not necessarily require that an offender have HIV/AIDS or that the disease be transmitted.[59] In June 2002, Uganda passed the Anti-Terrorism Act, which authorized a mandatory

52 Uganda Const. art. 18(1) (1962), quoted in Fernandez, *supra* note 6 at 5. The 1967 constitution contained a similar clause at Article 8. *Id.* at 6; Uganda Const. art. 8 (1967).

53 Fernandez, *supra* note 6 at 6–7.

54 *Id.* at 8–9.

55 *Id.* at 9.

56 *Id.* at 10.

57 Penal Code Act, §189 (murder), §286(2) (aggravated robbery), L. of Uganda, ch. 120.

58 Penal Code Act, §23, L. of Uganda, ch. 120.

59 Apollo N. Makubuya, *The Constitutionality of the Death Penalty in Uganda: A Critical Inquiry*, 6 East Afr. J. Peace & Hum. Rts. 222, 238 (2000).

death sentence for terrorist-related offenses.[60] Murder convicts constitute the majority of the convicted death row population, 333 out of 501 as of July 2005.[61] Capital armed robbery sentences are less common: about 166 or one-third of the total death row population as of July 2005. By contrast, treason charges rarely lead to a conviction or a death sentence. As of July 2005, only six death row prisoners had been convicted of treason.[62] Even more starkly, only two prisoners were given a death sentence for crimes where a judge had discretion to substitute a lesser sentence, both for kidnapping with intent to murder. No prisoners were serving a death sentence for rape, defilement, or smuggling of deadly weapons. This is further evidence of judicial reluctance to execute convicts.[63]

The constitution of Uganda provides a clemency process in which the President consults with the Advisory Committee on the Prerogative of Mercy. When the Supreme Court upholds a death sentence, the accused person writes an appeal for mercy to the President, which is transmitted to the Advisory Committee. Typically, before sending a warrant for execution to the President for his signature, the secretary of the Advisory Committee consults with the inhabitants of the village where the prisoner lived. Prison staff may also report to the Committee on the external behavior of the prisoners.[64] Article 121(2) disqualifies certain categories of individuals from appointment to the Advisory Committee, including members of parliament, practicing lawyers, and local government officials.[65] The attorney general presides as chairman and members serve for four year terms. In reviewing capital cases, the Advisory Committee is to review a report of the trial judge (or, if unavailable, the chief justice) about the case and any other relevant information. Upon a recommendation, the president may choose to sign the death warrant or grant clemency. Only one appeal for executive clemency had reportedly been successful between 1999 and 2004, suggesting the practice may be unusual.[66] The Ugandan constitution prohibits the Uganda Human Rights Commission from inquiring into any matter related to the exercise of the prerogative of mercy, such as an allegation that the power's exercise was discriminatory, arbitrary, or corrupt.[67]

More problematic is Uganda's retention of a wide array of military crimes, which do not always offer the due process protections available in the civilian court system. Uganda has an extensive military code of conduct, incorporated

60 Anti-Terrorism Act of 2002, Act 14 of 2002, Uganda Gazette, No. 33, Vol. XCV, June 7, 2002, cited by Fernandez, *supra* note 6 at 24.
61 Fernandez, *supra* note 6 at 15.
62 *Id.* at 18, 20–21.
63 *Id.* at 22–24.
64 Tarcisco Agostini, *May the State Kill? A Challenge to the Death Penalty*, 82–83 (2002).
65 Uganda Const. art. 121(2).
66 Fernandez, *supra* note 6 at 31.
67 Uganda Const. art. 53(4)(c).

into domestic law in 1992, that provides a mandatory death sentence for a wide range of offenses, including treason, murder, rape, and disobedience of a lawful order resulting in death, as well as a discretionary death sentence for desertion, cowardice, disobeying lawful orders, spreading harmful propaganda, and a large number of other offenses. For these cases, the offense is punishable by death only if it results in a failure of the military operation, leads to loss of life, and, for some offenses, if it causes defection to the enemy.[68] The cases have no appeal procedure, but soldiers have the right to legal representation by an army lawyer. Between 1987 and 2000, at least forty soldiers were executed by firing squad.[69] Executions by Field Court Martial typically take place immediately or within hours of a verdict.[70] For all military offenses, the President is advised on clemency by the military high command rather than by the Advisory Committee.[71]

President Museveni in particular has adamantly supported the death penalty for military offenses in relation to civilian killings committed in the ongoing operation in Northern Uganda.[72] Because a death sentence passed by a Court Martial or a Field Court Martial does not provide for an appeal to the Supreme Court as required by Article 22(1), carrying out such executions would be unconstitutional. Yet, the President's prerogative of mercy does not extend to death sentences passed by Field Court Martial.[73] To the extent that a death row prisoner has no right to seek clemency or pardon in Field Court Martial proceedings, Uganda is not in compliance with Article 6(4) of the ICCPR. In 2002, the Uganda Law Society brought a constitutional challenge against the public firing squad execution of two soldiers after a field court martial proceeding. The two men were tried without benefit of counsel and claimed they were not guilty. They attempted to withdraw their confessions. The execution occurred three hours after the conviction.[74] The Constitutional Court of Uganda found portions of the Uganda Peoples' Defence Forces Act of 2005 unconstitutional to the extent that it permitted civilians to be tried before military courts-martial for the crime of terrorism, a decision that was upheld on appeal.[75]

The Ugandan Supreme Court has found that banishment and adult corporal punishment constitute cruel and degrading punishment under Article 22.

68 Fernandez, *supra* note 6 at 32.
69 Makubuya, *supra* note 59 at 238–39.
70 Fernandez, *supra* note 6 at 35.
71 *Id.* at 33.
72 *Id.* at 33–34.
73 Makubuya, *supra* note 59 at 239.
74 Uganda Law Society and Jackson Karugaba v. Attorney General, Constitutional Petition No. 8 of 2002 (Uganda C.A.), cited in Margaret A. Burnham, *The Death Penalty in East Africa: Law and Transnational Advocacy*, in *Human Rights NGOs in East Africa: Political and Normative Tensions*, 263, 269–70 (Makau Mutua ed., 2009).
75 Uganda Law Society v Attorney General, [2006] UGCC 10 (January 30, 2006); Attorney General v Uganda Law Society, [2009] UGSC 2 (January 20, 2009).

In *Abuki v. Attorney General*, the Supreme Court of Uganda held that a ten-year term of banishment from the offender's home for the crime of witchcraft constituted unconstitutionally cruel and degrading punishment.[76] As Judge Mulenga wrote in a separate opinion, "the act of rendering a human being homeless is both inhuman and degrading," noting that such an experience is traumatizing.[77] In 2001, the Ugandan Constitutional Court found mandatory adult corporal punishment unconstitutional in *Kyamanywa v. Uganda*, a decision that was later confirmed by the Supreme Court.[78]

In 2001, the government established a Constitutional Review Commission to analyze a series of potential amendments, which specifically included consideration of death penalty abolition. Following a period of public consultation, the Commission noted that 42.5% of respondents favored abolition, while 57% favored retention, a noticeably closer result than during the 1992 constitutional consultations when 75% were in favor of capital punishment.[79] The findings also indicated that respondents favored limiting the number of capital offenses to murder, kidnapping, defilement, and intentional transmission of HIV. The Commission even received a submission from the Uganda Prisons Service calling for abolition, and senior corrections officials have been vocal in their opposition to executions.[80] Although the Commission recommended retention of the death penalty, it also advocated limiting the number of capital offenses and urged an alternative to hanging as a method of execution. A government White Paper published in late 2004 accepted in principle the Commission's recommendations on capital punishment.[81]

6. THE ABOLITION OF THE MANDATORY DEATH PENALTY

The primary avenue of attack on Uganda's death penalty has long been the removal of mandatory death sentences imposed by the penal code and other laws.[82] Makubuya explained that while the penal code used the more restrictive "shall suffer death" language for murder and other crimes, the offenses of rape, defilement, and kidnapping with intent to murder used the more flexible

76 Abuki v. Attorney General, [1997] UGCC 5; Attorney General v. Abuki, (2001) 1 L.R.C. 63 (Uganda S.C.).

77 *Id.*, quoted in Agostini, *supra* note 64 at 98.

78 Kyamanywa v. Uganda, Const. Ref. No. 10 of 2000 (December 14, 2001) (Uganda C.C.), confirmed in Oryem v. Uganda, [2003] UGSC 30 (September 16, 2003).

79 Fernandez, *supra* note 6 at 11; Benjamin Odoki, *The Search for a National Consensus: The Making of the 1995 Uganda Constitution*, 186 (2005).

80 Fernandez, *supra* note 6 at 12.

81 *Id.* at 12–13.

82 Makubuya, *supra* note 59 at 247.

"shall be liable to suffer death" language. For these offenses, judges exercising discretion rarely issued death sentences. The more flexible language was in keeping with the view that the death penalty "should only be retained as an option to be used in 'extreme' cases where there is no reasonable prospect of reformation and the objects of punishment would not otherwise be achieved by any other sentence."[83] In addition, judges interpreted "murder" narrowly in order to avoid a death sentence. Fernandez writes that because of the mandatory nature of the death penalty for murder, judges adopted a narrow interpretation of the concept of "malice aforethought" to exclude intention to cause grievous bodily harm, which has led to quashed murder convictions and resentencing to manslaughter on appeal. In addition, the judiciary has broadly interpreted the defense of provocation beyond the traditional common law rule. Both rules suggest a reluctance among judges to convict of murder in borderline cases.[84]

In 2005, the Ugandan Constitutional Court in *Kigula v. Attorney General* determined by a three to two majority that the mandatory death penalty and inordinate delay in carrying out executions violated the constitution, though it upheld a discretionary death penalty and hanging as a method of execution in an omnibus challenge.[85] The Court closely interpreted domestic precedent and engaged in a textual constitutional analysis. The concurring opinions used a range of constitutional interpretive methods, including cultural arguments, framers' intent, and popular opinion.[86] The dissents argued that the criminal justice system provided sufficient safeguards against arbitrariness, including legal aid for indigent defendants, the right of automatic appeal, and the right to petition for clemency.[87] Though the argument is more experimental, Article 24 of the Constitution of Uganda prohibits torture and cruel and degrading punishment, while Article 44 prohibits derogation from this right notwithstanding any other constitutional provision.[88] Some scholars have suggested that reading these two clauses together could allow a judge to find the death penalty *per se* is unconstitutional.[89] The Court did not accept the argument, relying on public opinion as justification for finding the death penalty constitutional, as expressed in a survey performed at the time the current constitution was in the drafting phase in which the majority was said to support

---

83 *Id.* at 248.

84 Fernandez, *supra* note 6 at 15–17.

85 Kigula et al. v. Attorney General, Constitutional Petition No. 6/2003 at 61–63 (2005) (Uganda C.C.).

86 *Id.* at 68–69, 116. See also, *id.* at 117–18 (Twinomujuni, J., concurring); 17–23 (Byamugisha, J., concurring).

87 *Id.* at 159–164, 169–173 (Mapagi-Bahigeine J, dissenting); 179 (Kavuma, J, dissenting).

88 Uganda Const. arts. 24, 44.

89 Agostini, *supra* note 64 at 79.

the death penalty.[90] As Justice Amos Twinomujuni wrote, "if the majority of Ugandans want violent crimes to be punished by death without any excuse so be it."[91]

Both parties cross-appealed the Constitutional Court decision to the Supreme Court of Uganda. The Supreme Court voted unanimously to uphold the death penalty *per se*, but to strike down the mandatory death sentence for murder and unconstitutional delay and conditions on death row.[92] The Court also voted six to one to turn away the challenge to hanging as a method of execution, emphasizing the conclusions of the Constitutional Review Commission ten years earlier as evidence of drafters' intent, finding that the "inclusion of the death penalty in the Constitution was therefore not accidental or a mere afterthought. It was carefully deliberated upon."[93] In addition to a savings clause, the Constitution contemplated existence of the death penalty through a right to legal representation for capital defendants at state expense and the right to seek clemency.[94]

The Supreme Court agreed with the lower court's finding that a fair trial included both conviction and sentencing stages and that a defendant was entitled to present mitigating evidence subject to appellate review.[95] The Court also addressed a novel separation of powers argument, finding that a mandatory death penalty tied the hands of judges in their inherent constitutional power to determine both conviction and sentence. Both the Constitutional Court and the Supreme Court interpreted domestic precedent on cruel and inhuman punishment closely, relying on *Kyamanywa*, which invalidated adult corporal punishment, and *Abuki*, which invalidated banishment as a penalty for witchcraft.[96] According to Fernandez, the Court's approach to the mandatory nature of the death penalty was "considerably more receptive to international developments" than its approach to the challenge against the death penalty *per se*.[97] Mujuzi explains that the Court's reliance on international and foreign legal sources has the potential to "enrich the jurisprudence of the Court."[98]

90 William Tumwine, *The Role of Public Opinion in Court Decisions on the Legality of the Death Penalty: A Look at Uganda and South Africa*, LL.M. Thesis, University of Ghana at Legon at 32 (October 27, 2006).

91 *Kigula* (C.C.), at 134.

92 Attorney General v. Kigula, [2009] 2 E.A.L.R. 1, 30 (Uganda S.C.).

93 *Id.* at 12.

94 Uganda Const. arts. 22(1), 28(3)(e), 121(5).

95 *Kigula*, [2009] 2 E.A.L.R. at 20, 22.

96 Abuki v. Attorney General, [1999] UGCC 5, aff'd *by* Attorney General v. Abuki, [2001] 1 L.R.C. 63 (Uganda S.C.); Kyamanywa v. Uganda, Const. Ref. No. 10 of 2000 (December 14, 2001) (Uganda C.C.) (referred from Uganda Supreme Court in Crim. App. No. 16 of 1999, dated July 4, 2000). *Kyamanywa* was confirmed by the Supreme Court in Oryem v. Uganda, [2003] UGSC 30 (September 16, 2003).

97 Fernandez, *supra* note 6 at 119.

98 Jamil Ddamulira Mujuzi, *International Human Rights Law and Foreign Case Law in Interpreting Constitutional Rights: The Supreme Court of Uganda and the Death Penalty Question*, 9 Afr. Hum. Rts. L.J. 576, 589 (2009).

He notes that both the Constitutional Court and the Supreme Court cited to the decisions of the UN Human Rights Committee, European Court of Human Rights, Constitutional Court of Malawi, High Court of Tanzania, Constitutional Court of South Africa, United States Supreme Court, and Supreme Court of Zimbabwe, among others. These authorities supported the proposition that a mandatory death sentence constitutes cruel and degrading punishment because it can be harsh or excessive for a crime.[99]

In accepting the argument concerning the death row syndrome, the Supreme Court looked in detail at "demeaning" prison conditions.[100] The Court found that the mandatory death penalty was a sentence in itself and consequently fell within the scope of *Abuki*, which laid out guidelines for determining whether a sentence constituted cruel and inhuman punishment. However, hanging was only a method of execution; consequently, *Abuki* did not apply. This distinction is not entirely rational and is in tension with the jurisprudence of the Judicial Committee of the Privy Council's Caribbean holdings that the mandatory death penalty is not a judicial punishment per se but rather simply a method of sentencing. The dissent by Justice Egonda-Ntende laid out in detail the harsh effects of hanging and argued that, like the mandatory nature of the death penalty, hanging was not specifically saved under the constitution and could be found unconstitutional.[101] As Twinomugisha wrote about the challenges to the constitutionality of the death penalty and to hanging, "the Supreme Court squandered an opportunity to creatively interpret the relevant constitutional provisions and declare the death penalty unconstitutional."[102]

One aspect of the Court's ruling is particularly controversial: the decision to dispose of prisoners on death row for longer than three years differently than more recent convicts. Hall notes that the Court essentially ruled that the applicants who appealed against their mandatory death sentences were to have their cases remitted for mitigation of sentence, but those who had been on death row for three years or more would have their sentences automatically commuted to life imprisonment without remission. This number comprised about 298 of the 417 applicants in *Kigula*.[103] Such a holding disallowed this latter group of prisoners the opportunity to mitigate their sentences.[104] Hall explains that this distinction is "highly questionable" and devoid of legal merit. The Supreme Court "usurped ... fair trial rights by imposing a blanket and indiscriminate sentence" which "equally does not permit of an assessment of either the offences

99 *Id.* at 581–89.
100 *Kigula*, [2009] 2 E.A.L.R. at 24.
101 *Id.* at 43–46 (Egonda-Ntende, J., dissenting).
102 Ben Kiromba Twinomugisha, *The Role of the Judiciary in the Promotion of Democracy in Uganda*, 9 Afr. Hum. Rts. L.J. 1, 21 (2009).
103 Hall, *supra* note 1 at 303, 305.
104 *Id.* at 302–03.

committed or the offenders' particularities," the same constitutional defect inherent in a mandatory death sentence.[105] Such a natural life sentence is not provided for in the Prisons Act and may be beyond the scope of the Court's constitutional authority.[106]

By ruling that all prisoners on death row for longer than three years should have their sentences commuted to life imprisonment "without remission," the Supreme Court's decision in *Kigula* created an interpretive problem since the Prisons Act defined "imprisonment for life" as twenty years' imprisonment rather than "whole life" imprisonment.[107] In addition to the twenty-year rule under the Prisons Act, prison officials retained some discretion to shorten the sentence for good behavior.[108] The Supreme Court squarely confronted the issue of the meaning of life imprisonment under Section 47(6) of the Prisons Act. In *Tigo Stephen v. Uganda*, the Supreme Court ruled that life imprisonment meant "natural life" and not a term of twenty years as defined by the Prisons Act.[109] In that case, the High Court sentenced the defendant to "life imprisonment (20 years)" for defilement, a sentence that was upheld by the Court of Appeal without further deliberation about the duration of a life sentence.[110] The Supreme Court indicated, however, that the Prisons Act was "meant to assist the Prison authorities in administering the prisons and in particular sentences imposed by the courts," but did not bind the judiciary.[111] Hall writes that this was clearly an *ultra vires* decision.[112] The Supreme Court specifically cited to the jurisprudence of the Supreme Court of India, which ruled that a sentence of life imprisonment presumptively meant natural life. According to the Ugandan court, judges were able to pass sentences of imprisonment longer than twenty years, so it would be "absurd" to assume that a life sentence was limited at twenty years. However, in the defendant's case, the Court assumed that "life imprisonment (20 years)" reflected an intention on the part of the trial judge to sentence the defendant to a period of twenty years' imprisonment rather than life.[113]

105 *Id.* at 303.
106 *Id.* at 303.
107 Jamil Ddamulira Mujuzi, *Life Imprisonment in International Criminal Tribunals and Selected African Jurisdictions – Mauritius, South Africa and Uganda*, LL.D. Thesis, University of the Western Cape (May 13, 2009), at 272–75.
108 Prisons Act, 2006, No. 17, §§84–86 (Uganda).
109 Tigo Stephen v. Uganda, [2011] UGSC 7 (May 10, 2011).
110 Tigo Stephen v. Uganda, [2009] UGCA 6 (March 22, 2009).
111 Tigo Stephen v. Uganda, [2011] UGSC 7 (May 10, 2011).
112 Hall, *supra* note 1 at 304.
113 Tigo Stephen v. Uganda, [2011] UGSC 7 (May 10, 2011). Hall notes a potentially worrying trend in which judges have started to sentence offenders to periods of imprisonment that far exceed a human lifespan. He points to an April 2012 sentence by a general court martial of 310 years for a host of charges, including murder. Hall, *supra* note 1 at 304. The present author has not found any reported case law doing this in civilian courts, but it would be a worrying trend if such sentences become more common.

The Supreme Court's holding in *Tigo* violated precedent, according to Mujuzi. In 1975, the Court of Appeal explained that the maximum sentence of imprisonment was life, "which we take to be equivalent to a sentence of 18 to 20 years."[114] In 1994, the Supreme Court overturned a sentence of eighteen years for manslaughter, holding that it was excessive because a life sentence in Uganda was twenty years.[115] Similarly, in 2003, the Court of Appeal again held that a life sentence was twenty years.[116] In 2006, Uganda enacted a new Prisons Act, but the amended legislation retained twenty years as the term in years of life imprisonment. As of September 2007, 43 prisoners were serving life sentences in Uganda, including five who were convicted of murder after *Kigula*.[117] Following abolition of the mandatory death penalty judges have imposed multiple life sentences. The number of such life sentences increased from 37 in 2008 to 329 in 2010.[118] As Mujuzi writes, the *Tigo* decision and subsequent trends conflict with a growing international trend to limit life imprisonment terms to a period of years rather than whole or natural life.[119]

Given the lack of clarity surrounding *Tigo*, it is unsurprising that lower courts have been inconsistent in applying it. In a 2014 case, the Court of Appeal upheld a sentence of life imprisonment, but specifically refused to state whether the sentence was for twenty years or for natural life, writing, "[w] e see no need to clarify whether the sentence remains for the remainder of the appellant's life or a sentence of twenty years' imprisonment. This is a matter for the Prisons department to resolve, in reliance on the Prisons Act and emerging jurisprudence," including the Supreme Court's decision in *Tigo*.[120] This type of hedging does not provide clarity to unsettled law and confirms Hall's conclusions that the uncertainty was "hopelessly unclear" for the 298 applicants in *Kigula* whose death sentences were commuted to life imprisonment because they had been on death row longer than three years.[121]

For newly sentenced convicts, however, *Kigula* has led to a revolution in criminal sentencing. The Supreme Court made clear that death sentences currently on appeal were required to be returned to the High Court for a sentencing hearing. Where the Court of Appeal had already confirmed a death

114 Jamil Ddamulira Mujuzi, *Why the Supreme Court of Uganda Should Reject the Constitutional Court's Understanding of Imprisonment for Life*, 8 Afr. Hum. Rts. L.J. 163, 166 (2008), citing Wasaja v. Uganda, [1975] E.A. 181, 184 (Uganda C.A.).

115 Mujuzi, *supra* note 114 at 166, citing Kakooza v. Uganda, [1994] 5 K.A.L.R. 54 (Uganda S.C.) [Kampala Law Reports].

116 Mujuzi, *supra* note 114 at 166.

117 *Id.* at 167.

118 Roger Hood & Carolyn Hoyle, *The Death Penalty: A Worldwide Perspective*, 482–83 (2015).

119 Mujuzi, *supra* note 107 at 283–290.

120 Sebuliba Siraji v. Uganda, [2014] UGCA 52 (December 18, 2014).

121 Hall, *supra* note 1 at 305.

sentence, the Supreme Court vacated the decision on sentencing.[122] The Court has given content to both aggravating and mitigating circumstances. Where an offender performed a killing in cold blood, dismembered a body, and removed organs, the Court of Appeal found that no mitigating circumstances were present. Consequently, it upheld a death sentence for the defendant.[123] The Court of Appeal upheld a life sentence for a revenge tribal killing in 2015, noting that the sentence was lawful and was neither manifestly excessive nor so low so as to amount to a miscarriage of justice.[124] In another case from 2015, the Court of Appeal reversed a death sentence where it was "harsh and excessive" given the defendant's advanced age and remorse, and substituted a sentence of life imprisonment.[125]

Recent case law has provided guidance on how to weigh mitigating and aggravating factors. In April 2010, the Ugandan Court of Appeal upheld two death sentences after considering mitigating factors such as a three-year delay in prison before trial, remorse for the murder of a relative, and dependents of the defendants.[126] In a similar case, the Court ruled that aggravating factors outweighed mitigating factors where the defendant violently murdered an elderly woman.[127] In mitigation, the defendant-appellant argued that he was a first-time offender, that he was on remand for four years before conviction, and that he had a wife and five children. He also raised defenses of intoxication and provocation, which were legal defenses raised at trial.

The Ugandan Court of Appeal reversed a death sentence in June 2010 where mitigating factors outweighed aggravating factors in the case of *Adama Jino v. Uganda*.[128] In that case, the defendant-appellant was convicted of armed robbery. He pleaded in his defense that he was a first-time offender, that he had been in prison for over three years before conviction, and that he had a wife and four children.[129] The Court found that the trial judge had properly convicted the defendant of armed robbery, but determined that a death sentence was inappropriate because even though three gunshots were fired, no life was lost.[130] In October 2011, the Ugandan newspaper *The Monitor* reported that the Ugandan High Court reduced three death sentences for convicts in aggravated robbery

122 Ambaa Jacob v. Uganda, [2012] UGSC 1 (May 16, 2012). In Yoda Atiku v. Uganda, [2012] UGSC 9 (July 3, 2012), the Supreme Court faulted the Court of Appeal for upholding a death sentence without remanding the case back to the High Court for an initial sentencing determination.

123 Mugabe v. Uganda, [2014] UGCA 66 (December 18, 2014).

124 Sunday v. Uganda, [2015] UGCA 67 (June 2, 2015).

125 Okada v. Uganda, [2015] UGCA 100 (May 27, 2015).

126 Calvin Omasige and James Okia v. Uganda, Crim. App. No. 179 of 2003 (April 6, 2010) (Uganda C.A.).

127 Yasin Feni v. Uganda, Crim. App. No. 51 of 2006 (June 28, 2010) (Uganda C.A.).

128 Adama Jino v. Uganda, Crim. App. No. 50 of 2006 (June 23, 2010) (Uganda C.A.).

129 *Id.* at 3.

130 *Id.* at 8.

trials to imprisonment of fifteen and twenty years, respectively, evidencing the Court's continued skepticism of death sentences for non-murder crimes.[131]

The Court of Appeal has made clear that a trial judge must have regard to the length of time that a defendant spent in pretrial detention when calculating a sentence. Analogizing to the delay holding of the *Kigula* case, the Court of Appeal ruled that "the fact that a person has spent an unusually long period in pretrial detention, delaying to bring such a person to trial may itself mitigate against the imposition of a death penalty."[132] In 2014 the Court of Appeal ruled that a trial judge must have regard to the length of pretrial detention in considering a defendant's sentence, but does not explicitly have to make a calculation subtracting it.[133] It appears now to be routine to include the time spent in pretrial detention in calculating the sentence length. In one case, the Court of Appeal listed as mitigating factors the defendant's youth, lack of prior convictions, and two and a half years spent on remand in custody, to be weighed against the brutality of the murder as an aggravating circumstance.[134]

In 2012, the High Court overturned a previously mandatory death sentence in a sentencing hearing in *Uganda v. Sekamatte* after finding that the aggravating factors considered by the trial court were not adequately proven in the record. According to the Court, "the onus to prove aggravating circumstances beyond reasonable doubt lies with the state, as does the onus to disprove mitigating circumstances to the same standard."[135] The High Court found that the defendant was "so consumed by anger" that he was driven to kill his own child, and therefore had a mental state tantamount to diminished responsibility. However, the Court extended the length of the defendant's prison term based on the frailty of the child and a father's position of trust, which were aggravating factors. The Court noted that the defendant was capable of reform and therefore did not deserve a death sentence, but that the severity of the crime warranted a retributive sentence of 32 years in prison.[136] On appeal, the Court of Appeal held that sentencing fell within the discretion of a trial judge, and the appellate court could "only interfere with that discretion when it is apparent that the Judge acted on a wrong principle or overlooked a material fact or if the sentence is illegal" or if the "sentence is manifestly harsh and excessive."[137] The Court upheld the 32-year sentence in a

131 Anthony Wesaka, *Three Convicts on Death Row Survive Hangman*, The Monitor, October 20, 2011. On the other hand, the Ugandan High Court has handed out discretionary death sentences after consideration of mitigating circumstances in an armed robbery case. See, e.g., Uganda v. Aurien, Crim. Case No. 12/2010, [2010] UGHC 102.

132 Muhwezi v. Uganda, [2014] UGCA 52 (December 18, 2014).

133 Sande v. Uganda, [2014] UGCA 11 (March 24, 2014).

134 Kasaija v. Uganda, [2014] UGCA 47 (November 20, 2014).

135 Uganda v. Sekamatte, [2012] UGHC 186 (September 20, 2012).

136 *Id.*

137 Sekamatte v. Uganda, [2015] UGCA 98 (May 27, 2015).

two-to-one vote, but backdated the sentence to the date of the original mandatory death sentence and not to the date of the sentencing hearing.[138]

Although no empirical studies have been undertaken to confirm the existence of sentencing disparities, the Uganda Law Reform Commission and the former Chief Justice Benjamin Odoki have indicated the existence of wide disparities among different trial judges and magistrates, threatening public confidence in the sentencing process.[139] To this end, Chief Justice Odoki appointed a Sentencing Guidelines Taskforce, which promulgated official sentencing guidelines in April 2013, after reviewing similar approaches in the United States, England and Wales, and South Africa.[140] In Uganda, judges have *prima facie* wide discretionary power to select a sentence from a wide range of sentencing options, provided that the sentence is lawful. For murder, this can range from a community service order or probation to any length of custodial sentence to the death penalty. Not only is the spectrum broad, but judges "are permitted to take into consideration any factors that may relate to the offender's character, antecedents, age, mental health, familial responsibilities, prevalence of the offense in the community, or any other factor that the court may deem relevant."[141] Dennison notes the importance of restorative justice as a sentencing principle; the guidelines permit judges to consider the impact of an offense on a victim and on the community and to apply sentences that emphasize reconciliation. However, the guidelines themselves do not appear to specifically provide for payment of compensation to a victim or family.[142]

The guidelines cover both felony and misdemeanor offenses, but most importantly, all capital offenses. Like the sentencing guidelines of the United States and England and Wales, a range of penalties is provided for each offense, with sentencing principles delineated in narrative form.[143] According to the guidelines, a judge has the discretion to sentence an offender to between thirty years and life imprisonment, as well as a possible death sentence, for offenses in which death is the maximum sentence. The guidelines explicitly discourage judges from sentencing prisoners to death, emphasizing that the penalty is only for the "rarest of the rare" cases.[144] The guidelines are voluntary and non-binding; consequently, a judge is not obligated to provide written reasons for departing from them. The guidelines provide a range of different

---

138 *Id.*

139 Juliet Kamuzze, *An Insight Into Uganda's New Sentencing Guidelines: A Replica of Individualization?*, 27 Fed. Sent'g Rep. 47, 47 (2014).

140 *Id., citing* Constitution (Sentencing Guidelines for Courts of Judicature) Practice Directions of 2013.

141 *Id.* at 47–48.

142 D. Brian Dennison, *Uganda's New Sentencing Guidelines: Introduction, Initial Assessment and Early Recommendations*, Uganda Christian Univ. L.Rev. (forthcoming).

143 Kamuzze, *supra* note 139 at 50.

144 Edward Ssekika & Sulaiman Kakaire, *Order, Certainty in New Sentencing Guide*, The Observer (Kampala), June 19, 2013 (retrieved from AllAfrica.com).

sentencing purposes that judges may look to and roughly scale offenses by seriousness, though for some offenses, such as aggravated defilement, the range is so broad (three years to life) that classifying the offense's seriousness becomes problematic.[145] All capital offenses are treated uniformly, so that the starting point is 35 years' imprisonment and the sentencing range is thirty years to death. For sentences with a broad range (up to life imprisonment), such as manslaughter or simple robbery, the guidelines suggest fifteen years as the starting point.[146]

7. THE PROPOSED ANTI-HOMOSEXUALITY BILL

In Uganda, the Anti-Homosexuality Bill of 2009 authorized a mandatory death sentence for persons convicted of "aggravated" sodomy or HIV transmission, eliciting worldwide condemnation despite the facial unconstitutionality of the mandatory death penalty provision after *Kigula*.[147] Although the bill was never likely to become law with the death penalty provisions intact, these provisions have attracted significant scholarly attention. The bill was proposed in fall 2009 by MP David Bahati, despite the existence of an anti-sodomy ban in Uganda's penal code. Quickly dubbed the "gay death penalty," the Anti-Homosexuality Bill garnered widespread media attention in Europe and the United States, sparking petition drives and mass protests both in Uganda and overseas. Although the Bill was tabled in 2010 as duplicative of current law, it was said to have incited a moral panic of homophobic violence against sexual minorities.[148] Notably, the Bill also criminalized failure to report an offense to authorities, so-called "promotion of homosexuality," and even actions taken outside Uganda's borders, conferring expansive jurisdiction on Ugandan authorities to carry out prosecutions.[149]

The Bill was proposed despite expansive protections of fundamental rights in Uganda's constitution, such as the freedom of expression and equal protection, though an increasingly authoritarian executive in President Museveni is associated with a political environment in which journalists, political activists, and opposition leaders do not operate freely. Museveni has disregarded rulings

---

145 Kamuzze, *supra* note 139 at 50–51.

146 *Id.* at 52–53.

147 Anti-Homosexuality Bill, No. 18 of 2009, Uganda Gazette No. 47, September 25, 2009. See also, Cecilia Strand, *Kill Bill! Ugandan Human Rights Organizations' Attempts to Influence the Media's Coverage of the Anti-Homosexuality Bill*, 13 Culture, Health & Sexuality 917, 917–19 (2011).

148 Kristen Cheney, *Locating Neocolonialism, "Tradition," and Human Rights in Uganda's "Gay Death Penalty,"* 55 Afr. Stud. Rev. 77, 78–79 (2012).

149 Sylvia Tamale, *A Human Rights Impact Assessment of the Ugandan Anti-Homosexuality Bill 2009*, 4 Equal Rts. Rev. 49, 55–56 (2009).

from an assertive judiciary.[150] The Anti-Homosexuality Bill became a site of resistance to a Global North-driven human rights agenda. An editorial by MP Margaret Muhanga in a national Ugandan newspaper called the civil society organizations opposed to the Bill "slaves living under neocolonialism."[151] The Bill imperiled Uganda's relationship with its aid donors and public health advocates. The health consequences of such criminalization include heightened risk of HIV transmission and crippled access to medical care for men who have sex with men. Criminalization of homosexual activity is said to conflict with the best practices of major funding organizations such as the Global Fund for AIDS and the U.S. President's Emergency Plan for AIDS Relief (PEPFAR).[152]

The Act is premised on the view that same-sex intimacy is foreign to Uganda and a Western, neo-colonial imposition.[153] The best historical evidence suggests that far from being "un-African," homosexuality existed in precolonial and modern society in Uganda, just as it did everywhere, despite colonial missionary attempts to suppress it. Ethnographic texts have documented same-sex social and sexual relationships in many of Uganda's ethnic communities, and in none of them was such behavior deemed sinful or unhealthy prior to the onset of colonial rule.[154] As Rao explains, during the reign of Mwanga II as King of Buganda in the 1880s, conflict erupted between the monarch and missionaries about suppressing sodomy and homosexual acts. The tension resulted in a series of ritual killings in 1885 and 1886, culminating in the martyrdom of several missionaries and the abdication of Mwanga II. Mass public executions of both innocent and guilty persons were carried out in precolonial Buganda to showcase the power of the king and to confirm his vitality.[155] As Cheney explains, viewing homosexuality as a form of acquiescence to "imperial" forces has its roots in colonial times, when fundamentalist religious evangelicalism became a form of resistance and nationalism to Britain and the established Anglican Church. This base of longstanding evangelical religious belief is fodder for alliances with missionaries from the United States, at least some of whom support political legislation like the Anti-Homosexuality Bill and play into personal insecurities caused by HIV/AIDS.[156] The Bill's popularity may also have

150 Daniel Englander, *Protecting the Human Rights of LGBT People in Uganda in the Wake of Uganda's "Anti-Homosexuality Bill, 2009*, 25 Emory Int'l L.Rev. 1263, 1279–80 (2011).

151 Quoted in Cheney, *supra* note 148 at 82.

152 Paul Semugoma, Chris Beyrer & Stefan Baral, *Assessing the Effects of Anti-Homosexuality Legislation in Uganda on HIV Prevention, Treatment, and Care Services*, 9 J. Soc. Aspects HIV/AIDS 173, 175 (2012).

153 Rahul Rao, *Re-membering Mwanga: Same-Sex Intimacy, Memory and Belonging in Postcolonial Uganda*, 9 J. Eastern Afr. Stud. 1, 1 (2015).

154 See Cheney, *supra* note 148 at 80–81; Stephen O. Murray, *Diversity and Identity: The Challenge of African Homosexualities*, in *Boy Wives and Female Husbands: Studies of African Homosexualities* (Stephen O. Murray & Will Roscoe eds., 1998).

155 *Id.* Rao, *supra* note 153 at 2–3.

156 Cheney, *supra* note 148 at 82, 84.

played into prevailing beliefs about the central role of family, the importance of child-bearing, an orientation toward communal values, and the perceived disintegration of traditional culture.[157]

On February 24, 2014, President Museveni signed the Anti-Homosexuality Act into law. The final text substituted life imprisonment for the death penalty and strengthened punishments for same-sex sexual conduct, same-sex marriage, and "promotion" of homosexuality. On August 1, 2014, the Ugandan Constitutional Court declared the Anti-Homosexuality Act of 2014 "null and void" on the technical ground that no quorum existed in parliament when the legislation was passed.[158] Ward describes the unity between mainline Christian groups, African spiritual leaders, and Evangelicals on the issue of homosexuality as historically fractious, as opinions have differed among them on many traditional sex and family issues such as polygamy, traditional marriage customs, and inheritance.[159] Should the bill be revived in the future, its passage would likely be as contentious as in 2009 and 2014.

8. PROSPECTS FOR ABOLITION

President Yoweri Museveni, who took office in 1986, attempted to renegotiate the careful constitutional balances that had fallen apart since independence. His "vision was to see a popular constitution evolved by the people themselves that would consolidate the fundamental change in the politics of Uganda."[160] In 1988, the government created the Uganda Constitutional Commission, which visited every district in the country and held seminars with local officials and representatives, eventually involving 10,000 people in the constitutional discussions.[161] The Commission received over 25,000 submissions, many from ordinary Ugandans.[162] A draft constitution was presented to President Museveni at the end of 1992, and elections to the Constituent Assembly took place in March 1994.[163] The assembly enacted the Constitution on September 22, 1995, and promulgated it on October 8.[164]

157 Lynn Healy & Hugo Kamya, *Ethics and International Discourse in Social Work: The Case of Uganda's Anti-Homosexuality Legislation*, 8 Ethics & Soc. Welfare 151, 156 (2014).

158 Oloka-Onyango v. Attorney General, [2014] UGCC 14 (August 1, 2014).

159 Kevin Ward, *The Role of the Anglican and Catholic Churches in Uganda in Public Discourse on Homosexuality and Ethics*, 9 J. Eastern Afr. Stud. 127, 141–42 (2015).

160 Odoki, *Constitution-Making*, *supra* note 50 at 267.

161 *Id.* at 271.

162 John Waliggo, *The Main Actors in the Constitution-Making Process in Uganda*, in *Constitution-Making and Democratisation in Africa*, 50–52 (Goran Hyden & Denis Venter, eds., 2001) (describing the submission process).

163 *Id.* at 57–62 (describing the election of the Assembly, its composition, and its activities).

164 *Id.* at 61–62.

The constitutional assembly considered a variety of views on the death penalty, but ultimately decided to retain it. Among the large number of submissions, an overwhelming three-to-one majority advocated retaining the death penalty.[165] During the negotiation process, the death penalty was among the more controversial issues, Odoki writes.[166] The Commission weighed contradicting testimony on deterrent effects of the death penalty and consequences of retention for human rights. In its final report the Commission remarked: "We have considered the arguments of both sides with care, critically analysed the international attitude to capital punishment and especially the praiseworthy campaign of Amnesty International for the abolition of the death penalty and considered the fact that the death penalty has been abolished in several countries," including in Africa.[167] The Commission concluded, "We have however not found sufficient reasons to justify going against the majority views expressed in submissions to us."[168]

Death is by hanging.[169] Uganda executed three prisoners in 1989, nine in 1991, twelve in 1992, and three in 1996, for the crimes of murder, aggravated robbery, and rape. During that same time, seventeen capital prisoners benefited from executive clemency in that period.[170] The last execution of a civilian took place in Uganda in 1999. The execution of 28 prisoners, some suspected to be political opponents of President Yoweri Museveni, took place over two days.[171] In addition, thirteen death row inmates received clemency that year.[172] However, 26 soldiers were publicly executed in 2002 and 2003 for crimes against military discipline, including killing civilians.[173] Some sources report that the last military executions occurred in 2006, for a total of 377 executions since 1938.[174] As of 2016, the country is now *de facto* abolitionist.

The large number of capital offenses in Uganda is troubling; these range from murder, aggravated robbery, defilement, terrorism, military crimes, and many others, which clearly conflicts with the prevailing interpretation of the ICCPR to progressively restrict capital punishment for the "most serious crimes," namely those that do not result in death.[175] The use of the death penalty for military crimes in particular has been subjected to significant abuse, including

165 Benjamin Odoki, *The Search for a National Consensus: The Making of the 1995 Uganda Constitution*, 186 (2005) (noting 75% of submissions favored retention).

166 *Id.* at 199, 202.

167 Quoted in *id.* at 203.

168 *Id.*

169 Hood & Hoyle, *supra* note 118 at 179.

170 Makubuya, *supra* note 59 at 223.

171 Burnham, *supra* note 74 at 268.

172 Makubuya, *supra* note 59 at 223.

173 Hood & Hoyle, *supra* note 118 at 94, 159, 193. The military executions in 2002 took place before about 1,000 people and those in 2003 occurred before about 200 people. *Id.* at 193.

174 See Hands Off Cain, *Uganda*, www.handsoffcain.info/bancadati/schedastato.php?idcontinente=25&nome=Uganda.

175 Hall, *supra* note 1 at 306.

101 executions for homicide (including at least one public execution) between 1986 and 1995. Most of these were passed by Field Courts Martial without any provision for counsel, opportunity for appeal, or fair trial guarantees.[176] The National Resistance Army Statute of 1992 attempts to provide a line of appeal to a Court Martial Appeal, but the appellate body is not obligated to take an appeal. In practice, the appeal mechanism is rarely used.[177] However, in 2009, Uganda signaled to the UN Human Rights Council that it sought to reform its criminal laws to abolish capital punishment for robbery, kidnapping, and rape that did not result in death.[178] That year, about 15% of persons on death row were reported to suffer from mental illness.[179]

The Museveni government's international and domestic posture favors death penalty retention. In 1999, Uganda joined a group of retentionist states in the UN General Assembly to oppose a European Union-sponsored resolution calling for a death penalty moratorium by signing an amendment stating that no global consensus existed on capital punishment.[180] However, other public officials, including the commissioner of prisons and the assistant commissioner of police have come out against the sentence.[181] Wrongful convictions have occurred in Uganda. In 1982, Eddie Mpagi was sentenced to death for murder. The victim turned up alive in 1989. Not until 2000 was he finally released for innocence following action by a presidential commission.[182] Uganda has faced legal aid shortages in post-*Kigula* challenges. A new initiative, developed in October 2011 and funded by the Uganda-based Foundation for Human Rights Initiatives and the British government, will provide free legal assistance to fifteen inmates on death row who are challenging their sentences.[183] Previously, Uganda followed the practice of assigning counsel for death row inmates for a minimal fee.[184] Uganda is planning to introduce a national comprehensive legal aid system embracing a mixed model encompassing both public and private resources. Now that capital defendants have an opportunity to reduce their sentences at mitigation hearings, post-conviction capital offenders are experiencing an acute shortage of legal assistance.[185]

176 Makubuya, *supra* note 59 at 250.
177 *Id.*
178 Hood & Hoyle, *supra* note 118 at 149–50.
179 *Id.* at 257.
180 William A. Schabas, *The United Nations and Abolition of the Death Penalty*, in *Against the Death Penalty: International Initiatives and Implications*, 9, 30–31 (2008).
181 Burnham, *supra* note 74 at 268.
182 Rose Karugonjo, *An Analysis of Capital Punishment in Uganda in Light of International Standards and Comparable Case Law*, LL.M. Thesis, University of the Western Cape, at 39 (October 31, 2003); Journey of Hope, *Edward Edmary Mpagi*, www.journeyofhope.org/who-we-are/exonerated-from-death-row/edward-edmary-mpagi.
183 Ephraim Kasozi and Betty Ndagire, *Death Sentence Inmates to Get Free Legal Services*, The Monitor, October 15, 2011.
184 Makubuya, *supra* note 59 at 251.
185 Hall, *supra* note 1 at 309–10.

Despite this apparent softening of public support, Uganda appears well behind Kenya in progress toward death penalty abolition. The country has shown few signs of seriously considering a formal moratorium on executions and has voted against UN resolutions calling for a death penalty moratorium in 2010 and 2012 – but it abstained in a 2014 vote.[186] Uganda has ratified the ICCPR and has accepted the First Optional Protocol to the ICCPR recognizing the jurisdiction of the UN Human Rights Committee. However, the country has not accepted the Second Optional Protocol on the abolition of the death penalty.[187] Like Botswana, another retentionist country, Uganda has ratified the Rome Statute of the International Criminal Court, placing it on record as supporting punishment less than death for the most serious crimes under international law.[188] As Hall acknowledges, the abolition of the mandatory death penalty in Uganda has greatly reduced the number of death sentences passed and the judiciary appears disinclined to pass the death sentence for crimes that do not result in death. Between 2009 when *Kigula* was decided and 2013, 64 death sentences were passed, all for murder.[189] Nonetheless, at the end of 2013, Uganda had a sizable death row population of 420.[190]

Later assessments of public opinion have provided more nuanced perspectives on capital punishment. In 2001, the Constitutional Review Commission "sounded out" opinions from various stakeholders on support for capital punishment, finding that 42% supported abolition of capital punishment while 57.7% were against abolition, down from 72% nine years earlier.[191] In 2004, public opinion appeared even closer in a subsequent survey published in the *African Journal of Legal Studies*. Of nearly 1,500 respondents, 50.4% thought that the death penalty should be abolished while 49.6% believed it should be retained. The survey showed no significant disparities as to support for the death penalty and urban/rural locale, gender, or age.[192] Some of Uganda's communities, especially those victimized by long-running conflict, prefer a restorative justice approach to serious crime. The Acholi people of Northern Uganda, who have endured a long-running conflict between the government and the guerilla forces of the Lord's Resistance Army, avoid retributive justice and the death penalty in particular. As Murithi explains, the Acholi have a sense that the death penalty

186 Hood & Hoyle, *supra* note 118 at 95; Hall, *supra* note 1 at 300.
187 Hall, *supra* note 1 at 300.
188 Karimunda, *supra* note 11 at 191.
189 Hall, *supra* note 1 at 307.
190 Hood & Hoyle, *supra* note 118 at 203.
191 Hood & Hoyle, *supra* note 118 at 436–37 (noting that the methodology for these results is unclear).
192 John Cantius Mubangizi, *The Protection of Human Rights in Uganda: Public Awareness and Perceptions*, 1 Afr. J. Legal Stud. 166, 180 (2005).

multiplies suffering in the community and ultimately undermines the possibility of reestablishing harmony.[193]

9. CONCLUSION

Uganda professes a commitment to legal capital punishment in both the domestic and international settings, though it has recently fallen into the category of *de facto* abolitionist, having not carried out an execution since 2006. Penal populism, most notably with the Anti-Homosexuality Bill of 2009, creates an opportunity to expand the scope of capital punishment under the guise of popular support. Despite this commitment, however, a constitutional challenge to mandatory capital punishment has dramatically decreased the number of death sentences and established new legal frameworks for judicial capital sentencing discretion. This decision has had collateral consequences, including uncertainty over the appropriateness of life imprisonment as an alternative to the death penalty, which accentuates resource shortages and prison overcrowding. Like Kenya, capital punishment was used in the precolonial, colonial, and postcolonial periods, including suppression of political dissent under one-party rule after independence. While Kenya's capital punishment regime still suffers from mandatory application and therefore a large number of death sentences, Uganda faces a different problem: an overly broad array of capital crimes that conflict with international norms restricting application of capital punishment to only the most serious crimes. Incremental abolition that focuses on narrowing this list of crimes would help accord Uganda with prevailing international norms.

193 Timothy Murithi, *Rebuilding Social Trust in Northern Uganda*, 14 Peace Rev.: J. Soc. Just. 291, 294 (2002).

INDEX

www.ingramcontent.com/pod-product-compliance
Ingram Content Group UK Ltd.
Pitfield, Milton Keynes, MK11 3LW, UK
UKHW051922100926
8556IPUK00021B/1326

9 781780 682945